1964

THE ART OF GREEK COMEDY

THE ART OF GREEK COMEDY

by

KATHERINE LEVER

METHUEN & CO. LTD.
36 Essex Street, Strand, London W.C. 2

First published in 1956

CATALOGUE NO. 5832/U

Printed in Great Britain
by T. and A. CONSTABLE LTD., Hopetoun Street,
Printers to the University of Edinburgh

In Memory of

JOHN MEDBURY LEVER

PREFACE

Comedy no less than tragedy is concerned with the fundamental problems of human life. The problems the dramatist chooses for comic or tragic treatment differ in nature rather than in importance. The tragic poet is concerned with the relations of human beings to those forces which lie beyond their control: God or the gods, fate, chance, prophecies, immutable laws of religion and morality, inheritance, a man's own passions or the diabolical wickedness of others. The characters in tragedy are caught in circumstances in which they must make choices, bringing their wills and desires into conflict with these uncontrollable forces. Often this conflict becomes internal when the character recognizes the superior power or reasonableness of the force while at the same time he believes in the goodness of his own desires. So Oedipus recognizes the power of Apollo's prophecy even as his moral nature rebels against it. The result of the tragic conflict is inevitably the defeat of the protagonist, although his nobility in suffering, his insight into reality, and sometimes his perception of goodness may lead to a spiritual victory.

The comic poet, on the other hand, is concerned with the relations of human beings to forces or conditions which do lie within their control: political corruption, social and economic injustice, aggressiveness in individuals and countries, war, sexual desires and romantic yearnings, degeneration of literary taste, petty vexations and tensions, foibles and eccentricities of character. In the world of comedy, man has no need to fear. The supernatural world is beneficent. The natural world is amusing and friendly. The authorities who rule over us—officials, teachers, parents, 'people'—are strong and evil in appearance only; in the dramatic fray they show themselves weaker or kinder than we first thought. Our own worries can be resolved without permanent harm. Nor need man pity himself or others. We all have within our control powers of reason, will, and imagination strong enough to extricate ourselves from our difficulties. The protagonist in comedy thus emerges from his conflict strengthened by his fight and joyful in victory.

This division of comedy and tragedy holds true in my opinion for all drama in the Western tradition, but the dividing-line was more strongly and clearly drawn by the Greeks than by modern dramatists. No Greek poet attempted to write both tragedy and comedy (the satyr-play was a distinct genre), with the result that Greek comedy exists in a pure form, detached from tragedy although related to it. We have the perspective now to look back at Greek comedy, to trace its origins, to watch its changing forms, and to evaluate the solutions it offered to human problems. We have gained this perspective through time, and through time also we have lost much valuable evidence. Greek comedy, with the exception of eleven comedies by Aristophanes, survives only in fragments; but we do have the comedies of Aristophanes, substantial portions of the comedies of Menander, and sufficient fragments to reconstruct the whole history of comedy. Many points are necessarily conjectural, but the main trend is reasonably clear.

In the formative stages of Greek comic poetry, poets, dancers, and actors worked separately on particular comic problems. It was the glory of Old Comedy as exemplified by Aristophanes to fuse the functions of poetry, dance, and drama into one artistic whole. Aristophanes tackled all the comic problems from political corruption through the degeneration of literary taste to eccentricity of character. He used all the methods of attack developed by his predecessors: among them ridicule, constructive suggestions based on a sympathetic and rational analysis, fanciful reduction to the absurd, and the creation of a world of beauty and joy through song, dance, and costume. When conditions in Athens grew progressively worse during and after the Peloponnesian War, Aristophanes realized that the comic poet was powerless to alter conditions; all he could do for his fellow sufferers was offer them escape through the imagination. The pattern of his plays changed from fight to flight. This change heralded the Middle Comedy. The dominant theme of fourth-century comedies became escape from trouble through fantasy. By the last quarter of the fourth century, audience and dramatists alike had apparently become dissatisfied with a solution for life's problems which was less a solution than a resigned endurance. Menander and his contemporaries again sought to solve comic problems, choosing family life as a sphere in which they believed man could control his destiny. Happy marriage and legitimate children became the goals of the characters, and the means were self-knowledge and faith in a spirit of good working always to bring good results from seemingly evil events.

I have written this book for those who share my interests in these varied solutions for the problems of everyday life, for those who are fascinated as I am by Greek culture, one so very different from our own and yet so curiously like it, and for those who wish as students of modern literature to compare our drama with the ancient. Quite simply, too, Greek comic poetry is intrinsically delightful, and the pleasure it gives is sufficient justification for its re-creation by critic and reader. Fellow students of English drama may find in this book a springboard for their own comparisons: the likenesses and differences between a religious drama inspired by Dionysos and that inspired by Christianity; between the religious, political, and educational problems dramatized by Bishop Bale, John Skelton, and John Redford in the sixteenth century and the problems dramatized by Aristophanes; between the romanticism of Lyly, Greene, and Shakespeare and that of Antiphanes and Alexis, between the treatment of family life by Wycherley and Congreve or by Steele, Goldsmith, and Sheridan and its treatment by Menander. Students of other modern literatures may find significant points for comparison in the satire of Machiavelli, German school plays and moralities, Lope de Vega's romances, Molière's comedies of manners.

For every reader, whatever his previous knowledge of Greek literature, I have tried to provide a clear and readable text. Greek words are transliterated; quotations are translated. The main line of the development of Greek comedy is kept in view, but each chapter is planned as a structural unit so that the reader may, if he wishes, read only about the type of comedy in which he is interested. The very nature of comedy calls for an understanding of its full context—political, economic, and social conditions, current ideas of religion, philosophy, and education, concomitant state of the arts of music, dance, art, theatrical architecture, non-dramatic poetry, and tragedy. To the extent that I have been able within the scope of one book, I have attempted to provide this context through a synthesis of the work of other scholars. Such a synthesis can, of course, reveal only the highlights; for those readers with the time and interest to pursue the subjects further, references have been given in the notes to the original sources, to scholarly works in special fields, and to articles representing varied opinions on controversial subjects.

My debt to other scholars is only partially acknowledged in the notes. Many who have been helpful to me are left uncited, and others have contributed far more to my understanding of Greek comic poetry than brief mentions might indicate. The two scholars to whom I am clearly the most indebted are the two I should like to thank in person, but, since this is no longer possible, I can only express my gratitude here. They are Sir Arthur Pickard-Cambridge and Gilbert Norwood. Within my own circle of friends I am particularly grateful to Professor L. R. Shero of Swarthmore College and to Professors Rhys Carpenter, Samuel C. Chew, and Arthur C. Sprague of Bryn Mawr College for their continuing interest in my study of the drama. If she were alive, I know that Ethel H. Brewster would be among their number. Finally, I wish to thank those many men and women unknown to me who have demonstrated their belief in the value of the liberal arts by their support of colleges and universities, especially those responsible for the Faculty Fellowship of Wellesley College and the Sterling Library of Yale University, because they gave me the opportunity to write this book.

Chapter 7 was published under the title of "Middle Comedy, Neither Old nor New but Contemporary" in *The Classical Journal*, XLIX (1954), 167-81.

Wellesley College
February 10, 1956

CONTENTS

CHAPTER I

ARCHAIC GREEK COMEDY: 600 TO 530 B.C.

THE beginning of Greek comedy is lost in the misty times of primitive man, if by beginning of comedy we mean the very earliest mimetic performances [1]. Vestiges of prehistoric tribal rites and ritual dances have been discovered by archaeologists; and anthropologists have reconstructed primitive cults by comparison with other tribes and by study of literary remains. Wherever one searches, thousands of years back in time or thousands of miles away in space, one finds tribal man dancing in honour of his god. When, as so often happens, the dancers wear masks, use gestures, sing or are accompanied by singing, and communicate to the worshippers a myth or to the god thanksgiving, praise, or entreaty, then the religious cult is hardly to be distinguished from the religious drama. When the dancer loses his identity as a worshipper and impersonates a character, he becomes an actor; and his actions, becoming imitative rather than self-expressive, are dramatic.

Is tribal cult, then, the origin of acting and thus of the drama? Aristotle sought the origin of drama beyond cult in the nature of man and found that imitation is instinctive in human beings. Laughter, the other major component of comedy, is also inherent. Indeed, man has sometimes been defined as the animal who laughs. The origin of comedy might be investigated more appropriately by the psychologists than by the anthropologists [2]. By studying people of all types to-day, the psychologists might discover the nature and the source of the comic spirit and dramatic form. From one point of view, the fountainhead of comedy is internal and not external, and comedy is born anew with every clown and spectator.

Even if the psychologists should succeed in explaining the human love of imitation and laughter, the origin of comedy would still elude us because of the difference between dramatic literature and theatrical performance. Theatrical performances of an impromptu or ritualistic kind—actors who sang, danced, mimicked, improvised a few words or simple incident —might well have arisen and developed separately from dramatic literature—the comic treatment of character or situation in poetry or prose. We might then say that true comedy originated at the moment when a dramatist first composed words and designated action for others to convey to an audience. If such a moment ever existed, no trace of it remains. Like the explanations of the anthropologists and psychologists, it is hypothetical and not historical.

A seemingly more substantial starting-point would be the eleven extant comedies of Aristophanes. Beginning with his characters, plots, comic devices, costumes, masks, metres, and vocabulary, we could trace them back to their sources in the earlier comedies and in non-dramatic poetry and prose, dancing, music, and art. Next, his ideas would need to be studied in relation to contemporary Greek culture and to his artistic intention. The dangers of this method are that indebtedness may be stressed to the exclusion of originality, and history may be distorted through the reversal of its natural direction. The early history of Greek comedy should guide us toward the understanding of Aristophanes. The problem then still remains. At what point does a history of Greek comedy begin?

A practical solution may be found by accepting an inscription that a man named Susarion invented the first comic chorus early in the sixth century. If one stops to question who Susarion was and where he lived and how or in what sense he invented a comic chorus and what the comic chorus was like, the solution crumbles into controversy. But, after acknowledging the uncertainties and obscurities, one may still find a modicum of probability sufficient for a starting-point. A turning-point would perhaps be a more accurate phrase, for Susarion could have been a comic dramatist only because seventh-century poets had already composed in a comic vein, semi-dramatic performances had already been common in Greece, and the time was ripe.

The sixth century was one of social and political revolution and great artistic and intellectual advance. By 600 B.C. the Mediterranean world had been explored and most of the Greek colonies which encircled the Mediterranean and Black Seas had been established. Trade routes connected the cities on the mainland and the Ionian coast with their colonies in Spain, southern France, Italy, Sicily, Thrace, southern Russia, Egypt, and Africa. With the trading of raw for manufactured products and with more extensive commerce, barter became impracticable; and coinage spread rapidly throughout Greece in the sixth century. Industry grew and flourished, but the changing values caused agricultural unrest with the small farmers, in particular, oppressed by debts and the injustice of aristocratic landowners. A few attempts were made in the seventh century to relieve their distress by legislation, but no lasting reform was accomplished in Attica until Solon. A few tyrants, too, had gained power in the seventh century, perhaps by means of the rising usefulness of money, but the most famous lived in the sixth century [3].

By 600 B.C. most of the forms and metres of Greek poetry had been created. The myths and legends of the Greek peoples were being transformed into epic poetry. The *Iliad* and *Odyssey* as separate and individual epic poems were probably in existence though their form and provenance are a tangled and thorny thicket of controversy which cannot be entered here. More is known of Hesiod, for he tells us in his *Works and Days* of the miserable village, Ascra in Boeotia, in which he lives, of the wickedness of his brother, of the deceitfulness of women, and of all the hardships farmers encounter. His *Theogony*, with its lists of gods and their attributes and its many myths, is one of our most valuable sources of information about early Greek religion [4]. These four poems in dactylic hexameter—two epic and two didactic—became the Bible of later Greece, the storehouse of wisdom to which one looked for advice about war and farming, political statecraft, and daily conduct [5]. Even the comic poet turned to them for themes and characters [6].

For comedy, the most important early poet is Archilochus [7]. He lived in the late eighth century in Paros, a soldier of fortune and a servant of the war god Ares. He sang that his spear was bread and wine and bed (frr. 1, 2). He also 'knew the gifts of the Muses' and was renowned in later Greece for his musical innovations and metrical versatility [8]. Though he did not create the elegiac and iambic measures, his genius created the mood they retained for centuries. In fact, the iambic metre became synonymous with invective, and the name Archilochus proverbial for those who practised invective [9].

Only fragments of his poetry remain, but even in these few words and lines we can perceive the bitter scorn and ridicule which reputedly caused the suicide of one victim. He objects to generals who are tall, straddling, and vain and to lewd, fat-ankled women (frr. 58, 184). In another verse form he invokes an elaborate curse upon an untrustworthy friend:

> driven out of his course by the waves; and at Salmydessus may the top-knotted Thracians seize him bare of friendly [kinsfolk] there to eat the bread of servitude and fill the measure of many ills, seize him frozen with the cold; and may he have upon him much tangle of the surges, and his teeth be chattering, as he lies on his belly like a dog, helpless on the edge of the surf, spewing out the wave. This I fain would behold, because he wronged me and trod a covenant underfoot, he that was once my friend [10].

Nor does he hesitate to mention by name Lycambes and Hipponax (frr. 94, 97B).

The wit of Archilochus has overshadowed both in ancient days and in our own his moral earnestness and religious fervour [11]. He calls upon his desolate townsmen to listen to his words (fr. 50); and in other fragments counsels endurance of grief, trust in the gods, modesty in victory and patience in defeat (frr. 9-13, 56, 66, 104B). Athena, Ares, Hera, Demeter, and Poseidon are all mentioned, and he beseeches Hephaestus to listen to his supplications, (fr. 75). Zeus he addresses as Father of the Olympians, Ruler of Heaven, who sees the righteous and unrighteous deeds of men and beasts alike and brings all things to fulfilment (frr. 74, 88). The family of Archilochus had been closely associated with the worship of Demeter, and Archilochus himself composed a hymn to Heracles which became the victory chant of the Olympian games [12]. He also says that he can lead the Lesbian Paean, the hymn of Apollo, and 'the beautiful song of the lord Dionysos, the dithyramb', when 'his mind had been struck with the thunderbolt of wine' (frr. 76, 77).

The leader of a Greek chorus was not simply a poet. He

needed to be a musician and dancer as well. The close association of poetry with music and the dance from the earliest times in Greece cannot be sufficiently emphasized. The flute or lyre accompanied the singing or recitation of elegiac and iambic verses, and almost all the Greek poets were known in later days as much for their contributions to musical knowledge as for their words. Choral lyrics were more fully developed in Sparta and in other Dorian states than in the Ionian cities, but Homer mentions five—the dirge, hymn to Apollo, processional wedding song, the hyporcheme, and a maiden-song—others were popular later [13]. Like other forms of Greek poetry, these choral lyrics were largely religious in origin [14]. Even the iambic invective, which in its scurrility seems to us wholly secular, was intended to purify the community by driving out wrongdoers and by averting evil.

Apollo, the patron god of poetry, is the archetype of Greek poets [15]. He is the god of music, to whom the lyre is particularly sacred, and the god of the dance, especially the hyporcheme (a song accompanied by a mimetic dance). He is also the god of prophecy, foretelling what is good and warning of evil. Above all, he is the god of healing [16]. The Greek poet was a medicine-man, not only soothing personal anxiety but strengthening and advising the people in a time of national distress [17]. In these manifold tasks he was guided by the Muses, upon whom he called for inspiration and support with sincere religious belief. The occasions for which he composed were usually religious, for the national festivals were dedicated to the gods, and marriages, funerals, and even banquets were religious ceremonies. The poet naturally, therefore, sang of the myths of the gods and invoked their presence [18]. The immorality of some of these myths strikes the Christian reader perhaps as blasphemous; but the Greeks with their anthropomorphic gods would consider only as blasphemous and atheistical the denial of the traditional attributes of the gods. The craftiness of Hermes was accepted much as was the skill of Hephaestus.

The poetry of the seventh century amply illustrates these manifold functions of the poet. In Sparta, at her cultural apogee during this century, two poets won renown though both were said to have come from foreign lands. Tyrtaeus, the lame school-master from Athens (?), stimulated the soldiers to valour and was credited with the victory over the Messenians [19]. His elegiac praises of martial prowess were probably sung as the men marched to the flute. Alcman, a Lydian slave, wrote delicate and beautiful lyrics for Spartan maiden choruses (fr. 1). His description of the sleeping mountains reveals his sensitivity to nature (fr. 36). More significant for the history of comedy are three less well-known fragments. In two fragments he personifies rather than deifies abstractions, a step toward drama from the myth. Fortune is 'the sister of Good Order and Persuasion and the daughter of Forethought' (fr. 66). His taste for metaphor took a comic turn when he said that the name for a man was 'Say-Much', and for a woman 'Glad-at-Everything' (fr. 27) [20].

In Ionia the most important follower of Archilochus was Semonides of Amorgos, who wrote elegiac reflections on the evils and shortness of life in somewhat the same manner as Mimnermus of Colophon, but is best known for his denunciation of women [21]. He not only echoed Hesiod's statement that nothing is better than a good wife nor worse than a poor one (fr. 6); he also wrote a long iambic poem in which he compared types of women to a pig, a vixen, a bitch, earth, sea, a she-ass, a cat, a mare, an ape, and a bee (fr. 7). The last, at least, is complimentary to the sex, but Semonides concludes with the generality, 'Zeus has made this the greatest evil, women', and with a description of the harm wives do their husbands.

SUSARION

The poetry described above was the literary heritage of Susarion, born into a world slowly emerging from a closed village economy and hereditary power into commerce with distant lands and personal independence leading to democracy. The earliest record of him is on the Parian Marble, *c.* 260 B.C. [22]. Here it is stated that a chorus of kômôdoi (comic actors or comic poets) was established in Athens by Icarians, Susarion having been the inventor, and that the first prize was a basket of dried figs and gallons of wine. Icaria is a small Attic village. The date for Susarion is between 581-560 B.C. The Greek competitive spirit made a prize indispensable, and no more suitable one could be found for revellers than wine.

The fragment ascribed to Susarion and other references to him are found only in somewhat dubious sources of our era. This is the fragment:

> Listen people! Susarion says these things,
> The son of Philinus of Megara, a Tripodiscian,
> Evil are women. But nevertheless, fellow demesmen,
> It is not possible to live in a home without evil,
> For both to marry and not to marry is evil [23].

According to one late writer, Susarion was married to a faithless woman who deserted him. He went into the theatre during a Dionysiac festival and recited four of the above lines. Other authorities credit Susarion with the invention of iambic, paralleling the invention of comedy by Epicharmus and tragedy by Thespis. One even substitutes Susarion for Epicharmus [24].

The historicity of Susarion and the authenticity of his lines have both been denied, and with reason. He is not mentioned by Aristotle; he is not named by anyone until three hundred years after his lifetime; and all other notices are centuries later. Moreover, our records are inconsistent. The Parian Marble calls him an Icarian, and the Ionic dialect of the fragment would confirm his Attic origin, but the second line says that he is a Megarian. Perhaps he was a Megarian who moved to Icaria, but more probably the second line was added later by Megarians to bolster their claim to be the inventors of comedy. The last line is without doubt a later addition, for it is preserved in only one document.

Another account of the origin of comedy, popular among late writers and sometimes connected with Susarion, describes an early rustic comedy of social protest [25]. A group of farmers had been treated unjustly by the citizens of the town. One night soon after the townsmen had gone to bed, these farmers came into the streets in which the malefactors lived and accused them of their crimes, though without mentioning their names. The next day the neighbours, discussing what they had heard on the previous night, decided that the culprits should be openly reproached in order that they might be ashamed and cease from evil-doing. They compelled the accusers to speak in the theatre for the good of the city. The country people, through modesty and fear, rubbed wine lees on their faces as disguise, and then publicly denounced their oppressors. The undertaking was successful, for it brought the injustices to an end.

These late and dubious sources have been presented, because they indicate clearly the type of evidence with which the historian of early Greek comedy must deal. Vase-paintings are early, but they need interpretation. Aristotle in the fourth century should be our most reliable witness; yet he was aware of several theories current in his day and confessed his ignorance of the early history of comedy. To treat any evidence as incontrovertible truth is impossible; but to reject it as merely fiction would leave us empty-handed. All evidence must be accepted for what it is—legend which may contain a kernel of truth though the shell is not historical fact. If the meaning of our documents is consistent with what we know of the sixth century, we are as near to an accurate picture of early Greek comedy as we can come.

The legends about Susarion I interpret as follows: early in the sixth century crude rustic performances were enacted in the market-place of the Attic village, Icaria; similar performances were held in Megara; and these performances consisted of iambic invective arising from private grudge or social protest. To test the truth of this interpretation, we should discover everything possible about Icaria, Megarian drama, iambic poetry, and agrarian discontent.

THE DIONYSIAC RELIGION

Icaria, a small village in central Attica, was historically unimportant, but closely linked with the early history of the drama through Thespis, the reputed founder of tragedy, and through one myth. The god, Dionysos, under whose auspices all Athenian plays were produced, was first welcomed to Attica by Icarius, the eponymous hero of the village [26]. Icarius suffered martyrdom at the hands of those who had drunk the wine of Dionysos and had been maddened by it. Later, another and this time successful attempt was made to introduce the god to Athens. Pegasos of Eleutherae, a small village on the road from Boeotia to Athens, was the apostle of the god. The Athenians at first resisted, but when they were stricken with disease they appealed to the oracle at Delphi for help. Apollo advised them to accept Dionysos, reminding them of the former visitation of the god at Icaria [27].

Dionysos played such an important part in the history of Greek drama that a knowledge of his myths and worship is essential for an understanding of comedy. He was in origin a Thraco-Phrygian god, son of Semele and Zeus. According to an Orphic legend, he was twice-born. First he was born of Semele and Zeus. Then in his infancy he was torn to pieces and eaten by the Titans, but was reborn from the thigh of Zeus. As a grown god he is usually portrayed richly dressed in a long chiton with himation, holding a cantharus or wine-cup, and encircled with the fertile vine. All accounts indicate that he arrived late in Greece, perhaps about 500 B.C., and that his worship was accepted by the Greeks only after violent opposition.

Dionysos is rarely mentioned in the earliest literature. Hesiod describes him in the *Theogony* (940-7) as the 'brilliant' and 'gladsome' son of Semele and Zeus and 'golden-haired' husband of Ariadne: in the *Works and Days* nothing is said of him even in discussions of wine [28]. Homer, too, knows little of him, recounting only the myth of Lycurgus in a passage which may well be a late interpolation. Even so, it is worth quoting in full because it is typical of the myths and legends which circulated in Greece during the sixth century.

> The son of Dryas did not live for long, the strong Lycurgus, who fought with the heavenly gods. Lycurgus pursued the nurses of the maddened Dionysos over the hallowed mountain Nysa. They all together cast down to the ground the sacred objects of Bacchic worship, stricken by the ox-whip of the murderous Lycurgus. Dionysos in terror dove beneath the waves of the sea, and Thetis received him into her bosom. Strong trembling seized him because of the loud shouting of that mortal. (*Iliad*, VI, 130-7.)

The cowardice of Dionysos, which seems so ungodlike to us, is consistent with his character. He is a god of ecstasy, sensitive and highly emotional, who naturally could not endure the whip and loud shouts of an unimaginative and brutal man. This god of joy appealed particularly to women. In the quotation above they are called nurses, but elsewhere Maenads (mad women). Men, on the other hand, especially those in authority, were opposed to his worship and tried to keep the women from it [29].

The opposition of the authorities is not surprising, for the Maenads went up into the mountains at night with torches and practised strange rites. From Athens and Thebes, Sparta and Argos, the same story is told of the introduction of Dionysiac worship and its consequences, an echo perhaps of actual occurrences. Pentheus of Thebes was murdered by his frenzied mother and her comrades in punishment of his *hybris* in resisting the god. The daughters of Eleuther were driven mad by the god and released only when their father instituted rites in his honour. The daughters of Proetus were also maddened, some say by Dionysos, but healed by Melampous, a priest of Dionysos, who was most famous for his cure of the Argive women. Stricken with insanity, they wandered around the countryside until the desperate Argives hired Melampous to heal them despite his demand for half the kingdom. This Melampous, according to Herodotus, taught the Greeks the name and rites of Dionysos and the procession of the phallus [30].

Dionysos appears in these legends in two distinctive but closely linked roles. As Bacchus, he leads human beings into madness; this madness is the ecstasy of communion with the god and the essence of his worship. In the emotional excitement aroused by wine, song, and dance on the dark mountainsides, the worshipper loses himself and partakes of divinity. In contrast, as Dionysos Lysios he releases his followers from the madness he has himself sent; he is the Deliverer [31]. This ecstasy of communion must not be confused with the madness which strikes the god's opponents. This is *ate*, folly or delusion, and *hybris*, insolence, which being evil work for destruction and may cause death.

The growth of the drama out of this religion is not difficult to understand. The loss of identity which the worshipper of the god feels in his devotion is a counterpart of the loss of identity the actor necessarily must experience in order to assume successfully the personality of a dramatic character. Imitation is thus the basis of religion as well as drama. Moreover, both comedy and tragedy spring naturally from the worship of Dionysos. To his followers the god brings the wild self-abandonment and joy which are essential for the comic outlook upon life; to his opponents he brings punishment and pain for their defiance, the tragic flaw which leads to downfall. Thus Dionysos may well be considered the spiritual origin and psychological source of Greek drama [32].

Dionysos might never have conquered Greece if he had not had the support of Apollo [33]. He was worshipped with Apollo at Delphi, sharing his temple and acting as the chief deity in residence for the three winter months. He may indeed have preceded Apollo, and later, Hellenized by the most Hellenic of the gods, become more acceptable to a civilized society. At any rate, in historic times these two gods, seemingly poles apart in disposition and attributes, were often united. They shared the paean and the dithyramb, and the arts of healing and purification [34]. Song, dance, and acting thus were linked in religious cult long before they were united in plays, and ecstasy and serenity were linked with one another [35].

The Delphic oracle by its recommendations could encourage the Greek states to institute new cults. Athens, for example, refused to accept Dionysos until commanded to do so by the oracle. Later, Athenian Thyiades, women votaries of Dionysos, went to Delphi to join the Delphian Thyiades in the trieteric festival of the god [36]. At Athens itself the union of the state with the new god was symbolized by the marriage of the Queen Archon to Dionysos, performed at the Anthesteria each spring [37].

When once the cult of Dionysos was accepted by the authorities and incorporated into the state religion, his worship was expressed mainly through choruses and processions. The phallus, symbol of fertility, played an important role in Dionysiac worship. Herodotus (II, 49) says that Melampous introduced the phallic procession into Greece from Egypt with other Dionysiac practices. The Egyptian origin is unacceptable, but the Egyptian rite described is authentic. A flute-player led the way, followed by women singing to Dionysos and carrying a human puppet with a large phallus. This tallies with the phallic procession which constituted a large part of the Rural Dionysia in Attica. In the *Acharnians* of Aristophanes Dicaeopolis celebrates the Rural Dionysia with his family. His daughter goes first carrying a basket with the sacrifice: then comes the slave Xanthias bearing the phallus; and finally Dicaeopolis brings up the rear singing the phallic song. He addresses Phales, comrade of Bacchus and fellow-reveller, and asks him for release from troubles and from battle and for peace.

Two phallic choruses illustrate even more clearly than the processions the religious character of these Dionysiac rites. The Ithyphalloi, wearing the masks of drunken men, garlands, and a special tunic, marched in behind the phallus and sang a song asking the worshippers to make room for the god. The Phallophoroi wore garlands of ivy and pansies but not masks. In iambics they promised to sing a new song for Bacchus and then scoffed at the bystanders [38].

These phallic rites were not in origin obscene; they were deeply religious, though in a manner alien to the modern Christian. They had the double function of increasing human fertility and purifying the community [39]. Their importance in the history of comedy is attested by Aristotle, who said that comedy originated with the leader of the phallic chorus (*Poetics*, 1449a). Though these choruses were not dramatic, because the members of the chorus did not lose their identity nor act in accordance with an assumed character, the seeds of later comedy were there: the procession, costume, song, and satire.

Tragedy as well as comedy was a product of the Dionysiac religion. Although our knowledge of the forerunners of tragedy is scanty, we do catch glimpses in the sixth century of dithyrambs, satyr-plays, and tragic choruses performed in honour of the god. The dithyramb, in Athens a circular chorus of fifty men or boys, was particularly sacred to Dionysos, but was also associated with the paean of Apollo and with Apolline centres like Delos and Delphi [40]. The Greeks believed that the word *dithyramb* meant 'through two doors', referring to the double birth of the god, and that its original purpose was to celebrate the god's births—first from Semele and secondly from the thigh of Zeus [41]. However, from the remark of Archilochus that he knew how to lead the dithyramb (fr. 77) and from other evidence, we may suppose that it began 'as a revel song after wine' [42].

Probably in the days of Archilochus this revel song was spontaneous, because, according to Herodotus (I, 23), Arion in the late seventh and early sixth centuries was the first to compose dithyrambs, to name them, and to teach them in Corinth. Arion came from Aeolian Lesbos to Periander's court in Corinth. The role of the Greek tyrants in attracting foreign poets and in encouraging Dionysiac cult is worthy of note. The sixth century was an age of tyrants, and much of the artistic and intellectual achievement of the period was attained under their aegis.

Arion is also said to have been the first to introduce tragedies [43]. Although his priority is doubtful, the early connection of dithyramb with tragedy is also attested by Aristotle's statement that tragedy had its origin in the leaders of the dithyramb (*Poetics*, 1449a9). Elsewhere Aristotle says the dithyramb has the same effects as the Phrygian mode and the flute—*ὀργιαστικὰ καὶ παθητικά* (*Politics*, VIII, vii, 1342a, b). These words cannot be merely transliterated as *orgiastic* and *pathetic*. The first means secret rites and was most commonly applied to the rites of Bacchus; the second means sensitive, passive, capable of feeling. A hymn of this nature could conceivably develop into tragedy.

That tragedy passed through a satyric stage, as Aristotle also says (*Poetics*, 1449a9), is less easily understood [44]. Does he mean that tragedy succeeded the satyr-play or that it was *like* a satyr-play—boisterous and obscene—in its early days? And what did Herodotus mean by 'tragic' when he tells us (V, 67) that Cleisthenes, the tyrant of Sicyon, early in the sixth century, transferred the 'tragic chorus' from honouring the dead hero, Adrastus, to the cult of Dionysos? Did Herodotus use 'tragic' in the sense common in his day of *serious* or in reference to the original meaning of *tragos—goat*? The goat was the sacrificial animal of Dionysos, and the prize for a winning tragedy so that one might expect early 'goat-choruses' to be danced in his honour: but, curiously enough, the satyrs in fifth-century Athenian plays had the legs and tails of horses, not goats.

What then can be the relations between goat-choruses in Sicyon and horse-choruses in Athens?

No answers satisfactory to all historians of tragedy have yet been found, but fortunately the understanding of comedy does not rest upon a solution to these vexatious problems [45]. It is sufficient to note that in the sixth century the precursors of tragedy—the dithyramb, satyr-play, and tragic chorus—whatever their relations were to each other or to the tragedy of Aeschylus, were at any rate related to Dionysos.

The vases of the sixth century provide us with the best evidence for the spirit of Dionysiac worship as it was expressed in revelry or the *kômos* [46]. Dionysos and his followers, the Maenads and satyrs, were very popular with the vase painters. Dionysos is pictured in his boat surrounded with dolphins, in his vineyard, with his consort Ariadne, with Hermes, holding a wine-cup or a bowl for mixing wine, and playing the cithara for dancing Maenads and satyrs. Maenads and satyrs are frequently portrayed dancing together in a continuous frieze around the vase or dancing in groups of two or three. An Athenian oinochoe (wine-jug) has preserved for us a vivid picture of a human *kômos*. In the centre a slave is dipping wine from a crater into a cantharus. On one side of him a bearded man is playing the double flute, while on the other a bearded man is dancing. Behind the latter sits a man drinking wine, and opposite him another man is reclining upon a cushion. At the extreme right a sick youth is being carried away. Doric vases are often decorated with bands of revellers, sometimes nude and ithyphallic, following a flute-player [47].

Dionysos was by nature the patron god of the drama. His life from the day of his birth was marked by conflict, the essence of the drama, and the spirit of communion and possession which he aroused in his worshippers was akin to the spirit which transforms a man into an actor. When the first wild frenzy sweeping over Greece had been subdued into cult, the choruses and processions in his honour contained the seeds of tragedy and comedy. The flute, the instrument with which Dionysos excited the emotions of his worshippers, accompanied not only the early dancers of the dithyramb and later tragedy and comedy but also the soldiers as they sang on the march or at a feast. The poets, composing these songs, looked to the intoxicating Dionysos for their inspiration. Thus poet and musician, dancer and actor, and the audience were all united under the patronage of Dionysos.

Nowhere is the influence of Dionysos more marked than in the words springing from his religion and still bearing unconscious testimony to his power. *Tragedy* is, in origin, the 'goat-song' sung at the sacrifice to the god [48]: *comedy* is the 'revel' danced by his followers. Dionysos is the god of death and of re-birth: he punishes the proud who refuse to sacrifice to him; he gives his devotees the ecstasy of joy—joy in music, dancing, and wine.

DORIC FARCE

A rival etymology for *comedy* was proposed by the Dorians in the fourth century in support of their claim that they were the originators of the drama. Aristotle presents their argument as follows:

> The Dorians lay claim to both tragedy and comedy. The Megarians in Greece say that comedy began during the days of the democracy: those in Sicily point out that Epicharmus was a poet there long before Chionides and Magnes. Some of the Dorians in the Peloponnese claim even tragedy. They make the names their proof. For they say that they call the villages *kômae* but the Athenians *demes* and that comedians are not derived from *kômazein* (to revel) but from *kômae* (villages) because comedians, being slightingly treated by the city people wandered out among the villages. Moreover, they say that their word for *do* is *dran*; the Athenians *prattein*. (*Poetics*, 1448a.)

Neither *drama* nor *comedy* comes from the Doric dialect, but the falsity of these etymologies does not discredit the existence of some kind of dramatic activity among the Dorians at an early time. Other sources indicate that primitive farces were frequently acted among the Dorians as early as the sixth century.

Among the Spartans the actors were called *deikelistai*, a word interpreted by later Greeks as *mime players* or *masks* [49]. Their exhibitions were primitive. 'Someone imitated in the vulgar tongue people stealing fruit or a foreign doctor speaking in dialect.' Similar low farces were performed in Thebes by *ethelontai* or *volunteers*; and later in Italy by *phlyakes* or *babblers*. Scenes from this Doric drama may have been depicted on sixth-century Corinthian vases. One vase, in particular, shows on one side four thieves rejoicing in the wine they have stolen while the owner threatens them with a stick. On the other side, two thieves lie in the stocks—wine-jugs near by, but out of reach. The costumes of the men on these Corinthian and most Doric vases are burlesqued by padding and indecently decorated with an exaggerated phallus [50]. The pictures may have been drawn from real life or mythology rather than from the theatre. We can only say for certain that the vases illustrate the Doric sense of humour.

Masks found in Sparta suggest another kind of performance. These masks, dating from the first half of the sixth century, have been discovered in the shrine of Artemis Orthia, a fertility goddess. They are probably votive copies of masks worn by participants in a ritualistic dance [51]. It may have been akin to the ritualistic dance in honour of Artemis in Elis called the *kordax*, a dance which later became lascivious. Aristophanes accuses Eupolis, a contemporary playwright, with having introduced a drunken old woman dancing the *kordax*, a character already used by another contemporary, Phrynichus (*Clouds*, 553 ff.). He boasts that he himself has never resorted to dragging in a *kordax*.

Megara was also a Dorian city, situated in mainland Greece between Attica and Corinth, with colonies in Sicily. Sicilian comedy will be discussed in the next chapter in connection with its first dramatist, Epicharmus. Mainland Megarians retained the tradition of comic performances in the days of the democracy which began in 581, a date which tallies closely with that of Susarion, also associated with Megara. Although there is no confirming evidence for this sixth-century Megarian farce, the freedom offered by a democracy makes the acting of comedy at that time not improbable [52].

In the fifth century this Megarian farce was viewed by the Attic playwrights with scorn. Ecphantides said, 'I am ashamed to make a Megarian comedy' (fr. 2). Eupolis describes a joke as 'licentious and Megarian and very cold' (fr. 244). Aristophanes tells the spectators not to expect any jokes stolen from Megara (*Wasps*, 57).

The relationships between Dorian farce and Attic comedy are difficult to determine because the farces were probably impromptu productions, the actors saying whatever they wished [53]. Probably they relied mainly upon action and gestures. Only in Sicily and Italy did dramatists give the dignity of written lines to these sketches, and even there the known authors of mimes and phlyakes, as these farces were called in later times, may be counted on the fingers of one hand —Epicharmus in the late sixth century, Sophron in the fifth, Rhinthon and Sopater in the fourth and third. Except for Epicharmus, these authors did not influence Attic comedy. No name was ever associated with the farces produced on the Greek mainland even by the ancients, who seldom missed an opportunity of attaching names to literary forms or events, no matter how erroneously.

The absence of names is all the more surprising because of the long history of farce. The costume of the padded body and large phallus reappears on third-century Italian vase paintings of the phlyakes actors, and the primitive childish humour depending upon indecency, deceit, physical abuse, mockery of foreigners, and the burlesque of myth was popular for centuries. Dramatists of any century might witness these productions, and, if they lacked invention or discrimination, might borrow characters, episodes, or costume. Thus the detection of similarities between comedy and farce yields no reliable clue to the date or manner in which comedy was contaminated. For example, the repudiation of Megarian farce by fifth-century Attic playwrights may be interpreted either as the departure from conventions inherited from a sixth-century influx of farce or as scorn for a vulgar, although unfortunately popular, contemporary drama in a rival city.

The least questionable testimony is that of vase paintings. In the early sixth century, Corinthian pottery was exported throughout the Greek world, carrying on it pictures of myths, scenes from daily life, and Doric revellers in their padded, phallic costumes [54]. Attic imports and imitations of these vases, fairly numerous early in the century, gradually gave way to the native black-figured ware which increased in popularity both at home and abroad, perhaps as a result of Solon's reforms [55]. The painters of this ware portrayed at first nude human revellers and then, turning to Ionia for inspiration, the Dionysiac *kômos* of Maenads, sileni, and satyrs [56]. The Doric figures disappeared from the Attic scene for a hundred and fifty years, reappearing on an Attic vase about 400 B.C. and shaped into terra-cotta statuettes of the fourth century [57]. Since at the same time the padded, phallic dancers and actors were favourite subjects for the terra-cotta manufacturers of Dorian Tanagra in Boeotia and the vase-painters of South Italy and Sicily, one wonders if Dorian influence might not have penetrated into Attica in the fourth century rather than surviving without record from early in the sixth [58].

Whatever may have been the exact relationship between Doric farce and Attic comedy throughout their long history, the farces in the sixth century certainly must have contributed to the development of Greek comedy. They familiarized the Greeks with dramatic performances; they provided clowns with the opportunity of perfecting the technique of comic acting; and they demonstrated the humorous possibilities of rudimentary situations, characters, and costumes. In a way they formed a testing-ground of popularity. Nowhere, however, do we find evidence that they contained seeds of growth or that they could be transformed into literature without the magic of some non-Doric artistry.

SIXTH-CENTURY POETRY

So much attention has been focused on native Attic *kômoi* and Doric farce that the culture of Lesbos, Sicily, and particularly of Ionia has been completely neglected by those looking for the origin of Attic comedy. Yet Ionia was the chief source of the materials and techniques used by the later comic poets. It was in Ionia that almost all the poetic forms were developed; and in Ionia philosophy and history began. The chief exceptions are the Aeolian Sappho and Alcaeus of Lesbos and a few Dorians. During the sixth century Ionians, fleeing from political difficulties within their cities or from invasions of hostile countries, travelled widely and emigrated in large numbers. The result was that toward the end of the century Ionic culture spread throughout Greece, Sicily, and lower Italy. Athens especially became a centre for this culture, for she had been the mother city of the Ionic migration centuries before and now welcomed back her emigrants [59].

From the Ionian epics, the *Iliad* and *Odyssey*, the dramatists learned much about characterization, plotting, suspense and discovery, and narrative technique. Aeschylus confessed his indebtedness, easy to perceive in his early plays which are more narrative than drama. The debt of comedy has been less commonly acknowledged though almost as important. The *Odyssey*, despite its tragic implications, is essentially comic in character and technique: the crafty hero, the romantic episodes, the humorous situations, and the structure with its repeated obstacles successfully overcome. The escape from Cyclops is the most obvious example of a humorous episode easily dramatized. The characters have the rudiments of a sense of humour although the objects are still primitive. Odysseus laughs at the tale of Ares and Aphrodite, and the suitors laugh at the discomfiture of Irus [60].

The epics were recited by rhapsodes before large audiences at the great religious festivals. This practice may have contributed to the growth of acting, for the rhapsodes and actors had much in common [61]. Both were interpreters of a poet's words; both wept or laughed to suit the feeling of the lines; and both in early days were themselves poets. Aeschylus was an actor and poet, for example, and the early rhapsodes composed preludes to their recitations. These preludes were usually short invocations to the gods, but sometimes the rhapsodes composed long hymns which could be recited independently of the epics. Some of the myths recounted in the Homeric Hymns suggest a changing concept of the gods. Dionysos, for example, is described as exacting a frightful vengeance upon pirates who kidnapped him. His transformation into a raging lion is accompanied by thunder and lightning [62]. He is as different here from the trembling god of the *Iliad* as the Dionysos of the *Frogs* is from his contemporary Dionysos of the *Bacchae*.

More important for comedy are the burlesques and parodies of myth. In the sixth century this burlesque was composed and received in the spirit of flippancy possible only to the true believer. The amusing hymn to Hermes, that babe in swaddling clothes who stole the sacred cattle of Apollo, is a good illustration of the humour the Greeks delighted in. Heracles is another comic favourite. One vase presents him killing

Egyptians by the dozen, and his gluttony became a stock joke, particularly in Dorian countries, for he was the tribal hero of the Dorians [63]. Odysseus was popular for his fertile imagination and easy plausibility. Two parodies of epic—the *Frogs and Mice* and the *Margites*—may be later in date; they are mentioned here because Aristotle believes that Homer wrote both the *Iliad* and the *Margites* (*Poetics*, 1448b). The Greeks had no difficulty in thinking that the same man could write a great tragic epic and a foolish comic parody, nor need we be surprised to find the Greek tragic dramatists finishing a trilogy with mythological burlesque in the form of a satyr-play.

The myths never failed to interest the Greeks, but they did not monopolize their attention. In the sixth century a personal poetry expressing the emotions and ideas of the poet emerged in full glory. The Aeolian Alcaeus and Sappho of Lesbos, Ionian Anacreon of Teos, Ibycus of Rhegium in Magna Graecia, Solon of Athens, and Theognis of Megara were poets of diverse countries, dialects, and personalities, but they had in common the Greek language, the varied metres of lyric, iambic and elegiac, and the desire to communicate their own feelings. Love was the favourite subject with most of them, but not to the exclusion of hatred and contempt, of religion, politics, and nature. The importance of their contribution to the art of the Athenian dramatists—both tragic and comic—should not be underestimated. These poets brought the art of self-expression to its zenith and left behind them not only a treasury of inspiring poems but a mine of metres, vocabulary, and imagery. The Aeolic use of the vernacular and of folk-songs, for example, formed a precedent for the later comic poets.

The lyric poets continued in the religious tradition of Greek poets. To Sappho, religion and love were as one, for she was a priestess of Aphrodite and leader of a thiasos in honour of the goddess. Her prayer to Aphrodite is an intense and vivid expression of the cult. Alcaeus, the poet, turned naturally to Apollo, the god of poetry, and to Hermes, the god of music, celebrating their lives in hymns. The light and witty Anacreon was drawn by nature and environment to Dionysos, for he was born at Teos, a centre of Dionysiac cult, and in exile went to Thrace, where he saw the Bassarids dancing in honour of the god. His religious poem is a prayer to Dionysos for help in a love affair. Finally, Ibycus the Sicilian, under the influence of his predecessor Stesichorus, composed lyrical narratives in which he retold the myths of gods and heroes. In other poems his gods were half turning into abstractions, portent of a change of great significance in the history of Greek literature [64].

Though these four poets were chiefly concerned with their own emotions, they could not escape involvement in the political upheavals of their native cities. Sappho fled to Sicily, probably when she was young, and Alcaeus to Egypt. Anacreon, after a short stay in Thrace, took refuge in Samos, at the court of Polycrates, whither Ibycus also came from Sicily. Alcaeus attacked Pittacus, the tyrant of Mytilene who had driven him out, with language more fitted for Archilochus, and Anacreon flayed a man named Artemon. Though Sappho did not to our knowledge write political poems, she was not above speaking contemptuously of her brother's mistress or wishing ill to some unknown woman. This invective is unpleasant to recall but as important to remember as those haunting lines of evening, the unpicked apple, the Pleiades, the nightingale, and violet, which seem in their natural beauty more fitting for these great lyric poets. Love and hatred, the natural world and the heavenly gods, were inextricably woven into the bright tapestry of Greek lyric poetry.

No important iambic poet succeeded Archilochus and Semonides until Hipponax at the end of the century with the possible exception of Phocylides. He is worth mentioning here only because his abuse of women and comparison of them with various animals echoes Semonides and parallels Susarion [65]. The seventh-century elegiac poets, however, found notable successors in Solon and Theognis. Elegy was in origin an Ionian metre, a song accompanied by the flute [66]. The combination of the rhythm and the flute music seemed to have been particularly appropriate for marching and for the gaiety of the soldiers' evening feast. (Since the flute accompanied fifth-century comedies, its early uses are worth noting.) In the sixth century Solon and Theognis were the pre-eminent elegists. They were aware of the Ionian elegiac tradition of conviviality as the amorous fragments ascribed to Theognis and a few of Solon's fragments show, but they also knew the didactic poems of Hesiod. Confronted with difficulties in their city states too serious for them to ignore, they converted the elegiac form into vehicles for their political opinions [67].

These difficulties originated in the increased use of money and the growing power of wealth, which revolutionized the political, economic, and social structure of most Greek states. In many Greek cities, tyrants with the help of money, the new moneyed classes, and the oppressed farmers seized control of the governments. In Megara the *demos* became strong enough to rule to the dismay of conservative aristocrats like Theognis. He had no love of tyranny, but he valued birth and thought wealth should be the prerogative of the noble. His poverty and the new democratic régime distressed him equally [68].

In Athens the plight of the small landowner and free labourer had become desperate. The farmer was obliged to mortgage his farm in order to obtain money for necessary purchases and thus became hopelessly indebted. The labourer, squeezed between stationary wages and rising prices, mortgaged his only possession—his body—and became enslaved. Revolution or tyranny would certainly have resulted had Solon not been made archon with extraordinary powers. This is not the place to discuss the value or extent of his reforms; he did alleviate the condition of the poor, ward off tyranny for a number of years, and mediate between the opposing forces [69].

As the first Athenian poet, Solon claims more of our attention. He had been nurtured in an Ionian culture, but he did not accept without question the Ionian philosophy of life when he adopted their dialect and metre. He enjoyed the pleasures of life for he wrote

> The works of the Cyprian [Aphrodite] are dear to me,
> And of Dionysos and the Muses who bring happiness to men.
> (fr. 20.)

yet he rejects the melancholy with which the famous Mimnermus had moaned the shortness of youth and the horror of old age [70]. He advised Mimnermus to hope that death would not come until he was eighty, and in his poem describing the ten stages of man's life he places the prime of life between the ages of forty-nine and sixty-three (fr. 27). During his own long and fruitful life as a soldier, reformer, and lawgiver, he spoke often to the Athenian people, exhorting them to fight for

Salamis, rebuking them for their lawless ways, warning them of the perils of greed, arrogance, and the false security of wealth. Concerned though he was with the welfare of his country, he was not without interest in his own reputation. His iambic lines contain a defence of his life and principles: his rejection of tyranny, his middle course between democracy and aristocracy, his just dealings with exiles, his own strength and firmness. Thus Athenian poetry began in public education and private justification yet not divorced from the joys bestowed on man by Aphrodite, Dionysos, and the Muses.

All these sixth-century poets were turning from the epic simile to the more dramatic metaphor. Homer and Hesiod used metaphors, but they preferred similes, and they deified ideas like Panic and Strife, instead of personifying them [71]. The difference between deification and personification is hard to perceive in Greek literature: it rests upon the distinction between mythology and metaphor, and in an anthropomorphic religion this distinction is seldom clear. Nevertheless, the two may be separated: for example, in Hesiod's *Theogony* (901), Eunomia, Dike, and Eirene (Good Order, Justice, and Peace) are said to be the daughters of Zeus and Themis and are treated as gods, while Solon speaks of Eunomia more as Good Order [72]. Personifications by other poets of the sixth century include Chance, Hope, Poverty, Wealth, Desire, Virtue, Time, Persuasion, and Satiety. The relationship between metaphor (particularly personification) and the drama is clear. Personification is idea embodied in human form. The dramatist's success depends upon his ability to communicate his invisible concepts through the medium of human beings. Thus, it was not an accident that Aeschylus, the first tragic dramatist, was the greatest master of metaphor in Greek literature with the exception of his contemporary, Pindar.

The fable, too, is a kind of allegory, the concrete representation of ideas not in human or divine form but in animal form [73]. These animal stories were great favourites with the Greeks because of their shrewd twists, clever characterization, and sound morals. Among the poets Hesiod, Archilochus, Solon, Stesichorus, Alcaeus, and Ibycus refer to fables indicating that fables were popular even before Aesop had become famous. Aesop was a Phrygian slave who lived during the middle of the sixth century. Few facts are known of his life, though many legends clustered about his name. He was supposed to have been a slave on Samos, then attached to the court of Croesus in Lydia, and finally a traveller in Greece. After his death, all Greek fables were ascribed to him and his name affixed to all the collections. The Greeks loved animals and observed their appearance and habits closely, as their art attests; they also used them as disguises for political advice and individual education.

No one could possibly hope to describe the rich complexity of the sixth century even if many volumes were at his disposal, and certainly these few pages can only suggest the swift pace, the extraordinary vitality, and the profundity of the period. The exhilarating new religion, the shock of economic revolution and sudden political upheavals, the slower growth of democracy and individualism, and the expansion of the intellectual world touched the lives of everyone. In the centre of this activity was the Greek poet, participating in the life around him as a priest, teacher, healer, prophet, and boon companion of his people.

These manifold functions of the Greek poet deeply affect the nature and form of later Athenian comedy. Anyone searching for the origin of Greek comedy would do well to begin with these functions and then examine the contributions made by lyric, elegy, and iambic to music, metre, and poetic diction, by epic, myth, allegory, and fable to the development of characters, episodes, and themes, and by Doric farce to dancing and acting. Next he might investigate the Dionysiac religion, its 'cultic' practices, the psychological phenomenon of ecstasy, and the manifestation of the comic spirit in burlesque, parody, and satire. Finally, he should study the first posing of the problems which were later to concern the Athenian dramatists: poverty, wealth, good government, democracy and aristocracy, tyranny, and women. In this multiplicity he might find the origin of comedy.

Where does Susarion, the first comic poet, fit into the complexities of the sixth century? He may have lived in a village connected by myth with the patron god of drama and the home of the first tragic actor, Thespis, or he may have lived in the home of Doric farce. Like the other iambic writers—Semonides and Phocylides—he used the Ionic dialect and spoke slightingly of women. The open venting of private grudge and public wrong was typical of the period. Of Susarion's wife we know nothing, but we do know that Attic villages during his lifetime were seething with justifiable discontent. We also know that simple little semi-dramatic performances were common all through the Greek country districts.

I say semi-dramatic advisedly, for as yet there is no trace of a dramatist. Susarion spoke in his own person, not as a dramatist does through characters. The Doric farces, too, were not composed by dramatists but improvised by the actors. There were no professional actors but only amateurs; no theatre but the market-place; only the beginning of an audience to take the place of fellow worshippers or revellers. The productions were still in the primitive artistic stage of the line and the circle—the procession and the circular chorus. Not until the end of the sixth century did a more advanced theatre develop and a comic dramatist appear—the theatre in Athens under the tyrant Peisistratus and the dramatist in Sicily under the tyrants Gelon and Hieron [74].

NOTES FOR CHAPTER 1

1. The most notable investigation into the origin of comedy is that of Sir Arthur Pickard-Cambridge, *Dithyramb, Tragedy and Comedy* (Oxford, 1927). He has collected all the ancient evidence and weighed it judiciously. Whether or not one agrees with his conclusions, he has done a great service to the study of early drama. I should like at once to acknowledge gratefully a debt which my notes will soon manifest. His last book, *The Dramatic Festivals of Athens* (Oxford, 1953), contains material pertinent to later chapters and will be cited there.

Since Pickard-Cambridge has not provided translations, either *The Greek Theater and Its Drama* (Chicago, 1936), by Roy C. Flickinger, or Gilbert Norwood's *Greek Comedy* (Boston, 1931) would be most helpful to the non-classical scholar. Mr Flickinger emphasizes the theatrical performances of the drama; Professor Norwood stresses the importance of the comic poets other than Aristophanes. Both present clearly the sources of our knowledge of early Greek comedy without reconstructing the role of drama in sixth-century civilization.

An entirely different approach to the problem is represented by F. M. Cornford, *The Origin of Attic Comedy* (London, 1914). He has followed the example of T. Zielinski, *Gliederung der altattischen Komoedie* (Leipzig, 1885) in seeking the origin of comedy through the analysis of the structure of Aristophanes's plays. His hypothesis, 'that this canonical plot-formula preserves the stereotyped action of a ritual or folk drama, older than literary Comedy, and of a pattern well known to us from other sources' (p. 3), is akin to the explanation of the origin of tragedy presented by Jane E. Harrison and Professor Gilbert Murray. My aim, premisses, and methods differ so radically from Mr Cornford's that comparison is not really possible. Those who wish to pursue the subject should in fairness read his book and then the comments of Pickard-Cambridge, pp. 329-49, and Norwood, p. 6, n. 2.

Sir William Ridgeway in 'An Appendix on the Origin of Greek Comedy', *The Dramas and Dramatic Dances of Non-European Races in Special Reference to the Origin of Greek Tragedy* (Cambridge, 1915), not only rejects Mr Cornford's hypothesis but also the belief that comedy was religious in origin.

2. Norwood believes that the origin of comedy is really the province of the psychologist and that we must begin with 'stating the time, place, and circumstances of the first comic drama reported by our authorities'. (pp. 1-2).

3. In addition to the standard histories, P. N. Ure's *The Origin of Tyranny* (Cambridge, 1922) and 'The Outer Greek World in the Sixth Century', *Cambridge Ancient History*, IV, 83-123, should be consulted for detailed accounts of the political, social, and economic background of the period.

4. *Hesiod, The Homeric Hymns, and Homerica* (trans. Hugh G. Evelyn-White, Loeb Classical Library, London, 1926).

5. Werner Jaeger, *Paideia: The Ideals of Greek Culture* (trans. Gilbert Highet, 1st ed., Oxford, 1939), I, 34, 73.

6. For example, the *Odyssês* by Cratinus.

7. *Elegy and Iambus* (ed. and trans. J. M. Edmonds, Loeb Classical Library, London, 1931), II, 82-209. For further details see A. Hauvette, *Archiloque: Sa Vie et Ses Poésies* (Paris, 1905).

8. Plutarch, *Musica*, 28, lists the metres Archilochus supposedly invented and speaks of his innovation of reciting some iambic lines and singing others, an innovation which influenced tragedy and dithyramb. Edmonds, II, 88-9.

9. Diogenes, *Proverbs*, 2.95. Quoted by Edmonds, II, 84-5. Also

Pindar, *Pyth.* II, 55 f., describes him as growing fat in his harsh-tongued hatred.

10. Fr. 97A, trans. Edmonds, II, 151.

11. Jaeger, I, 118, has demonstrated the importance of the 'parainetic, or hortatory, aspect' of Archilochus. He cites Heracleitus, fr. 42, as evidence that the Greeks believed he was an educator.

12. Fr. 119 from Pindar, *Ol.* 9, and Aristophanes, *Birds*, 1764, and their Scholia. Edmonds, II, 174-7.

13. C. M. Bowra, *Greek Lyric Poetry from Alcman to Simonides* (Oxford, 1936), pp. 4, 19. The relevant passages in Homer's works are *Iliad*, I, 472-4, XVIII, 50-1, 314-16, 493, and XXIV, 746-7; *Odyssey*, VI, 102-8, VIII, 256-65.

14. *Ibid.*, p. 10.

15. *Lyra Graeca* (ed. J. M. Edmonds, Loeb Classical Library, London, 1927), III, 610; Jaeger, I, 166; Bowra, *Lyric Poetry*, p. 4.

16. Walter Addison Jayne, *The Healing Gods of Ancient Civilization* (New Haven, 1925), says on p. 224, 'The earliest traditions of Greek healing cluster about the divinity Paian, the Centaur Cheiron, and the hero Asklepios, with Apollo as an oracular deity in an honorary capacity.'

17. W. R. Halliday, 'Some Notes on the Treatment of Disease in Antiquity', *Greek Poetry and Life* (Oxford, 1936), p. 279, writes, 'the seers of post-Homeric tradition, Melampous, Polyidus, and the rest are ἰατρομάντεις "medicine-men", persons inspired with magical powers employed for healing and prophecy'.

18. Bowra, *Lyric Poetry*, p. 12.

19. C. M. Bowra, *Early Greek Elegists* (Cambridge, Massachusetts, 1938), pp. 39-70.

20. Bowra, *Lyric Poetry*, pp. 16-76, particularly 67. The fragments are numbered as they are in *Lyra Graeca*. In fr. 70 Alcman says that he knows the tunes of all the birds.

21. *Elegy and Iambus*, I, 210-37.

22. The complete texts of ancient sources about Susarion have been published by George Kaibel, *Comicorum Graecorum Fragmenta* (Berlin, 1899), I, 77-8. Translations and discussions of our evidence about Susarion are to be found by A. Körte in *RE*, s.v. 'Susarion'; Pickard-Cambridge, pp. 280-4; and Norwood, pp. 13-15.

23. Pickard-Cambridge, pp. 282-3, and Norwood, p. 14, reject this verse as spurious on the grounds of its sentiment as well as its

lateness. Norwood says that the passage 'shows a jaded sophistication incredible at the only date possible for Susarion'. Compare Hesiod, 'If you trust women, you trust cheats' (*Works*, 375, *Theogony*, 585-93); also Semonides above.

24. Kaibel, p. 77.

25. Schol. Dion. Thrac. p. 747, 25, and in a parallel form in *περὶ τῆς κωμῳδίας* quoted by Kaibel, pp. 12 ff. Pickard-Cambridge thinks, 'It is possible that this absurd story may preserve a grain of genuine tradition . . . but the evidence is too poor to prove anything' (p. 282).

26. Lewis Richard Farnell, *The Cults of the Greek States* (Oxford, 1909), V, 114 and *passim*, for the myths and cult practices of Dionysos.

27. Farnell, V, 116, from Paus. I, 2, 5, and Schol., Aristophanes, *Ach.* 247.

28. In two somewhat later works in the Hesiodic school Dionysos is the wine-god who brings both joy and grief to mortals, *Shield of Heracles*, 400, and *Catalogues of Women*, fr. 87.

29. Erwin Rohde, *Psyche* (trans. W. B. Hillis, 8th ed., New York, 1925), pp. 282-7; Farnell, V, 108.

30. Rohde, p. 287. Ancient sources: Aelian *V. H.* iii, 42; Paus. II, 18.4, VIII, 18.7, X, 6.4; Hdt. IX, 34, II, 49.

31. Rohde, pp. 285-7. See Farnell, V, 108, 'the religion promised immortality and release from bondage to sanity and measure. . . .' Also Jane Ellen Harrison, *Prolegomena to the Study of Greek Religion* (Cambridge, 1903), p. 426, 'All intense sorrow or joy is to him obsession, possession.' Cp. George Thomson, *Aeschylus and Athens* (London, 1941), p. 377.

32. Rohde, pp. 285-7. Also Margarete Bieber, *The History of the Greek and Roman Theater* (Princeton, 1939), p. 15. The chorus, separating from the leader, may become the prototype of the audience. See Harrison, *Prolegomena*, p. 569, and *Themis: A Study of the Social Origins of Greek Religion* (Cambridge, 1912), p. 46.

33. H. W. Parke, *A History of the Delphic Oracle* (Oxford, 1939), gives a full account of Apollo's assistance to Dionysos. Rohde, p. 288.

34. Rohde, p. 294, 'The prophetic age of Greece must have seen the origin of what later became part of the regular duties of the "seer": the cure of diseases, especially those of the mind; the averting of evil of every kind by various strange means, and particularly the supply of help and counsel by "purifications" of a religious nature.' Dionysos was called *'Ιατρός* (Plut. *Symp.* 3.1.3.)

35. Athen. XIV, 628a. 'Philochorus says that the ancients do not always sing the dithyramb as they pour the libations; but, when they have poured it, they sing to Dionysos in wine and intoxication, to Apollo with peace and orderliness.'

36. Farnell, V, 153, from Paus. X, 6.4, and X, 32.7.

37. *Constitution of Athens*, III, 5.

38. Athen. XIV, 621d, e, 622a-d. Pickard-Cambridge, 228 ff.

39. Farnell, V, 197 ff. believes that Dionysos was a vegetation-deity and that his winter festivals were designed to waken the powers of the sleeping god. Purification through satire is described, pp. 211-12. Also Farnell, V, 205, writes, 'And no doubt the φαλλός, which is itself deified in the hymn sung by Dikaiopolis, was regarded as possessed with the "mana" or influence of the god of life and also as evoking it.' 'If we can trust Suidas' citation in all its details, the wagon-vituperation at Alexandria was intended very seriously, as a sort of commination-service; for the wagoners drew up at the doors of the citizens and told them nothing but painful hometruths: the truthfulness must have added to the cathartic effect: even Aristophanes's ribaldry may have occasionally been true '(V, 212).

40. Pickard-Cambridge, pp. 5-18, 48, and chap. i, *passim*.

41. Plato, *Laws*, III, 700b.

42. Pickard-Cambridge, pp. 12, 19.

43. Solon, (R. M. 1908, p. 150), quoted by W. W. How and J. Wells, *A Commentary on Herodotus* (Oxford, 1912), I, 64. See Pickard-Cambridge, pp. 131-5, for other sources and comment about Arion.

44. Gerald F. Else, 'Aristotle and Satyr-Play', *Trans. Proc. Amer. Phil. Assoc.*, LXX (1939), 139-57, gives a full account of the evidence and the controversy and also an ingenious solution to the problem.

45. This is hardly the place for a bibliography of modern theories of the origin of tragedy. The evidence available, the methods, and conclusions run parallel for tragedy and comedy. Bieber, p. 7, n. 11, summarizes conveniently the various hypotheses and their exponents.

46. Margarete Bieber has published in *The History of the Greek and Roman Theater* the finest collection of illustrations readily accessible. See figs. 7-19, 33, 39, 139. For the continuous frieze of dancing Maenads, see Joseph Clark Hopkin, *A Handbook of Greek Black-figured Vases* (Paris, 1924), pp. 233, 235, 239, 265, 277.

47. Adolf Greifenhagen, *Eine attische schwarzfigurige Vasengattung und die Darstellung des Komos im VI. Jahrhundert* (Königsberg, 1929),

pp. 64-5, concludes from his study of the vases that human revellers preceded Dionysos and his followers who became popular among Attic painters about the middle of the sixth century. For the human *kômos* see Hoppin, p. 145.

48. The varied interpretations of tragedy are cited by Pickard-Cambridge, pp. 149-66. He concludes, p. 165, 'and *τραγῳδός* may well mean (as has often been held) the "singer at the goat-sacrifice" or (a very ancient view) the "singer for the goat-prize" '.

49. Athen. XIV, 621-2, is our chief ancient source. He quotes from Sosibius of the fourth century B.C. and from Semus of the second. The choral phallic ritual and the farces are not distinguished by Athenaeus, although they are clearly different. In the former, the phallus is carried as a religious symbol; in the latter, it is worn and the religious symbolism is not apparent although it probably was religious in origin. For discussion of Doric farce, see Pickard-Cambridge, pp. 253-84, and Cornford, pp. 177-89. The *deikelistai* are interpreted by Pickard-Cambridge, pp. 228-31. Ancient sources are collected by Kaibel, pp. 73-6.

50. Bieber, pls. 84-5. Pl. 83 shows Dionysos returning with Hephaestus to Zeus.

The identity of the padded Doric dancers is a highly controversial subject. Humfry Payne, *Necrocorinthia* (Oxford, 1931), pp. 118 ff., presents the evidence, discusses the arguments for and against their being human beings, supernatural attendants on a deity, or personifications of a natural force (p. 120). He comes to the conclusions that the dancers were human beings, worshipping Dionysos (p. 121). Bieber, pp. 70-3, and Pickard-Cambridge, pp. 263-4, relying mainly on the names given the thieves, *Ὀφέλανδρος, Εὔνους*, and *Ὀμβρικός*, believe that they represent Dionysiac demons, perhaps the equivalent in the Peloponnese of 'the Ionic sileni and the Attic satyrs' (Bieber, pp. 70-1).

51. Pickard-Cambridge, p. 254. Heinz Schnabel, *Kordax: Archäologische Studien zur Geschichte eines antiken Tanzes und zum Ursprung der griechischen Komödie* (Munich, 1910), contends that the origin of comedy is to be sought in the Peloponnesian cult of Artemis and Dionysos. Charlotte Fränkel, 'Korinthische Posse', *Rheinisches Museum*, Second Series, LXVII (1912), 94-106, has examined this theory in detail and found it untenable.

52. Kaibel, p. 75, has collected the ancient evidence. In addition to the *Poetics*, quoted above, Aristotle speaks of it again in the *Nicomachean Ethics*, IV, 1123a21. The scholiast for this passsage is the source of the fragments quoted below.

53. Pickard-Cambridge believes that the iambic scenes in Old Comedy were derived from Dorian sources, but that the way in which Doric influence exerted itself cannot be traced (pp. 273-4). Cornford holds to the indigenous Attic origin of comedy with an ancient ritual the source of both comedy and farce. The fifth-century references to Megarian comedy he interprets as directed toward contemporary jokes rather than 'that they allude to any importation of Dorian Comedy into Attica a century or more before their time' (pp. 192-3). When Cornford wrote in 1914, he said that 'the present tendency is, thus, to derive nearly all the characteristic features of Aristophanic Comedy, except the *Parabasis* and *Exodus*, from foreign sources . . .' (p. 6). Cf. Bieber, p. 83. An exception is Greifenhagen, who questions Corinthian influence on Athens in the sixth century.

54. Ernst Pfuhl, *Masterpieces of Greek Drawing and Painting* (trans. J. D. Beazley, London, 1926), pp. 19-22.

55. Payne, *Necrocorinthia*, pp. 184 ff., with pls. 51 and 52 showing Attic imitations of Corinthian ware, including both naked and padded dancers. Payne writes, 'Padded dancers occur now and then on vases of other fabrics, but in some cases at least it seems natural to suppose that these non-Corinthian representations are the result of Corinthian influence in art and not in customs. . . . It is true that when we find them and their equivalents on Laconian vases we may suppose that they represent dances which actually took place at Sparta, for Laconia, as we know, was the home of burlesque dancing of various kinds' (p. 123). B. L. Bailey, 'The Export of Attic Black-figured Ware', *Journal of Hellenic Studies*, LX (1940), 60-70, suggests that Solon encouraged commerce and traces the spread of Attic vases during the sixth century.

56. Ernest Buschor, *Greek Vase-Painting* (trans. G. C. Richards, London, 1921), p. 66; Payne, *Necrocorinthia*, p. 124.

57. The Attic aryballos, now in Leningrad, is published by Bieber, who writes of it, 'In fact, an Attic vase painting of the fourth century (fig. 121) shows actors who might just as well have appeared in a Doric farce. Zeus is depicted with a follower who sits on his luggage, about which he is supposed to be making phortika, or low, vulgar, tiresome jokes. There is also represented a grotesque servant and two women' (p. 85). She has also published pictures of the terra-cotta statuettes, figs. 86-100 and 122-35.

58. T. B. L. Webster, 'South Italian Vases and Attic Drama', *Classical Quarterly*, XLII (1948), 15-27, is the most thorough study of the subject. His point is that the vases throw light on Middle

Comedy in Athens, either directly or through contemporary and analogous comic performances in Sicily. So far as I have been able to discover, all authorities agree that the actors in Attic comedies wore the Dorian costume with the phallus as a more or less frequent appendage, but there is no evidence that it was habitually worn as an inherited convention. It is grouped by Aristophanes in the *Clouds* with jokes about bald men, the *kordax*, an old man with a stick, torches, and cries of '*iou, iou!*', stale tricks used by his contemporaries and immediate predecessors. I believe that the vulgar farce with all its appurtenances of costume, character, situation, and jokes was a constant rival of the Attic comedy and that Attic comic poets yielded to its pressure and its proven popularity with one element among the Athenians with more or less frequency according to the weakness of their own originality and inventive powers.

Pickard-Cambridge in *The Dramatic Festivals of Athens* says, 'It is evident that the poets enjoyed complete freedom to clothe their choruses and their actors in accordance with the characters which they represented, but that the actor's dress often differed from that of real life by its gross indecency, the tight χιτών being cut short so as to show the phallos, and by the grotesque padding of the body' (p. 234). He cites literary evidence from the plays of Aristophanes and thinks his resolution of the *Clouds* did not last long.

59. Humfry Payne and Gerard Mackworth Young, *Archaic Marble Sculpture from the Acropolis* (London, n.d.), p. 56, write, 'In the decades immediately succeeding the year 550, the Ionian elements multiply; Ionian dress, in several forms, becomes universal; Ionian physical types, or at least an approximation to them, become common and Attic sculpture discovers an interest in surface decoration which can be traced far back in the East, but has no origin that we can detect in its own early tradition. And let us remember, at this point, that the time in question is the time of the first appearance of Ionic architecture in Athens; and of close political connections between Athens and Ionia.'

60. Walter Morris Hart, 'High Comedy in the Odyssey', *University of California Publications in Classical Philology*, XII (1943), 263-78.

61. Samuel Eliot Bassett, *The Poetry of Homer*, Sather Classical Lectures, XV (Berkeley, California, 1938), chap. iii. Ancient sources include Plato, *Ion*, 532d, *Republic* 395a, 602, 605; Aristotle, *Poetics*, 1462a15.

62. Homeric Hymn VII.

63. Gilbert Murray, 'Heracles, "The Best of Men"', *Greek Studies* (Oxford, 1946), pp. 106-26.

64. For texts, translations, and interpretations of Sappho, see Bowra, *Lyric Poetry*, pp. 186-247; of Alcaeus, pp. 141-85; of Ibycus, pp. 248-83; of Anacreon, pp. 284-316.

65. *Elegy and Iambus*, I, 168-81. In fr. 12 from Aristotle's *Politics*, he speaks of the city; in fr. 16 from the *Nicomachean Ethics* he says that all virtue is found in justice. The third fragment, from Stobaeus, a late source, compares women to dogs, bees, pigs, and horses. Phocylides foreshadows later thought in fr. 10, 'Seek your livelihood, and when you have your life, seek virtue.'

66. Bowra, *Greek Elegists*, pp. 5-6, 39.

67. Jaeger, I, 86.

68. *The Elegies of Theognis* (ed. T. Hudson-Williams, London, 1910).

69. E. E. Adcock, 'The Reform of the Athenian State', *Cambridge Ancient History*, IV, 26-58, and W. J. Woodhouse, *Solon the Liberator* (Oxford, 1938), p. 7.

70. J. M. Edmonds, 'An Account of Greek Lyric Poetry', *Lyra Graeca*, III, 614, says, 'The two streams Iambic and Elegiac unite for the last time in the first truly Athenian poet, the greatest instance of the poet as healer of public ills, Solon.' Also he comments that Solon's answer to Mimnermus points to the Ionian origins of Attic literature and represents the early use of poetry to criticize the poetry of another.

71. A. L. Keith, *Simile and Metaphor in Greek Poetry* (Menasha, Wisconsin, 1914), pp. 34-8.

72. Bowra, *Greek Elegists*, p. 85, Cf. p. 67 of *Lyric Poetry* and discussion of Alcman above.

73. *The Fables of Aesop* (ed. Joseph Jacobs, London, 1889), I, 204.

74. The date 530 is a round figure arbitrarily chosen to indicate a turning-point. It corresponds approximately to the founding of the Great Dionysia and to the birth of Epicharmus.

CHAPTER 2

ARCHAIC GREEK COMEDY: 530 TO 470 B.C.

THE semi-dramatic performances, the cults of the gods, the ideas and poetic forms of an earlier day did not cease to exist in any one year, nor were they even gradually supplanted during the last third of the century. Farces were enacted; Homer and Hesiod continued to be recited by rhapsodes; elegy and iambic retained their distinctive features. Yet the whole intellectual world was turning in new directions: turning on the one hand to purification of soul, body, and belief and on the other to observation of the world of nature and human life. The trend toward purification can be clearly discerned in iambic poetry, the new mystery cults, and the sceptical philosophers; the trend toward the immediate world is just as evident in occasional poetry, realistic vase paintings, political manipulation of religious festivals, and Ionian scientific investigations. Both these trends had far-reaching effects upon the nature and form of Greek comedy, directly through the Dionysiac festival and indirectly through the development of characters and technique.

Simonides, the great elegiac poet, and Hipponax, the virulent iambic poet, exemplify the changes which were taking place. They were both thoroughly conversant with the traditions of their art at the same time that they perceived new possibilities. Simonides, born on the Ionian island Ceos, travelled widely during his long life, visiting Thessaly, Athens, and Sicily [1]. His religion was the conventional one of respect for the Olympian gods, submission to fate and the mutability of life, and the recognition of the inevitability of toil, trouble, and death. In this he followed Mimnermus and earlier elegiac poets, but unlike them he wrote for specific occasions of new and diverse kinds. He was, in fact, the first known poet of victory and festal songs [2].

Throughout the sixth century national festivals had grown in popularity, until at the turn of the century Greeks from West and East participated eagerly in the contests. The most famous, were of course, the Olympic games; but the Isthmian, Nemean, and Pythian festivals were well attended also, for the Greeks loved athletics, chariot races, music and above all the excitement of rivalry and the honour due the victor. It is extremely important for the modern reader to understand this deeply ingrained national Greek habit of expressing grief and joy and reverence for the gods through contests in order that he may understand both the dramatic contests instituted by Peisistratus and the lyric poetry of the late sixth century. The victors were welcomed at their homes with choruses sung and danced in their honour, composed by Simonides, Pindar, Aeschylus, and Bacchylides—the finest poets of the day. These same poets also celebrated the great national victories of the Greeks over the Persians and Carthaginians in the fifth century and wrote the epitaphs of the men who won those victories.

In sharp contrast to these poems fostering national pride is the work of Hipponax, a snivelling beggar, who scarcely moved from his birthplace, Ephesus [3]. He seems like an unworthy successor of Archilochus, complaining of cold and hunger, begging Hermes for a cloak, carping at petty enemies (frr. 16, 17, 18, 11). But signs here and there of realistic caricature suggest that he may well have contributed to the art of Aristophanes, and his vocabulary confirms this. Words, not found before his time, crop up again and again in the fragments of Cratinus and later comic poets [4].

The chief contribution Hipponax made to the development of Greek comedy lies, however, in another direction. He was the first of the iambic poets to state explicitly the purpose behind iambic poetry—the purification of the city by the scourging of evil. In a remarkable series of fragments (4-10) he describes the ritual of the *pharmakós*, the scapegoat who is sacrificed for the atonement of others. The *pharmakós* stood with figs, bread, and cheese in his hands and was struck seven times upon the penis with branches and squills (fr. 10). Hipponax is the first to use the word *pharmakós* with this meaning and accent [5]. Earlier the word with another accent had simply meant a *medicine* and then a *cure*. Nothing marks more clearly the deep gulf between the conservative, aristocratic Simonides and the man of the street, Hipponax, than their use of this word. Simonides simply thinks of Zeus as the cure of all things without any perception of the need for purification (fr. 100), while Hipponax was conscious of a deeper level of human experience. Later comic writers found much to admire in the beauty and serenity of Simonides, but their art is deeply rooted in the tradition of Hipponax.

The growth of a moral conscience and a desire for personal salvation led to a dissatisfaction with the Homeric gods which persisted side by side with their worship as long as Greek culture lasted. This dissatisfaction was expressed in three ways; in the mystery cults, in the rejection of impurities by the philosophers, and in state organization and control. All three were influential in shaping the course of Greek comedy and must, therefore, be discussed here, though their full influence is not perhaps discernible until the plays of Aristophanes are read.

The religious revival took the form of two closely connected cults—Orphism and Pythagoreanism [6]. They resembled each other in the secrecy of their rites and books, which has prevented our full knowledge of their practices and beliefs, although we do know that they were never incorporated into the state religions and that their strongholds were Sicily, Italy, and Athens. Both promised the believer personal salvation and purification through abstinence. This purification should not be confused with Christian purity of heart. In Greek days it tended to be a physical matter of obeying such odd taboos as not eating beans.

The Orphics were particularly important for the history of comedy, for they worshipped the god Dionysos. To them he was not Dionysos Lysios, nor Bacchus, nor Iacchus, child-god of the Eleusinian mysteries, but Dionysos Zagreus. This is the cult name attached to the myth of the god's birth, death, and re-birth. According to this myth the Titans rended the son of Zeus and Persephone and ate the raw flesh. Zeus in his anger destroyed the Titans and then gave his child a second birth. Man grew from the ashes of the Titans with the mixed nature of the Titans and the god, doomed to repeated incarnations until he can be released from the wheel of birth. Orpheus was the legendary priest of the cult, an ancient poet and prophet about whom many stories were told. Like Dionysos he was said to have been torn to pieces by angry women, and like Apollo he was a musician. In historic times men imitated him by posing as prophets, by reciting oracles, and by selling charms. Aristophanes pictures them with disdain and even ridicules their rites of initiation, but many Greeks of note—Plato, Aeschylus, and Pindar for example—were deeply affected by the cult, even if they were not initiates [7].

Pythagoras, founder of the cult named for him, was an historical figure, an Ionian from Samos who settled in Italy about 540 B.C. [8]. He was primarily a philosopher, scientist, and musician, and the god of his cult was appropriately Apollo. For the mythology of the Orphics he substituted a theory of numbers and musical harmony and taught that purification came through music and science. There is no need to discuss the political connections of Pythagoras; it is sufficient to note that the religious fraternity he organized became very unpopular and that the house in which his followers gathered was set on fire. A reminiscence of this outrage may be preserved at the end of the *Clouds*.

These two attempts to heighten the spiritual values of Greek religion won as many opponents as adherents. Two Ionians particularly revolted against both the old religion and the new sects. The first was Xenophanes of Colophon, like Simonides long-lived, a traveller, and a writer of elegiacs, but the direct opposite of Simonides in tone and work [9]. He was a satirist who attacked the whole anthropomorphic concept of the gods.

There is one god among gods and men,
Not like mortals in form or understanding. (Fr. 23.)

He sees all over, he thinks all over, he hears all over. (Fr. 24.)

But mortals think the gods came into being,
Wear their clothes, and have a voice and form. (Fr. 14.)

But if oxen or lions or horses had hands and could draw
And could perform rites like human beings, the horses
Would draw their gods in the form of horses, the oxen
Like oxen, and they would give them bodies exactly like their own. (Fr. 15.)

Homer and Hesiod ascribe to the gods all those things
Which are a disgrace and reproach among men—stealing,
Adultery, and deceiving one another. (Fr. 11.)

Xenophanes was not an atheist in the modern sense of the word, for he did believe in the existence of a god, but his denial of the anthropomorphic gods was blasphemous to the Greeks. In this he was a forerunner of some fifth-century philosophers; and in his belief that certain knowledge is impossible and that opinion fashions all things, he foreshadowed the later sophists. Yet he should be considered perhaps more as a satirical poet than a philosopher and remembered for his picture of a Greek banquet and for his attack upon the athleticism of his day (fr. 1).

His younger contemporary, Heracleitus, an Ionian from Ephesus, was a philospher and one of the most profound of the pre-Socratics [10]. Of his predecessors—Thales, Anaximenes, and Anaximander—little needs to be said here beyond an acknowledgment of their investigations into the nature of the physical world and attempts to solve the fundamental problem of reality. Heracleitus is best known for his statement that one cannot step twice into the same river, a vivid illustration of his belief in eternal flux, less well known for his belief that war is father and king of all things (fr. 53). Strife or the tension of opposites—male and female for example—produces all goods (fr. 80). Is this doctrine the origin of dramatic conflict? No, merely another expression of a commonplace Greek attitude which tended naturally to perceive division and contention. Heracleitus, like Xenophanes, was disgusted with the pictures of the gods given by Homer and Hesiod; he even went further and denounced the impostors of the new mystery religions, the rites of Dionysos, and his contemporaries—Pythagoras, Xenophanes, and Hecataeus (frr. 14, 15, 42, 57). 'Much learning does not teach understanding,' he wrote of them (fr. 40).

This contempt for the intellectual powers of others is noticeable in the works of Hecataeus, an Ionian, who prepared the way for the fifth-century historian Herodotus [11]. He began his genealogies with the remark that the ideas of Greeks are many and laughable. The implication is plain that Hecataeus will correct their mistaken notions. His geography illustrates, too, the growing interest in the immediate world which we find again and again in the first crude gropings toward scientific observation of the heavens and earth.

These, then, were the two principal trends of the late archaic period: the turning *from* the world to find personal salvation through abstinence, and the turning *to* the world to find the meaning behind its appearance, to glorify important occasions in the lives of men, and to portray even the insignificant moment. And everywhere there was a rising tide of scepticism and doubt, not only about traditions and conventions but also about the very foundation of knowledge. Fortunately for the history of Greece, an equally strong force was at work—the growth of the democratic city-state. Ionian culture contributed ideas, material, and forms to later comedy, but only Athens provided the milieu in which comedy flourished.

ATHENS AND THE DIONYSIAC FESTIVAL

Almost every Greek city was ruled at one time or another by a tyrant, and Solon, seeing this and fearing a similar fate for Athens, had sought desperately to prevent it. He succeeded only in staving off the day, and lived to see Peisistratus rule Athens. Peisistratus was twice driven out of Athens before his final return in 540, but then he managed not only to hold power until his death in 527 but also to bequeath it to his sons, Hippias and Hipparchus. They ruled together until Hipparchus was murdered in 514 and Hippias was expelled in 510 [12].

During these thirty years Athens enjoyed comparative peace both at home and abroad. Some economic and social reforms within the state minimized strife and discontent, and expansion toward the Black Sea prepared the way for the empire of the fifth century. Attracted by the security and comforts Athens could offer, Ionian refugees and Peloponnesian artists gathered at the court of Peisistratus and his sons, who eagerly welcomed them. Anacreon and Simonides lived in Athens, and two Peloponnesian musicians—Lasus of Hermione and Pratinas of Phlius—composed for the tyrant and taught the principles of music to aspiring poets. The Theban Pindar is said to have come to Athens to study under Lasus. In general, though, Ionian culture had the most influence in Athens about this time, as we can see from the change in dress and style of the statues [13]. The new red-figured pottery with its increasing portrayal of scenes from every-day life is indicative of the quickening spirit of Athenian art.

The most decisive steps the tyrants took to enhance their power and make allegiance to the city-state prevail over clan, tribe, party, or individual desires were those directed toward state control of religion. Hardly a cult or rite was left untouched. Peisistratus superintended the purification of the island of Delos, sacred to Apollo, and he built a temple at Eleusis, centre of the great mystery cult of Demeter, Persephone, and Iacchus. He instituted the Panathenaia in honour of Athene, with its famous procession. At this festival the epics of Homer were to be recited, not at the whim of the rhapsode but in the order determined by a committee. Onomacritus, a member of this committee, was an Orphic, and with Hippias worked on the corpus of Orphic oracles [14]. The mystery religions as well as the greatest of the Olympic gods were being brought under state control.

The Great Dionysia was destined to be the most famous of the works begun during the reign of the Peisistratidae. Before this time Dionysos had been worshipped at the spring festival of the Anthesteria, which had only a slight connection with the drama, at the Rural Dionysia in December, and the Lenaea in January [15]. The Rural Dionysia has already been described with its phallic ritual. Less is known of the Lenaea, though its antiquity is attested by the fact that it was under the control of the king archon, an early religious official. It did not come under state control until 442, and even then greater licence was permitted the comic poets there than at the Great Dionysia [16].

The Great Dionysia was not created at a single stroke, nor did it remain static; it developed gradually, beginning in the late sixth century, and during the fifth and fourth centuries the number and kinds of performances were changed to suit the times [17]. The festival was, however, always celebrated in the spring month, Elaphebolion, which corresponds to our late March and early April. The archon eponymous, one of the most important city officials, was in charge of all the arrangements. The earliest feature of the Dionysia may well have been the procession in which the cult image of Dionysos Eleuthereus was taken from his temple near the Acropolis out on the road to Eleutherae. The reader may remember that

Dionysos was thought to have come to Athens from the village of Eleutherae bordering Boeotia. This procession was in the sixth-century tradition, gay with music and dancing, colourful and noisy.

> The image was escorted by the *épheboi* marching in armour and followed by a brilliant procession, which included animals for sacrifice, unmarried girls carrying on their heads baskets containing the sacrificial implements, and the general public, men and women, natives and foreigners, all gaily attired, the rich driving in chariots, many of them wearing crowns or masks. In the market-place a halt was made while a chorus performed before the statues of the Twelve Gods. Then the procession pursued its course as far as the Akademia. The image was deposited on a low altar, hymns were sung in praise of the god, and the animals were sacrificed. . . . The celebrants were also supplied with wine, and, after the feast was over, they reclined by the roadside on beds of ivy leaves, drinking and merry-making. At nightfall the procession returned to the city by torchlight, but instead of being restored to its temple, the image of Dionysus was escorted by the *épheboi* to the theatre and set up on an altar in the middle of the orchestra, where it remained until the end of the festival [18].

This procession is akin to the phallic chorus of Phallophoroi and Ithyphalloi described in Chapter 1.

The image and thus the god were honoured in the Greek way with contests, those appropriate to Dionysos being tragedy, the satyr-play, dithyramb, *kômos*, and comedy, added to the festival in that order. Tragedy came first about 534 B.C., when Thespis of Icaria made the initial step of assuming a character not his own and answering the chorus [19]. Set and memorized speeches now displaced improvisation, but actor and poet were still one, and the actor's speeches were probably no more than monologues. These early tragedies, before Aeschylus introduced the second actor and thus made dialogue possible, must have been operatic rather then dramatic—relying for effect upon music, lyric, and dance and not upon conflict of character [20].

The contest of satyr-plays began probably between 534 and 501, introduced into Athens by Pratinas, a Dorian from the Peloponnese [21]. In later times he was known primarily as a musician and writer of hyporchemes, a kind of dance-poem, but he was also a dramatist and wrote fifty plays, of which thirty-two were satyr-plays. One fragment of his satyr-plays has survived, described by a modern scholar as follows:

> As I conceive the situation, we have a satyric drama in which, at the point where our Fragment takes on, someone (the protagonistes?) has just brought to an end a lyric strain easily apprehended by the audience as a parody of the 'New Rhythmic'. (The element of parody suggests forcibly the Old Comedy.) Upon the dying cadences of this strain the Chorus bursts in tumultuously, and deluges the protagonistes with invective bordering—to my mind; but we shall see—upon ribaldry [22].

The satyr-plays were usually lusty mythological burlesques full of primitive wood-spirits [23]. Favourite themes were the gluttony of Heracles, the slyness of Autolycus, and the free abandonment of the satyrs, particularly in their behaviour toward Iris, Pandora, and other maidens. One prominent theme is the freeing of those bound, betokening the god who liberates. Because the chorus was always composed of satyrs, the satyr-play retained its Dionysiac character longer than the tragedies and comedies. Its intense religious conservatism prevented growth or change with the result that the origin and history of the genre are obscure and only one complete play, the *Cyclops* of Euripides, has been preserved.

In 510 B.C. Hippias was expelled with the aid of the Spartans and the counter-revolution of Isagoras defeated. Cleisthenes came into power, as a democratic leader not a tyrant, and set to work reorganizing the political system of Athens. The old Ionian tribes, four in number, were replaced by ten tribes based on geographical units instead of birth. Other changes are of no concern here, but these new tribes provided choruses for the dithyrambic contests instituted in 510-9 or 509-8. Five choruses of fifty boys and five of fifty men competed, singing and dancing to the accompaniment of a flute in a circle around the altar. The dithyramb was always sacred to Dionysos and probably had originally dealt exclusively with his myths, but by the end of the sixth century the myths of other gods and heroes were celebrated.

The greatest poets of the period composed dithyrambs for these Athenian contests—Simonides, his nephew Bacchylides, and Pindar. From early in the history of the Dionysiac festival the Greeks were accustomed to hearing the finest lyric poetry side by side with the tragedies. Inevitably they must have compared the dithyrambic choruses with the tragic and later the comic choruses. A high standard of excellence was set which the dramatists could not ignore, though they were not in direct competition with the dithyrambic choruses. Only fragments of the dithyrambs of Simonides have been preserved, a misfortune in the light of his ancient fame. Simonides says that he won fifty-six dithyrambic contests, an astonishing achievement when we remember that he taught the chorus to sing as well as composed the words they sang. Moreover, he faced a formidable rival in Lasus of Hermione who had introduced dithyrambs in Athens [24].

After the dithyramb, the *kômos* was made an official part of the City Dionysia perhaps in 501 [25]. Reconstructions of the *kômos* have been attempted, but we actually know little of it beyond the slight evidence afforded by four Attic vases, 540-490 [26]. These vases depict revellers dressed as cocks and birds, as warriors upon dolphins and ostriches, and as knights on men disguised as horses. The choruses of Aristophanes's *Birds* and *Knights* have an honourable ancestry, which may be traced back to these sixth-century *kômoi*, although the actual appearance of the choruses in the theatre did not necessarily copy the pictures on the vases. The 'horses' would have found it difficult to dance with knights upon their backs. Perhaps the form and contents of the choral songs have the same origin as the animal costumes. (For example, the *kômos* may have taken the form of a choral parodos (entrance), a semi-histrionic *agon*, then a parabasis, and finally a recessional.)

The *agon*—a ritual fight or conflict—might have taken place between leaders of half-choruses before real actors were assigned to comedies [27]. The parabasis of Old Comedy may with greater probability be an inheritance from these early revellings. In the parabasis, current political and literary problems were tackled in a humorous way and individuals of notoriety assailed by name. Unfortunately, in the absence of any direct evidence about the nature of the *kômos*, it cannot with certainty be said to have contributed anything more than the animal choruses to the later comedies.

Not until 487-6 B.C. were comedies granted official recognition [28]. Even then the comedies, judging by their names, were hardly more than *kômoi*; and the two earliest Athenian comic poets, Chionides and Magnes, are shadowy figures [29]. Magnes wrote plays called *Birds*, *Gallflies*, *Frogs*, plainly reminiscent of the *kômoi*, and a play about Dionysos, patron god of the festival [30]. Of the *Harpers* and the *Grasscutters* we know nothing, and conjecture seems profitless; but his *Lycians* plainly points to the contemporary wars waged by the Greeks against the eastern peoples. Magnes was not a great playwright; and, though once popular, he could not hold public favour. Two new playwrights began to produce comedies—Cratinus about 453 and Crates about 450—and with them Old Comedy as a distinctive form came into existence.

Comedy was the last addition to the City Dionysia. After 487 B.C. the component parts of the great spring festival remained the same: the procession with the image of Dionysos Eleuthereus, dithyrambs, tragedies, satyr-plays, comedies, and the *kômos* [31]. The length of the festival is uncertain and may have varied from three to five days. The number of plays produced also varied. For most of the fifth century, however, four tragic poets produced three tragedies, and a satyr-play apiece, and five comic poets a comedy each. Whether the comedies were all presented on a single day preceding the tragedies or in the afternoons following the tragedies in the morning is a controversial question [32]. But whatever the number or order, the plays were always produced in competition. Judges were chosen by an elaborate method to ensure fairness, and prizes were awarded for first, second, and third place. The honour of victory promoted a keen spirit of rivalry, unashamedly manifest in the comedies.

The theatre of Dionysos, now visible on the side of the Acropolis, was built in the fourth century, but archaeologists have been able by their excavations to learn something about the sixth-century theatre. Warning, however, should be given that the history of the theatre is obscure and that little can be said of it with certainty. Probably before 500 B.C. the auditorium had not been built and the theatre consisted only of a large orchestra (dancing-place), a steep approach, and a small temple to Dionysos [33]. The contribution to the development of the theatre made by the archaic period was the orchestra—

an appropriate contribution for a people who held the chorus and the procession in such great honour.

The years 530-480 were certainly critical ones in the history of Athens. The tyrants, who did so much for the cultural and religious life of the city, were succeeded by Cleisthenes, who laid the foundations for the democracy with his political and social reforms. The great battles of Marathon, Salamis, and Plataea, in which the Persians were finally and decisively repulsed, brought Athens to the forefront as a leader of the Greeks and started her on the road to empire. As more and more citizens shared the responsibilities of government, the splendour of national festivals, and the glory of great victories, the city-state grew in importance until it satisfied all the needs of men. On these foundations Athens rose to the height of power and grandeur during the fifty years 480-430, mistress of an empire, unrivalled in the beauty of her architecture, sculpture, and drama. But before we turn to this period and Old Comedy, we must consider the life and works of the first comic poet, who was, oddly enough, not an Athenian but a Sicilian.

EPICHARMUS AND SICILY

The brilliance of Athens in the fifth century has cast a shadow upon the cultural achievements of other parts of the Greek world: Sparta in the seventh century, the Ionian coastal cities in the sixth, and Sicily in the first half of the fifth. The history of Sicily and particularly of Syracuse, a Corinthian colony, runs roughly parallel to that of Athens. During the sixth century the Greek cities in Sicily and Italy grew rapidly, and in their growth seriously threatened the economic power of the Carthaginians in North Africa. The invasion of Sicily by the Carthaginians in 480 B.C. coincided with the Persian invasion of the Greek mainland and met with a similar fate at the Battle of Himera. The decisive defeat of the barbarians gave a new freedom and security to the Greeks in Sicily and made possible a continued cultural advance [34].

The Greek cities were not ever, of course, free from war and political strife, but under the tyrants, Gelon and his successor Hieron, Syracuse gained sufficient strength to crush her adversaries and to achieve comparative peace within her borders. Before this time Sicily and southern Italy had not been devoid of a native culture. Stesichorus of Himera had converted mythological and epic material into choral odes, Ibycus of Rhegium had sung his lyrics, and Aristoxenus of Selinus composed iambic lampoons [35]. But the Ionian emigrants of the sixth century and the visitors at the Syracusan court in the fifth were chiefly responsible for the brilliance of west Greek civilization. Pythagoras, for example, came to Italy from Samos; Cynaethus, the rhapsode, recited Homer in 504 B.C. for the first time in the West, if we can believe the tradition [36]; and Ionian influence is apparent in Sicilian art.

The wealth of the Syracusan tyrants attracted poets from all over Greece. The wandering Ionian, Simonides, came, his nephew Bacchylides, and the Theban Pindar. They wrote odes celebrating the victories of the tyrants in the chariot races at Olympia and the other national festivals. Aeschylus came from Athens, bringing with him his tragedies. The philosopher and elegiac poet, Xenophanes of Colophon, spent much of his life in the West, part of it doubtless in Syracuse. Thus, though the city was Dorian—necessarily as a colony of Corinth—and the dialect spoken was Dorian, the culture of the court was Ionian. This was the court in which Epicharmus, the first known comic poet, lived; these his associates with whom he talked and for whom he wrote; and his work can only be understood in terms of this brilliant but imported civilization.

Little is known for certain of Epicharmus's life [37]. He was born probably about 530 B.C., but the place is variously reported as Samos, Cos, Megara Hyblaea, and Crastus. He might have been, then, an Ionian brought to Sicily as a child, or a child of a Greek colonist from Megara, or less likely a native Sicilian. Without doubt his early life was spent in Megara Hyblaea, a colony of mainland Megara, and he may have written his first plays there. The city was destroyed by Gelon in 483 B.C., and its inhabitants moved to Syracuse. Just when Epicharmus went to Syracuse is not known, but most of his life probably was spent there. The date of his death has been placed anywhere from 480 to 440 B.C.

Epicharmus was primarily a comic poet, and yet he was always closely associated with philosophers. He was said to have been a student of Pythagoras, a not unlikely story, though his plays offer no proof [38]. Only a few fragments of these plays have survived. They do show familiarity with the theories of his contemporaries, Heracleitus and Xenophanes [39]. Plato ranks him as supreme in comic poetry as Homer was with tragic; he must have read the plays with attention [40]. In fact, Plato was later accused by Alcimus of plagiarizing the ideas of Epicharmus [41]. The accusation rests upon forgeries, mistakes, and malice but confirms the impression that the plays were intellectual as well as humorous. Aristotle mentions Epicharmus twice in the *Poetics*, once in support of the Megarian theory about the origin of comedy and once as the first comic dramatist to develop plots. Late authorities ascribe to Epicharmus six forgeries, including poems on nature, medicine, and a collection of maxims made by Axiopistis. Though Epicharmus without doubt wrote only plays, the forgeries are plausible only if Epicharmus was something of a philosopher as well as comic poet [42].

Unfortunately, nothing is known of the circumstances under which his plays were produced. The Sicilian theatre, finished about 460 B.C., was similar to the one at Athens. It was there that *Women of Aetna*, by Aeschylus, was produced. But comedies do not seem to have been performed there [43]. Presumably, the plays were short sketches, needing few properties and no setting, acted by two or three men in the dining-halls of the tyrants, but this is merely presumption in the absence of definite information. Presumably, also, they resembled the farces acted in the Dorian cities of the mainland—Megara, Corinth, and Sparta. The facts that Epicharmus was claimed by the Megarians, that Syracuse was a Dorian city, and that the dialect of the plays is Dorian, all point toward the influence of Dorian farces on these plays.

Moreover, many of the plays are mythological burlesques, a form popular among Dorian peoples. Heracles, the great Dorian hero, is the subject of five plays by Epicharmus—*Alcyoneus*, *Busiris*, *Hebe's Wedding*, *Heracles and the Girdle*, and *Heracles aganist Pholos*. The fight of Heracles with the Egyptian king Busiris has already been mentioned in connection with vase paintings [44]. Three plays were about the crafty Odysseus—*Odysseus the Deserter*, *Odysseus Shipwrecked*, and the

Sirens. The first of these recounted the story of Odysseus's attempt to penetrate Troy before its capture and his decision to fabricate a story for the Greeks rather than risk his life. Other mythological burlesques include the *Philoctetes*, *Cyclops*, *Trojans*, *Amykos*, *Pyrrha and Prometheus*, *Skiron*, *Sphinx*, *Atalantae*, and *Revellers*. This last play was based on a myth also portrayed by vase painters. Hera had banished her son Hephaestus. In revenge he sent her a chair so cleverly fashioned that Hera was held in it. She sent for Hephaestus to loose her, but he refused. Finally, Dionysos went after Hephaestus, made him intoxicated, and escorted him back to heaven [45]. Two plays, the *Bacchae* and *Dionysoi*, were about the patron god of drama [46].

About half of Epicharmus's known plays fall into the classification of mythological burlesque, but this statement may give undue emphasis to his indebtedness to Dorian farce. Parody and mock heroism had been long popular in Ionia, and the work of Hipponax may have come West with the tide of Ionian culture [47]. Certainly the *Odyssey*, *Iliad*, epic cycle, and Homeric Hymns offered the comic poet endless material for his mythological burlesque, and he needed only to look about him to see real models for craft and gluttony. The Dorian farce may have contributed a technique, but its importance has been exaggerated. The true significance of these plays lies in the training they gave the dramatist when comedy was still in its infancy. With the characters and plots ready to his hand, he could concentrate his attention wholly on dramatic technique and language.

The other main classification into which the plays may be divided is the allegorical. Most of the remaining plays suggest by their titles that the characters were either abstractions or types. The two most obvious are *Earth and Sea* and *Logos and Logina* (*Masculine and Feminine Argument*). These must have consisted of arguments between the abstractions concerning their respective merits. The titles *Hope or Wealth*, the *Feast*, *The Islands*, and the *Pots* also suggest that the characters may not have been human. Judging the contents of plays by their titles is not a secure mode of procedure to be sure, but in the absence of significant fragments it is our only recourse. The *Rustic*, the *Megarian Woman*, and the *Ape* may have been comedies of type characters, and the following surely were: the *Snatchers*, and *Citizens* [48]. Three plays were perhaps religious in content if not in treatment—the *Choreutae*, *Pilgrims*, and *Victory*. The *Hip-joint* and the *Thirty Days* are enigmas.

In composing these plays Epicharmus had to rely entirely upon his own observations and reflection, so that they represent a decided step forward in the art of dramatic composition. To project an idea into human form, to make an inanimate object talk and act like a human being, to concentrate the distinctive features of a group of individuals into one typical character requires imagination and dramatic ability. Plots had to be constructed; and, while they were probably very simple and may have been merely a single conflict or series of conflicts, still they were original and not second-hand. Epicharmus was the first to compose new plots, as we learn from Aristotle (*Poetics*, 1449b5); and we should remember that this talent was first exercised in plays with abstractions and types.

Epicharmus was not, of course, the first poet to use abstractions. They had already been in vogue with Hesiod, Solon, and the lyric poets. Wealth and Hope were familiar personifications by the end of the sixth century, though Logos and Logina seem to have been invented by Epicharmus. The use of metaphor and personification was rising like a tide, and at the crest of the wave were Pindar and Aeschylus. At least eighteen personifications may be found in Pindar's poems and many more in the tragedies of Aeschylus [49]. Ideas and emotions—Fear, Truth, Courage, Shame, Desire, Satiety, Justice, Peace, Impiety, Sedition, and Good Order among others—gained new dimensions and new importance.

Pindar and Aeschylus were not the only exponents of personifications. It was an age of allegory and personification. Athens had deified Persuasion and Necessity according to Themistocles [50]. Simonides made a spirit of Tomorrow and was the first to personify Time [51]. Bacchylides speaks also of Time and of Pride, Justice, and Peace [52]. Even the philosophers were affected. The longest fragment surviving from the works of Parmenides, an Italian philosopher, is an allegory of the two ways open to man; and the two creative forces in the universe according to Empedocles are Strife and Love. Epicharmus must have known the poetry of the first four poets, and may have been familiar with the two philosophers, but he did not necessarily imitate their methods. Rather, the likelihood is that he thought with them in the current mode, and expressed himself in the metaphorical and allegorical terms of the day.

The use of one abstraction will illustrate this point. In the mythological burlesque, *Odysseus the Deserter*, Epicharmus wrote,

> Peace, the charming woman,
> Lives near to Moderation. (Fr. 101.)

The word here translated *peace* is not *eirene*, the opposite of war, but *hesychia*, the opposite of motion. It might better be rendered as *rest* or *quietness*. The Greek word *sophrosyne* cannot be adequately translated by Moderation, for it includes many of the connotations of chastity, prudence, temperance, not necessarily implied in the English word *moderation*. Sophrosyne is too common a Greek abstraction to be helpful; *hesychia* is rarer and more enlightening. Pindar uses it three times. He addresses Hesychia as a goddess at the opening of the eighth Pythian ode:

> Friendly Quietness, daughter of Justice which makes cities blest, holding the keys of council and of war, receive from Aristomenes the honour appropriate for a Pythian victory. You understand both how to give and to receive with gentleness and in true measure.
>
> But you, whenever anyone drives deep into his heart a relentless anger, step forth to meet him with rough hostility and thrust with power Arrogance into the brine.

The word appears again in a fragment:

> Anyone who wishes to make genial the community of citizens should seek for the bright face of great-hearted Quietness, driving from his heart hateful strife, for strife breeds poverty and nurses youth in hostility. (Fr. 109.)

Finally, Hesychia is twice invoked by Aristophanes, both times with the adjective *aganophronos* (of gentle mood) [53]. The Chorus in the *Birds* asks,

> What fine thing does not dwell here in the city with this man? Wisdom, Desire, Ambrosia, the Graces, and the lovely face of Peace with the gentle mood. (1318.)

This seeming digression has been necessary to show the quality of the personifications. They are not cold, lifeless, and dull, as we are inclined sometimes to consider abstractions; they are, on the contrary, 'manly' or lovely, graceful maidens with sisters, fathers, and mothers, with homes and activities. Pindar, for example, wrote of Corinth:

> Good Order dwells within and her sisters, the strong foundation for cities, Justice and Peace, the treasurers of man's wealth, the golden children of wise Themis. They ward off Arrogance, the rough-speaking mother of Insolence. (*Ol. XIII*, 6-10)

It was but a step from these poetic personifications to the dramatic characters of Epicharmus.

The reputation of Epicharmus as a philosopher rests upon fragments not drawn from known plays. This throws some doubt on their authenticity, though most scholars accept them. In one fragment he contradicts Xenophanes, who had written (presumably of his single god), 'He sees all over, he thinks all over, he hears all over' (fr. 24). Epicharmus countered with the line, 'The mind sees and the mind hears; other things are dumb and blind' (fr. 249) [54]. In a second fragment a character in Socratic fashion questions another, thus eliciting the Heracleitean doctrine of the flux—that men are never the same from day to day (fr. 170). The use of odd and even numbers as proof looks back to Pythagoras and forward to Socrates. The humble illustrations of the cock and hen and the flute-player are similar to ones used by Plato. That does not necessarily imply plagiarism. Both the dramatist and the philosopher must have recognized the value of concrete examples for clarity and vividness.

Epicharmus was, of course, essentially a comic poet, not a philosopher. The quotations referred to above are not part of a systematic belief but parodies of contemporary philosophies. He also parodied the poetry of Aeschylus according to a late notice, and perhaps of other poets (fr. 214). Though little trace remains, an interest in parody would complement his interest in burlesque, and the requisite feeling for words is clearly apparent in the surviving fragments. He is even accredited with the invention of the rhetorical figure, *climax* or *ladder*. Step by step one is led from festival to feasting, from feasting to drinking, from drinking to revelry, from revelry to swinishness, from swinishness to a lawsuit, from a lawsuit to a counter-lawsuit, and finally to chains, the stocks, and punishment (fr. 148). Thus does the laudable religious festival end in disgrace.

Almost all the verbal comic devices may be found in the fragments: puns, lists, comic names, long words and diminutives, oaths, and anachronisms [55]. They no longer seem very witty to-day even in Greek, and in English they are meaningless or dull; yet perhaps if we stretch our imaginations we can picture the ancient Syracusans laughing heartily at the oath 'by the cabbage', at the tripod with four legs, at the foolish fellow who mistook *g'eranon*, lover, for *geranon*, crane, and at the picture of Heracles devouring his dinner with a great rumble and clashing of jaws (frr. 25, 149, 87, 21). Food was a popular subject with Epicharmus, though the fact that most of these fragments came from a food anthology may partially explain this popularity. He mentions walnuts, almonds, kidneybeans, lentil soup, porridge, pumpkin, mushrooms, and lots of greens such as lettuce, fennel, cactus, and sorrel. Quotable epigrams like, 'You are not clever at speaking, but unable to be silent' (fr. 272), have become attached to the name of Epicharmus, and with them moral aphorisms so dear to the Greek heart, such as 'The gods sell good things to mortals at the price of toil' (fr. 287). How many of these are genuine, it is now hard to say, but it is not unlikely that he and his audience enjoyed pithy sayings both clever and moral.

The Greeks always spoke of Epicharmus as a comic poet, but they called his plays *dramas* and not comedies [56]. They clearly realized that these dramas were not comedies in the sense in which the word was applied to the work of Aristophanes and Menander. This distinction is justifiable when we consider how much the plays of Epicharmus lacked which is to be found in the Old Comedy of Athens. First of all, they seem to have been neither spectacular nor lyric. There was no chorus or *kômos*, very little if any dancing, only occasionally music. So far as we know, the metres used were iambic, trochaic tetrameter, and anapaestic, but no lyric metres at all [57]. Moreover, the plays were non-religious and non-political. The phallus, the indecency, the personal scurrility, which are signs of the ancient rituals and the traditional iambic purification, are entirely lacking. Political problems and important contemporaries are rarely mentioned [58]. Finally, the plays were not even completely dramatic. One fragment indicates that three characters were present on the stage at the same time, but the rest of the fragments are either monologues or duologues. The action seems often to have been reported in narrative rather than presented directly to the audience.

The plays of Epicharmus were not, then, comedies in a technical sense, but humorous sketches—burlesques of myths and legends, parodies of current philosophical ideas, portrayals of familiar character types, vehicles of comic word-play. He fused the two elements of Sicilian culture into artistic wholes: from the Ionians he took ideas, parody, and mythological and legendary material; from the Dorians he took the broad physical humour of farce; and he plaited these two strands into plays which caught and held Greek fancy for centuries.

His influence was not felt immediately in Sicily: Phormis, a contemporary, is hardly more than a name, and Deinolochus, said to have been either the son or student of Epicharmus, wrote only a few mock tragedies [59]. The later phlyakes are continuations of the Dorian mime and seem to show no signs of the civilizing influence of Epicharmus [60]. Theocritus in the third century, an admirer as his graceful epigram indicates, was his only true successor in his native land.

In Athens, however, Crates followed in his footsteps, and through him Epicharmus influenced the development of Old Attic Comedy. Other dramatic and comic performances—the *kômos*, satyr-play, phallic choruses, farce, and burlesque—were static, continuing for generations, even centuries, without change [61]. Only Athenian comedy was dynamic enough to transform itself from early ritual to political extravaganza, through mythological burlesque into a comedy of ethics. From Epicharmus to Menander, the history of Greek comic poetry is the history of Athenian comedy; therefore, we must now turn our attention to the formation of Old Comedy in Athens from 487 to 430 B.C.

NOTES FOR CHAPTER 2

1. *Lyra Graeca* (ed. J. M. Edmonds, Loeb Classical Library, London, 1931), II, 246-417; C. M. Bowra, *Greek Lyric Poetry from Alcman to Simonides* (Oxford, 1936), pp. 317 ff. Particularly important for comedy are his political views admirably set forth by C. M. Bowra, 'Simonides and Scopas', *Classical Philology*, XXIX (1934), 230-9. Bowra writes that Simonides 'absorbed the constructive ideas of his generation and preached them boldly to ears which he may well have found deaf to such an ethical appeal' (p. 239). In his *Lyric Poetry*, Bowra says, 'Simonides regarded himself seriously as a teacher' (p. 399). Some illuminating fragments follow. Fr. 32: 'No one without the gods seizes virtue, neither a city nor a mortal.' Fr. 95: 'The city teaches the man.' Fr. 100: 'Zeus alone is the cure of all things.' He was not without a sense of humour, as fr. 109, with its play on the letter *s*, proves.

2. See Sir Richard Jebb, *Bacchylides* (Cambridge, 1905), pp. 34-8.

3. The fragments have been published by Theodore Bergk, *Poetae Elegiaci et Iambographi* (Leipzig, 1915), II, 460-500. Cf. *Anthologia Lyrica Graeca* (3rd ed. Ernst Diehl, Leipzig, 1923-). Friedrich Jung, *Hipponax redivivus* (Bonn, 1929), points out the relations between Hipponax and Archilochus and Attic comedy. Cf. Gerhard in *RE*, s.v. 'Hipponax'. T. B. L. Webster, *Greek Art and Literature* (Oxford, 1939), p. 5, writes, 'At the beginning of our period realism and caricature are found in Hipponax of Ephesus, whose descriptions of everyday life form an intermediate stage between his predecessor Archilochus and the later writers of Sicilian mime and Athenian comedy.'

4. See the notes in Bergk following fragments 33, 35, 36, 38, 39, 41, 50, 59, 66, 70, 71, 74, 76, 84, citing parallels between Hipponax and Cratinus, Eupolis, and Aristophanes.

5. S.v. *φαρμακός*, *A Greek-English Lexicon* (compiled by H. G. Liddell and Sir Robert Scott, revised by Sir Henry Stuart Jones and Roderick McKenzie, Oxford, 1925-40). See Lewis Richard Farnell, *The Cults of the Greek States* (Oxford, 1909), V, 212, for katharsis and purification rites.

6. W. K. C. Guthrie, *Orpheus and Greek Religion* (London, 1935), *passim*, but particularly pp. 41, 46, 82, 115, 201, 204. Also Jane E. Harrison, *Prolegomena to the Study of Greek Religion* (Cambridge, 1903), chaps. 9-10.

7. *Clouds*, 250 ff., discussed by Guthrie, pp. 210 ff., and Harrison,

Prolegomena, pp. 512 ff. George Thomson, *Aeschylus and Athens: A Study in the Social Origins of Drama* (London, 1941), chap. 9, offers a full account of the cult in Athens and its relation to tragedy.

8. Fragments relating to the life and philosophy of Pythagoras are to be found in *Die Fragmente der Vorsokratiker* (ed. Hermann Diels, 5th ed. by Walther Kranz, Berlin, 1934), I, 96-105. Translations and comment are available in Kathleen Freeman, *The Pre-Socratic Philosophers, A Companion to Diels, Fragmente der Vorsokratiker* (Oxford, 1946), pp. 73-83. Also see John Burnet, *Early Greek Philosophy* (4th ed., London, 1930), chap. 2.

9. Diels-Kranz, I, 113-39; Freeman, pp. 88-104. C. M. Bowra, *Early Greek Elegists* (Cambridge, Mass., 1938), p. 107, writes, 'In Xenophanes of Colophon the Ionian intellectual movement found its poet, a man who put into verse a serious criticism of predominant beliefs and institutions and approached his subject with a fine appreciation of the human issues at stake.' Freeman, p. 90, says that Xenophanes was a 'travelling rhapsodist, and made his living in that way'. Her note for this follows: 'Burnet (EGP[4], p. 115) rejects this too lightly. If Xenophanes was not a professional rhapsodist, why did he complain of the excessive reward of the athlete "who is not deserving like me"? (B2).'

10. Diels-Kranz, I, 139-90; Freeman, pp. 104-32.

11. *Die Fragmente der Griechischen Historiker* (ed. Felix Jacoby, Berlin, 1923-43), I, 7, fr. 1. Cf. Herodotus, V, 36.

12. Herodotus is our chief ancient source for this period. For modern interpretation, see F. E. Adcock, 'Athens under the Tyrants', *Cambridge Ancient History*, IV, 59-82.

13. Adcock, p. 70, writes, 'The Athenians became more ready to assert their kinship with the Ionians. A hint of this may be seen in the fact that the figure of Theseus, the symbol of Athenian race-consciousness, appears more and more often on Attic vases.'

14. Herodotus, VII, 6; Pausanias, VIII, xxxvii, 5. Thomson says, 'It would seem therefore that Orphism was carried to Attica, as it had been to Corinth and the west, in the wake of industry and trade. It was an outgrowth of the urban revolution' (p. 154). 'For these reasons the Orphic movement is likely to have reflected the outlook of a dispossessed peasantry' (p. 155).

15. For the Anthesteria, see Sir Arthur Pickard-Cambridge, *The Dramatic Festivals of Athens* (Oxford, 1953), pp. 1-22; for the Rural Dionysia, pp. 40-52.

16. The festival of the Lenaea took place in the Attic month

Gamelion, our January and February. In the Ionic states Gamelion was named Lenaion. The festival was thus clearly of Ionic origin. The word is derived from *lenai*, mad women, equivalent of the Maenads. See Pickard-Cambridge, *The Dramatic Festivals*, pp. 22-40; Farnell, V, 108, 212-13; Arthur Bernard Cook, *Zeus: A Study in Ancient Religion* (Cambridge, 1914), I, 666 ff. Cook thinks that tragedy originated at this festival, p. 678. Cook's suggestion 'that Dionysos was conceived at the City Dionysia and born at the Lenaia' (p. 681), and again, 'a conception at the Anthesteria, a birth at the Rural Dionysia' (pp. 683-4), is not supported by sufficient evidence. See A. W. Pickard-Cambridge, *Dithyramb, Tragedy and Comedy* (Oxford, 1927), pp. 208-18, for criticism.

17. Pickard-Cambridge, *The Dramatic Festivals*, pp. 55-106.

18. Thomson, pp. 165-6.

19. The evidence for Thespis is presented by Pickard-Cambridge, *Dithyramb, Tragedy and Comedy*, pp. 97-121. The Marmor Parium is the source for the date of the first victory of Thespis. Plutarch, *Solon*, chap. xxix, tells an anecdote about Solon and Thespis, which, if true, must have taken place about 560 B.C. Solon objected to the lies Thespis was telling. Thespis was, thus, an actor as well as dramatist. Compare with Susarion.

20. Phrynichus was one of these early tragic poets, a predecessor of Aeschylus. Agathon in Aristophanes's *Thesmophoriazusae*, 160 ff., comments on the beauty of his person and his dramas. He also links him with the lyric poets Ibycus, Anacreon, and Alcaeus who, he says, were Ionic in dress and manner. In the *Wasps*, Aristophanes speaks of the μελισιδωνοφρυνιχήρατα (l. 220).

21. Ancient sources include Plutarch, *De Musica*, chap. xxxi; Pausanias, II, xiii, 5, and Suidas. Illustrations of satyrs and later satyr-actors are to be found in Margarete Bieber, *The History of the Greek and Roman Theater* (Princeton, 1939), figs. 20, 23-6. For modern comment, see Pickard-Cambridge, *Dithyramb, Tragedy and Comedy*, pp. 92-7, and Aly in *RE*, s.v. 'Satyrspiel'.

22. H. W. Garrod, 'The Hyporcheme of Pratinas'. *Classical Review*, XXXIV (1920), 134. Garrod has also published the text of the fragment. The works of Pratinas are also published in *Lyra Graeca*, III, 46-55.

23. Aly in *RE*, s.v. 'Satyrspiel', p. 246.

24. Pickard-Cambridge, *Dithyramb, Tragedy and Comedy*, p. 25, writes, 'Simonides was probably the most famous and successful of all the ancient writers of dithyrambs. In an extant epigram he claims to have won fifty-six dithyrambic victories.' Bowra, *Lyric*

Poetry, p. 334, says of Simonides and his dithyrambic victories, 'He was himself the teacher of the choir, as well as the poet. His choir was composed of men, not of boys. The natural assumption is that the majority of these victories were at Athens, since it was there that Lasos, under the patronage of the Peisistratids, had inaugurated dithyrambic competitions.' Cp. *Wasps*, 1410-11, for a hint of controversy between Simonides and Lasos.

25. This date depends on the interpretation of the inscription, *C.I.A.* ii, 971; iv, 971, on which the victories of the City Dionysia were recorded. Edward Capps, *The Introduction of Comedy into the City Dionysia* (The Decennial Publications, University of Chicago, 1903), p. 29, believes that the word *kômoi* means 'celebrations' and refers to the whole festival rather than to one part. What was new, then, in 502-1 was the choregic system, since dithyrambs and tragedies had earlier been produced. Pickard-Cambridge, *Dithyramb, Tragedy and Comedy*, pp. 94-5, thinks this likely if not certain. For further discussion, see Pickard-Cambridge, *The Dramatic Festivals*, p. 103 f.

26. Bieber, pp. 65-6, figs. 76-9.

27. This is the hypothesis of Pickard-Cambridge, *Dithyramb, Tragedy and Comedy*, pp. 240-53. 'Now it must be admitted without reserve that we have no direct evidence for the existence of the exact κῶμος which we want to explain the epirrhematic parts of comedy: but in truth the existence of a form so persistent in type as that of the Parodos-Agon-Parabasis structure can almost itself be taken as evidence for the existence of a κῶμος of a similar type before the Old Comedy (which combines this with scenes of a quite different origin) was produced: and along with this κῶμος sequence, we must postulate the existence of a conventional epirrhematic form—surely a very simple and natural form—associated with it.' (p. 243). Cp. Roy C. Flickinger, *The Greek Theater and Its Drama* (4th ed., Chicago, 1936), p. 46. Octave Navarre, 'Les Origines et la Structure Technique de la Comédie Ancienne', *Revue des Etudes Anciennes*, XIII (1911), 245-95, believes that a double *agon* was the essential feature of the *kômos*.

28. Capps, p. 29.

29. For texts of the fragments see *Comicorum Atticorum Fragmenta* (ed. Theodore Kock, Leipzig, 1880-88), I, 4-9. For discussion, see Gilbert Norwood, *Greek Comedy* (Boston, 1931), pp. 15-17.

30. Aristophanes, *Knights*, 518-25. tells us most about Magnes, citing him as an example of a comic poet who could not hold the Athenian audience, and transforming the titles of his plays into verbs.

31. Demosthenes, *in Meid.* 10, 'and in the City Dionysia the procession and the boys [the dithyrambs] and the *kômos* and the comedies and the tragedies'.

32. This controversy is ably discussed by James Turney Allen, 'On the Program of the City Dionysia during the Peloponnesian War', *University of California Publications in Classical Philology*, XII (1938), 35-42.

33. Bieber, p. 103. See also A. W. Pickard-Cambridge, *The Theatre of Dionysus in Athens* (Oxford, 1946), pp. 1-15.

34. J. B. Bury, *A History of Greece* (3rd ed. by Russell Meiggs, London, 1951), pp. 296-311.

35. For Stesichorus and Ibycus, see Bowra, *Lyric Poetry*. The two late notices about Aristoxenus are quoted by George Kaibel, *Comicorum Graecorum Fragmenta* (Berlin, 1899), I, 87. Epicharmus, fr. 3 (Kaibel) p. 107, mentions Aristoxenus. Nothing is known of him.

36. The evidence in favour of this date is presented by H. T. Wade-Gery, 'Kynaithos', *Greek Poetry and Life* (Oxford, 1936), pp. 56-78.

37. The ancient sources for the life of Epicharmus have been published by Diels-Kranz, I, 190 ff., and Kaibel, I, 88-90. For modern accounts, see Freeman, pp. 132 ff.; Pickard-Cambridge, *Dithyramb, Tragedy and Comedy*, pp. 353-63; and Norwood, pp. 83-6.

38. Pickard-Cambridge, *Dithyramb, Tragedy and Comedy*, pp. 356-7, quotes Plutarch and Diogenes Laertes as evidence. Freeman, p. 133, says, 'Epicharmus, one of the originators of comedy, has no claim to be considered a philosopher. He is said to have attended Pythagorean lectures as an "exoteric" student, though he did not join the inner fellowship, and to have expressed Pythagorean doctrines in his comedies, disguising them because of the tyranny of Hiero; but the surviving fragments of Epicharmus do not exhibit Pythagorean doctrine (the fragment quoted by Clement of Alexandria is clearly a very poor forgery), nor is there any reason to believe that the expression of philosophical views was dangerous under Hiero's regime.'

39. Frr. 1, 2, interpreted by Pickard-Cambridge, *Dithyramb, Tragedy and Comedy*, pp. 372 ff., and fr. 173.

40. *Theaetetus*, 152e.

41. Diels-Kranz, I, 195 ff. Cf. Pickard-Cambridge, *Dithyramb, Tragedy and Comedy*, pp. 377 ff., and Norwood, pp. 87 ff.

42. The forgeries are discussed by Pickard-Cambridge, *Dithyramb, Tragedy and Comedy*, pp. 363 ff., and by Norwood, pp. 90 ff.

43. Bieber, p. 258.

44. Pickard-Cambridge, *Dithyramb, Tragedy and Comedy*, figs. 47, 48, 49.

45. Bieber, fig. 83. See Pickard-Cambridge, *Dithyramb, Tragedy and Comedy*, pp. 390-1, for the representation of this story in art and literature.

46. Fr. 132, 'The dithyramb cannot be composed by a water-drinker,' links the god of wine with his song.

47. Athenaeus, XV, 698c, says that Hipponax invented parody and that Epicharmus, the Sicilian, used it a little in some of his dramas. Webster, p. 6, writes, 'From Ionia the tradition of realistic caricature spreads westward. Epicharmus, the Sicilian comic poet, is neither so sharp nor so stinging as Anacreon, but his description of a parasite is in the same line.'

48. Fr. 35, from *Hope or Wealth*, is spoken by a parasite, the first appearance of that long-lived character, Athenaeus, VI, 235e, f. The same source, X, 429a, says that Epicharmus first introduced a drunken man on the stage. See Pickard-Cambridge, *Dithyramb, Tragedy and Comedy*, p. 407, and Norwood, pp. 104-5.

49. Lewis Richards Farnell, *Pindar, Critical Commentary* (London, 1932), II, 467-8. Also Arthur Leslie Keith, *Simile and Metaphor in Greek Poetry* (Menasha, Wisconsin, 1914), pp. 79-133.

50. Herodotus, VIII, 111, 2.

51. *Lyra Graeca*, fr. 22; Keith, p. 72; Bowra, *Lyric Poetry*, p. 396 f.

52. Keith, p. 102. *Bacchylides*, ed. Sir Richard C. Jebb (Cambridge, 1905), pp. 175 ff., 296-7, 350-3.

53. Gilbert Norwood, *Pindar* (Sather Classical Lectures, XIX, Berkeley and Los Angeles, 1945), p. 266, n. 26, mentions the use of *hesychia* as one evidence that Pindar knew Epicharmus. The later history of this word is also significant. John H. Finley, *Thucydides* (Cambridge, Mass., 1942), p. 122, writes, 'Pindar uses the word, which means literally "tranquillity", to connote the poised and dignified way of life that is built on established position[1] and with two other virtually synonymous terms, σωφροσύνη and δικαιοσύνη, "moderation" and "justice", it has much this same connotation in the *History*. But it had also come to signify the oligarchic quietism just mentioned which offered an ever-increasing

[1] *Pyth.* VIII, 1; fr. 99 (Bowra).

contrast to the creativity of democratic Athens.' Similarly, R. A. Neil, 'Political Use of Moral Terms', *The Knights of Aristophanes* (Cambridge, 1901), pp. 208-9.

54. But Epicharmus, fr. 173 (Kaibel), seems to agree with Xenophanes, when he says, 'A dog would appear finest to a dog, a cow to a cow, a donkey to a donkey, a pig to a pig.' Werner Jaeger, *The Theology of the Early Greek Philosophers* (Oxford, 1947), p. 55, writes, 'The Sicilian Epicharmus . . . has left us some clever verbal fencing over the origin of things, in which one of his characters shrewdly criticizes the venerable Hesiodic *Theogony* because it speaks of Chaos, the ultimate beginning itself, as having come into being.'

55. Cp. a similar list in Pickard-Cambridge, *Dithyramb, Tragedy and Comedy*, p. 408.

56. Pickard-Cambridge thinks this accidental. 'The word *δρᾶμα* appears not to be used in Attic of the classical period in application to Attic Comedy, but in a fragment of Ecphantides there is a mention of a *δρᾶμα Μεγαρικόν*, which was evidently a comic performance, and it is possible that the word was also used of comedy and similar performances in Sicily. This would agree with Aristotle's statement in *Poet.* iii that some people regarded *δρᾶμα* as a Dorian word. What is highly probable, is that the performances of Epicharmus were not especially associated with a Dionysiac *κῶμος*, and that there would accordingly have been no ground for calling them *κωμῳδίαι* in Sicily itself; but that the ancients recognized them as belonging to the same general type as *κωμῳδίαι* can hardly be disputed.' (*Dithyramb, Tragedy and Comedy*, p. 403.) This evidence, though slight, seems to me to confirm my hypothesis that Attic comedy owed more to Ionia and the *kômos* than to Dorian drama as practised in Megara and Sicily.

57. *Ibid.*, p. 409.

58. Pickard-Cambridge, *Dithyramb, Tragedy and Comedy*, p. 396, writes 'The *Πέρσαι* has only its title to speak for it; but this, and the certainty that the *Νᾶσοι* referred to a political event of 477-6 B.C. imply that political subjects were not altogether barred to Sicilian comedy.'

59. Kaibel for Phormis, p. 148; for Deinolochus, p. 149. Pickard-Cambridge, *Dithyramb, Tragedy and Comedy*, pp. 413-15.

60. In this I disagree with Norwood, p. 113, and with Pickard-Cambridge, *Dithyramb, Tragedy and Comedy*, p. 412. Although they recognize our lack of evidence and can state no specific influence,

they still believe Epicharmus must have left marks on later Sicilian dramas.

61. Pickard-Cambridge, *Dithyramb, Tragedy and Comedy*, p. 363, says 'that political comedy was a special extravaganza peculiar to Athens and does not lie in the main stream of the development of the art'. I see no traces of 'development' except in Athens.

CHAPTER 3

ATHENIAN OLD COMEDY: 487 TO 430 B.C.

COMEDY was officially recognized as a part of the City Dionysia in 487-6 B.C. when the archon granted the comic poet a chorus. Volunteer actors and impromptu lines now gave way to professional performances, a development of interest and importance about which we know nothing. Even Aristotle confessed his ignorance of the early history of comedy, saying that no one thought seriously of comedy and, therefore, no one recorded the names of those who first introduced actors, masks, prologues, and similar matters (*Poetics*, 1449b) [1]. The early playwrights are no more than names—Chionides, Euxenides, Myllus—though Magnes is rescued from oblivion by Aristophanes [2]. Without doubt the native *kômos* continued to hold the stage with its picturesque choruses of animals, birds, or other exotic creatures who could, from behind their protecting disguise, safely mock at individuals and enact the ancient iambic ritual of purification. But no true playwrights emerge from this darkness until 453, when Cratinus won his first victory, closely followed by his rival, Crates, in 450.

ATHENS, 487 TO 453

Yet these thirty-four years are not to be lightly dismissed. Events were taking place which transformed the Athens of Solon and Peisistratus from a small agricultural community into a great commercial empire, from an aristocracy to a democracy, from a people who appreciated the thought and art of others into a people who created an unsurpassed culture. This transformation had such a penetrating effect upon later comedy that it might almost be said that the history of comedy in the fifth century is the history of Athens. And the history of Athens is in essence the growing intensity of conflicts—some old and some new—into bitter opposites without hope or possibility of reconciliation.

The war against the Persian invaders, victoriously finished at Salamis in 480 and Plataea in 479, preserved Greek freedom from barbarian aggression, but it did not unify the Greek world. It deepened, rather, the chasm between the Ionians, who clustered around Athens, and the Dorians, who followed the leadership of Sparta. Athens, with an expanding navy, became the bulwark of the Ionian islands, which banded together in the Delian League. Founded originally in 478-7 to drive the Persians from the Aegean, the League gradually changed into an Athenian empire. This change was completed in 454-3 when the treasury was shifted from Delos to Athens. From then on the tribute paid by the allies became the property of Athens, which thought it not improper to use the money for the Parthenon and the glorification of the city so long as the promised security was not threatened. On the mainland, too, Athens embarked on a career of conquest of initial success but not long duration. The Spartans, though aware of their rival's growing power, took but few steps to check it until finally their fear forced them to combat it openly in the Peloponnesian War [3].

Within Athens the deep-rooted struggle between the aristocratic and democratic parties continued with the democratic parties gaining strength. An aristocrat, Cimon, won fame and support by his naval victories in the first years of the Delian League, but he was ostracized in 461, and though later recalled never regained power before his death in 449. His opponent was Pericles, also of an aristocratic family and spirit, but democratic in tendency either through expediency or sympathy. Pericles ruled Athens until his death in 429, elected yearly as one of the ten generals. During these years, the government of Athens became constitutionally more democratic by the introduction of two new principles—election by lot and payment for services. The old Areopagus, a conservative aristocratic council, was stripped of its authority and reduced to a court for homicide. The archonship was opened to the lower classes, and the archons, the Council of the Five Hundred, and the judges were paid and elected by lot. This meant that the poorer citizens could afford to hold office and that the wealthy aristocrats could not take political advantage of their leisure or prestige. It also meant that the man who could best persuade the Assembly to follow his advice could control the policy of Athens. Pericles was a great orator, and in that gift lay his power [4].

His skill in speaking had been increased by the tutelage of his teacher and companion, Anaxagoras of Clazomenae, an Ionian philosopher, who brought to Athens the Ionian spirit of scientific research and free inquiry [5]. During his long residence in Athens (*c.* 480-450), Anaxagoras conducted the cosmological investigations which resulted in his trial for impiety and forced return to Ionia. His scientific studies of the moon, sun, stars, and so forth led him to seek natural causes for natural phenomena and to declare that the sun was a red-hot stone (Plato, *Apology*, 26d). He ran counter to accepted belief: first, by denying the divinity of heavenly bodies and thus undermining the mythological structure of the Greek world; and secondly, by exposing the superstitions on which the current modes of divination were based [6]. He was a stimulating but dangerous friend for Pericles.

Pericles was not the only intellectual in Athens attracted by the brilliance of the Ionian philosopher. Socrates heard tell of Anaxagoras's theory that Mind or *Nous* was the cause of all things. In haste, Socrates bought the book of Anaxagoras, eager to learn more, but he was disappointed by the lack of development of this promising idea [7]. Socrates in his youth seems to have been a student of contemporary philosophies, talking with the visiting philosophers and perusing their works. For these pursuits he had unusual opportunities.

Athens was an intellectual crossroads—the one Greek city in which the Ionian philosophy of rational and scientific investigation met head on the Western philosophy of dialectic and mysticism [8]. From Italy came Parmenides and Zeno, with whom Socrates conversed about the middle of the century. Parmenides, in rebellion against the Ionian explanations of the world, declared that the world was a continuous, indivisible plenum without motion [9]. This challenge to the senses was defended by Zeno, who developed dialectic, the art of demolishing your antagonists by accepting their premisses and reducing their systems to absurdity.

Another great Western philosopher, the Sicilian Empedocles, may have visited Athens at the time of the founding of Thourioi, an Athenian colony, or his successor, Hippon of Rhegium, may have brought his philosophy to Athens [10]. Empedocles was versatile and eccentric. He claimed to be a god and wrote a book called *Purifications* to help the citizens who had asked him the way to gain money and to cure sickness (fr. 112). He invented rhetoric, according to Aristotle, and founded a school of medicine [11]. Yet, primarily perhaps, he should be thought of as a poet, for his works are in verse, and his ideas are expressed metaphorically. The four roots of all things (the fundamental stuff of the world) are given mythological names, and Love and Strife are the causes of change and motion. His writings abound with abstractions: Discord, Harmony, Truth, Uncertainty, Silence, and Voice [12].

Both Parmenides and Empedocles were poets who expressed themselves allegorically; both were intimately connected with Pythagoreanism, either as apostates or disciples [13]. They are the direct antithesis of Anaxagoras, with his clipped prose, scientific leanings, and religious scepticism. This conflict of theory and attitude stimulated the youthful Socrates and his contemporaries to seek answers for the perplexing problems they heard discussed, but the many contradictory philosophies current in Athens also led to scepticism and popular distrust of these 'wise men'. As the century proceeded, the philosophical disputes became more bitter, and the gulf between the 'wise men' and the populace deepened into an unbridgeable chasm.

TRAGEDY AND SATYR-PLAY

During these years, so dark in the history of comedy, tragedy was making rapid strides [14]. Aeschylus, who won his first victory in 484 B.C., was at the height of his career, culminating with the *Oresteia* in 458, produced in Athens just two years before his death in Sicily [15]. It is obviously impossible to do justice to this great dramatist and poet in a few sentences, but some suggestion of the scope of his interests may be valuable. He fashioned the myths of heroes and gods into trilogies in which he could trace the working of divine law through three generations or, in the Prometheus legend, in aeons of time. The hereditary curse of the houses of Laius and Atreus brought murder and pollution to Oedipus and Agamemnon and to their children. Aeschylus was essentially concerned with the reconciliation of conflicting decrees of the gods—Avenge your father's death! Do not murder your mother!—and the purification of the guilty.

This religion of Aeschylus was intimately related to his patriotism, to his love for Athens, and his desire to protect and glorify her. The *Oresteia* shows this clearly. In the first part, Agamemnon returns from the Trojan War and is killed by his wife, Clytemnestra, and her paramour, partly in revenge for Agamemnon's sacrifice of his daughter. In the second play, Orestes returns from exile and murders his mother and Aegisthus in revenge. In the last play of the triology, Orestes maddened by his guilt, pursued by the Furies for the crime of matricide, seeks purification first at Delphi and finally at Athens. A trial is held, and Orestes is acquitted with the help of Apollo and Athena. At the end of the play the Areopagus is founded as a court to try homicidal cases. Thus the hereditary curse is ended, the guilty purified, divine decrees reconciled, and Athens and her institutions glorified.

Aeschylus's patriotism is also shown by his active service in the Persian War, particularly in the battle of Salamis. Shortly after that victory he composed the *Persians*, in which the queen of Persia, Atossa, welcomes home her vanquished husband, Xerxes. Since the dramatization of the myths was the principal form of Greek tragedy, we forget sometimes the rarer plays in which contemporary events were portrayed. Phrynichus wrote two of this kind: the first, *The Fall of Miletus*, was performed in 494 soon after the event and aroused a storm of protest because it was so painfully real; the second, the *Phoenicians*, was about the battle of Salamis and was produced in 476 with Themistocles perhaps as choregus [16]. Comedy was not the only Athenian dramatic form which portrayed contemporaneous life.

The second of the three greatest Greek tragedians was Sophocles, who began his dramatic career in 469-8 and continued writing until his death in 406 [17]. He did not construct his three tragedies into a unified trilogy, but brought to perfection the single play. His *Antigone*, 442 B.C., is a good example of the balance which characterizes his writing. Character contrasts with character, episode with episode, and even emotional balance is achieved at the end when Antigone recognizes the claims of human law and Creon those of divine law [18]. Sophocles perceived the tragedy of individuals caught between conflicting loyalties or in a web of circumstance, noble people who suffer and thus gain a greater nobility [19].

The third great tragic poet, Euripides, produced his first plays in 455 at just the same time that a recognizable comedy was emerging [20]. Of the first twenty-four years of his career we know little; because his first extant play, the *Medea*, was not produced until 431, discussion will be postponed. We do know that the *Telephus* of 438 deeply impressed the Athenians, for Aristophanes parodies this tragedy in his first extant comedy, the *Acharnians* of 425. Euripides had chosen to dramatize a legend in which a king disguises himself as a beggar, and the realism of the disguise offended the conservative Greek audience. His only other early play of interest is the *Alcestis*, which he substituted for the satyr-play in 438.

The satyr-plays, which rounded off the set of three tragedies presented by each competing poet, are usually neglected in histories of Greek drama because they are neither tragedy nor comedy. They were written by the tragic poets, but they were certainly not tragic. On the other hand, the Greeks did not think they were comedies, for they assumed almost as a self-evident truth that no tragic poet could write comedies [21]. Two examples of this anomalous form have survived, the complete *Cyclops* of Euripides and a large portion of the *Ichneutae* of Sophocles.

The *Cyclops* is a dramatization of a well-known episode in the *Odyssey* [22]. Odysseus, seized with his comrades and imprisoned by the cannibalistic Polyphemus, escapes by blinding the giant. The satyr-play opens with a prologue by Silenus, telling of his attempt to rescue Dionysos from the pirates, an attempt which had, instead, ended in his enslavement with his satyrs to the dreadful Cyclops. A chorus of satyrs enter driving their sheep, just before the entrance of Odysseus seeking food. The whole plot does not need to be outlined; but the strong Dionysiac flavour should be noted. Silenus and the satyrs long for their master Dionysos and for his wine; Polyphemus is won over from hatred of the god to subservience, and desires in his drunkenness to join his fellow cyclopes in a *kômos*; and at the end Silenus and the satyrs leave with Odysseus, saying, 'We shall be fellow-travellers with Odysseus, being for the future the slaves of Bacchus' [23].

Sophocles in the *Ichneutae* has dramatized the myth recounted in the Homeric Hymn to Hermes [24]. Apollo offers a reward for his cattle, mysteriously stolen. Silenus and his satyrs accept his challenge and track the cattle to the cave in which the infant Hermes lies. His nurse, a mountain nymph, tries to protect the child from the accusations hurled by Silenus, but in her description of the newly invented lyre she lets slip the fact that cowhide has been used. Our fragment breaks off before the end of the play.

From these brief descriptions the reader can quickly perceive that these plays are neither tragic in theme nor in treatment; they are not even burlesques of tragedies. They seem in fact, comic in every way. The characters are humorous—braggart, thief, and detective; the plots and situations are amusing—the bully outwitted, the baby thief discovered; and the dialogue is witty with much repartee and obscenity. Why did the Greeks not consider them comedies?

If we remember that the dramas of Epicharmus were never called comedies, we can see that the same explanation holds for both kinds of plays: neither the dramas nor the satyr-plays had the *kômos* element of iambic ritual purification. The satyr-plays had a chorus of satyrs and the spirit of Dionysiac revelry, but no personal invective or contemporary application. The Greeks with their sensitive feeling for form recognized subtle differences of type. To-day we use the word 'comedy' for any amusing play or even one with a happy ending, but the Greeks used their terms with greater nicety [25].

Two changes of the greatest importance took place in theatrical production during the first half of the fifth century, changes intimately related to the new interests of the time: the number of actors was raised from one to three and a scene building was erected [26]. According to Aristotle, Aeschylus increased the number of actors from one to two, thus making conflict between individuals a dramatic possibility. Sophocles added a third actor. We hear nothing from Aristotle of a fourth actor. In view of the competition for prizes among the actors as well as the poets, the state officials probably in fairness did limit each poet to three actors for each tragedy. By skilful manipulation the poet could make use of a large number of characters. During the choral interludes the actors could easily assume new masks and new costumes. Extra actors were apparently available to play mute characters or children. As interest in the individual characters and their problems grew, the tragic chorus gradually lost its position as the centre of attention. It was transferred to the periphery, where it became a spectator rather than an active participant in the drama.

The theatre reflected this change of emphasis from the chorus to the actor. At some point during the early fifth century the site of the theatre was shifted. The orchestra, dancing-circle for the chorus, was reduced in size, leaving room at the edge of the hillside for a scene-building. The size, shape, and appearance of this building are controversial problems seemingly insoluble with our limited information, but the building's usefulness and importance are clear. It provided entrances and exits for the actors, dressing-rooms for swift changes of costumes, and a sounding board for the acoustics.

Above all, the scene-building served as a background, suggesting to the audience the place of action. The following account of the nature of the scenery in these years seems to me as positive as our evidence permits.

> In the preceding chapter it has been shown to be probable that while the earliest plays of Aeschylus required only the simplest setting, greater elaboration had become necessary by 458 B.C., when the *Oresteia* demanded a palace- or temple-front as a façade, with the provision of (probably) three doors and the enclosure of the actors' territory by paraskenia. Not many years after this the 'Periclean' theatre doubtless provided the necessary framework for the erection of backgrounds of this and of the other types which seem to have been recurrent throughout the rest of the fifth century. These all had in common a central opening, serving for the entrance to a palace or temple, or the door of a house, or the mouth of a cave. It would be easy to adapt it for any of these purposes and to close or cover up or disguise any of the other entrances which were not required for a particular play. As about two-thirds of the extant tragedies were played before a palace or a temple, it may be that this, if any, was the permanent or semi-permanent background. That it was taken down be-

> tween one festival and another is very likely; a wooden structure would hardly have been left in position all the year. But it may have remained through each Dionysiac festival, and been subjected between the plays to such modifications as would be necessary (e.g.) to differentiate palace from temple, or to transform the façade (perhaps by the use of painted canvas or screens or panels, which could be easily moved into position) into a representation of one, two, or three tents, or a country district (indicated in the simplest possible way), with or without a central cave, or of the seashore and cliffs, or in Comedy, of private houses. Probably there were, as has been suggested, 'sets' for each type of scene, easily transferable so that when (e.g.) in 431 B.C. Euripides presented the *Medea*, the *Philoctetes*, the *Dictys*, and the satyric *Theristai*, the changes of background from palace to sea-shore and from sea-shore to country could be quickly effected [27].

The dramatist depended upon his poetry to convey the feeling of a time and place rather than upon physical properties.

From all of these dramatic and theatrical improvements, comedy benefited. By watching performances and writing burlesques, the comic poets learned through imitation what the tragic poets learned through experiment: the handling of actors on the stage, entrances and exits, the subordination of narrative to dramatic crises, the right tempo with which to lead up to a climax and then away to a conclusion, the effective linking of chorus with action and theme, and the adaptation of epic and myth to the stage. No wonder Aristotle did not know who introduced into comedy the masks or prologues or when the number of actors was changed. The tragic poets were the true innovators; the comic the beneficiaries [28].

ATHENIAN COMEDY: 453 TO 431 B.C.

At the middle of the fifth century Aeschylus was dead, though his plays were not; Sophocles was an established playwright and Euripides was just beginning to write; the treasury had been moved from Delos to Athens, and Athens was both a great land and sea power; Pericles was in control, though powerful enemies still threatened his supremacy; and Athens was to become in the next fifty years an intellectual and cultural centre unrivalled in the history of the world. These fifty years coincided with the full bloom of Old Comedy [29]. Exact dates for literary types are, of course, impossible; but we do know that the first victory of the first comic playwright of whom we know anything fell in 453 and that the last extant play of Aristophanes, fully in the spirit of Old Comedy, was the *Frogs* of 405. His two fourth-century comedies, though they retain much of the old, herald a new type.

Cratinus and Crates are the best known of the older generation of comic poets. They, in a sense, created Old Comedy, for they brought to the native *kômos* the two most active and fruitful comic influences then in existence. Cratinus looked to Ionia and to the iambic poetry of Archilochus, Semonides, and Hipponax. Crates turned to Sicily, to the plays of Epicharmus —mythological burlesque and allegorical debates. Aristophanes was heir of a double legacy.

Cratinus, the older of the two playwrights, was born about 490 and died about 420 [30]. He wrote twenty-one plays according to ancient reports, though twenty-eight titles have survived [31]. Almost half of his plays were successful, for he won nine victories—six at the City Dionysia and three at the Lenaea. One of these victories is particularly significant, because it meant defeat for the *Clouds* of Aristophanes!

He was famous throughout antiquity for the bitterness of his invective and the harshness of his style [32]. In this he was following his master, Archilochus. His debt to that great iambic poet is well established not only by ancient testimony but also by his play, *Archilochoi*, and by a parody, 'Oh desolate citizens, hear my words' [33]. This call to the people indicates again the serious intention which lies behind iambic scurrility. Aristophanes links him closely to Dionysiac worship. The cleansing of the city was one of the motives for his attacks upon private citizens for poverty, bribery, boastfulness, effeminacy, and adultery [34]. He was scornful, too, of the sophists or wisemen: Hippon, the follower of Empedocles; Chaerephon, a companion of Socrates; and Euathlos, a friend of the famous Protagoras (frr. 155, 202, 75). Public men like Xenophon and Cleon were also rebuked, but he directed his most savage abuse at Pericles and Aspasia [35].

Pericles, as the foremost man in the state following the death of Cimon, might well expect the comic poets to comment on his appearance, and doubtless was unmoved by references to his 'squill-head', which he tried to disguise with a helmet [36]. Nor would he have been much upset by praise of his rival Cimon, whom Cratinus lauds (fr. 1). Moreover, he was probably accustomed to the title 'Olympian' and might have been secretly pleased by comparison of him with Zeus. But must he not have been galled by lewd remarks about his mistress, Aspasia? Could he have endured without rebuke such a statement as 'Brutal Lust bore Hera to him and Aspasia, dog-eyed courtesan' (fr. 241)?

Whatever the private feelings of Pericles may have been, we know that as soon as he had gained complete power after the exile of Thucydides, son of Melesias, his last serious rival, the festival of the Lenaea was brought under state control. Comedies were an essential part of this ancient festival. Moreover, two years later a law was passed forbidding the satirizing of individuals. This Law of Morychides was instituted in 440 at the time of the Samian Revolt, which may have been used as a pretext or may have been the authentic cause for the law, and lasted three years [37]. With its repeal in 437, the comic poets hurled their reproaches with fresh vigour and without legal opposition. Pericles continued to be a target, and with him all his associates: Aspasia, Anaxagoras, Lampon, who helped with the founding of Thurioi, and others [38]. This antagonism culminated in the charges brought against Aspasia by Hermippus, a comic poet, in 430 [39]. Pericles himself was brought to trial, deposed, and fined, though later returned to office [40].

Cratinus was thus not alone in his opposition to Pericles. Hermippus, Telecleides, and even Aristophanes attacked him, alive and dead. How can we explain this abuse of a man acknowledged by both contemporaries and Athenians to be the greatest citizen of Athens? The answer need not be sought in party politics or personal dislike; it can be found simply in the popular voice. Those very people who deposed Pericles had elevated him, and the comic poets merely expressed the sentiments freely aired in the streets.

The claims of art were not neglected by Cratinus; in fact, nothing can be more fatal to an understanding of Old Comedy than an exclusively sociological or political interpretation.

Cratinus wrote a whole play about citharode players, the *Euneidae*, and parodied the poetry of Hesiod, Theognis, Archilochus, Pindar, Sophocles, and Euripides (frr. 317, 15, 10, 198). Of these, he praises Sophocles. He mentions Aristophanes, Ecphantides, and Callias, all fellow comic poets (frr. 300, 307, 324, 334-5). No doubt this list would be greatly extended if any complete plays were extant, for Cratinus was evidently a well-read and cultured man.

Some plays seem to have been given over entirely to parody, but most of them were either mythological burlesques or allegories. In both of these, invective played its part, conveyed either by the chorus or as incidental jests in the dialogue; yet we need not suppose that it dominated the action. Scoffing at individuals was a comic device or a ritualistic survival; it was not a type of play.

The mythological burlesques include not only the familiar story of Odysseus and the Cyclops but the famous legend of Paris, Helen, and Agamemnon [41]. The plot of this last play, *Dionysalexandros*, is known from a papyrus fragment, a lucky find.

> These [the chorus of satyrs] address the audience concerning the poets, and when Dionysus appears they mock and jeer at him. Dionysus, being offered by Hera unshaken sovereignty, by Athena success in war, and by Aphrodite the possession of charm and surpassing beauty, adjudges the victory to Aphrodite. Next he sails to Sparta, abducts Helen, and returns to Mt. Ida. But soon, hearing that the Greeks are ravaging the land, he flees to Alexander, hides Helen in a basket as (a goose?), disguises himself as a ram, and awaits the upshot. Alexander arrives, detects them both, and orders them to be taken to the ships, intending to hand them over to the Greeks. But Helen objects; he takes pity on her and withholds her, to make her his wife, but Dionysus he despatches to be handed over. The satyrs escort Dionysus with encouragement and assurances that they will never desert him. In the play Pericles is most convincingly satirized by innuendo as having involved the Athenians in the war [42].

Here we have an exciting romantic story with all the devices of the romance—the abduction of a beautiful woman, flight in disguise, pursuit, danger, and finally rescue by a young hero. We might almost think this an Elizabethan comedy if it were not for the clear signs of Old Comedy—the chorus of satyrs, their address to the audience, their discussion of poetry, the mocking of the god, and the political satire. The satire may have been conveyed through occasional jests, or the whole play may have been an allegory with Pericles represented by Dionysos, Thucydides the son of Melesias by Alexander, and Athens by Helen [43]. We cannot know certainly since the play is lost.

The *Nemesis* was another mythological burlesque and political commentary [44]. It recounted the myths of Helen's birth. Zeus (Pericles) pursued Nemesis (Aspasia), who eluded her lover by changing forms. Finally, as swans, they mated. The egg laid by Nemesis was taken to Sparta by Hermes, where Helen was hatched by Leda. There is no doubt in my mind of the identifications of Zeus with Pericles, Nemesis with Aspasia, but the significance of the egg, Helen, and Leda has been obscured by time.

In other plays Cratinus was frankly allegorical without recourse to a mythological disguise. He was the first of a long line of comic poets to celebrate the glories of a Golden Age, a theme which can be traced back to Hesiod. The *Ploutoi* or *Riches* contained a line about the days of Cronos when men played dice with bread (fr. 165), and both the *Laws* and *Cheirons* extol Solon and the period in which men lived 'gentled in mood with sweet-tongued Wisdom, very beautiful among mortals' (fr. 238).

Yet Cratinus himself was far from sweet-tongued. Aristophanes compares him to a rushing river, sweeping all before it (*Knights*, 526 ff.). One late critic says that Cratinus wrote in the 'austere' style without the grace in which Aristophanes cloaked his jests. Another admires the openings of his plays for their cleverness, but finds fault with the endings because they are not consistent [45]. His bitter lampooning and uneven construction are sharp contrasts to the laughable merriness and constructive powers of Crates, who furnished his audience with 'dainty tidbits' and general plots.

Crates was a contemporary of Cratinus; indeed, he was said to have begun his career in the theatre by acting in the comedies of Cratinus [46]. Disgusted with his parts, he turned to writing. He probably won his first victory in 450, but he was neither so prolific nor popular as Cratinus. He won only three victories altogether and wrote but a few more comedies. Fourteen titles are known, but four of these are doubtfully assigned to Crates, and three are merely names without fragments or explanatory notes.

He would be a most insignificant figure in the history of comedy if Aristotle had not told us that the making of plots had come originally from Sicily and that Crates 'was the first of the Athenians to abandon the iambic form, making general themes and plots' (*Poetics*, 1449b7). Epicharmus must be the Sicilian meant. As we have seen in the previous chapter, his dramas were either mythological burlesques or allegorical debates. The plots of either of these would fit Aristotle's statement. If Aristotle meant that Epicharmus had been the first to write plays with plots, the mythological burlesques with their use of preconstructed myths would be ample evidence. If Aristotle meant that Epicharmus had first invented plots from his own head, then his independently created allegories would be examples. Secondly, the general themes or *logoi* might well refer to the ideas which formed the basis of the allegorical plays of Epicharmus [47].

The plays themselves give us very little information. The *Beasts* was a picture of the Golden Age in the manner of Cratinus's *Riches*. No one was a slave of another man, and dinners cooked themselves (fr. 14). One needed only to bid the bowl climb upon the table, and the fish roast himself. Such plays as *Dionysos*, *Birds*, and *Speakers* are similar in title, at any rate, to other plays of the Old Comedy. But the evidence is only negative and can neither confirm nor refute any theory.

Aristotle's statement that Crates had abandoned the iambic form or *idea* needs more detailed explanation. Obviously he is not referring to the iambic metre, nor to a type of play (the word is not used by Aristotle in that sense) nor to the epirrhematic structure. The word *idea* is used in works on rhetoric for *topic* or *element* [48]. In other words, Crates abandoned the iambic element—the lampooning. This is substantiated by the absence of any mention of names in the few surviving fragments and positively by other ancient critics who comment upon this surprising omission. This omission seems to have been the result of Crates' temperament and style. Aristophanes calls his designs *asteiotatas*, a word which may be translated *witty*, *polite*, *dainty*, *graceful*, *clever*, or *elegant* (*Knights*, 539). To such a man the crude thrusts of a Cratinus would be anathema and the jibes of Archilochus distasteful. He would turn naturally to the philosopher and poet, Epicharmus, with his Sicilian wit and charm and fanciful inventions [49].

Two minor playwrights of this period are worthy of note, less for their own sakes than for their resemblance to Cratinus and Crates. Pherecrates, who was first an actor, as Crates had been, followed his lead and refrained from abuse and politics [50]. Unfortunately, the more interesting of his plays are of doubtful authorship, and fragments are few. Three plays may have dealt with revolts of women in the manner of the fourth-century *Ecclesiazusae* of Aristophanes [51], and *Corianno*, the name of a courtesan, suggests the Middle rather than the Old Comedy. On the other hand, *The Deserters* contained a political allusion to the Argives in the Peloponnesian War, and he speaks with scorn of Alcibiades (fr. 155). The Golden Age, a favourite theme at this time, was pictured in the *Persians* and *Miners*, though both are not with certainty ascribed to Pherecrates. A long fragment has been preserved from the *Miners*, which describes in detail rivers of soup and other edible marvels (fr. 108). In contrast, *The Savages* ridicules the idea of a noble primitive race [52]. *Chiron*, a title reminiscent of Cratinus's *Chirons*, seems to have been composed of parodies, poetic and musical. Hesiod and Homer are parodied, and Music in a dialogue with Justice complains of her treatment at the hands of the dithyrambic poets, Melanippides, Cinesias, and Timotheus [53].

The other playwright, Telecleides, was more nearly a contemporary and follower of Cratinus. His first victory, about 446, was succeeded by seven more, three at the City Dionysia and five at the Lenaea [54]. His political interests are shown by his portraying life in the days of Themistocles as luxurious in contrast to the present when the people had turned over to Pericles 'the income from the cities, even the cities themselves to fetter or set loose, the stone walls to construct or destroy, treaties, power, force, peace, wealth, and happiness' (fr. 42). The shape of Pericles' head comes in for its share of mockery (fr. 44). He accuses Charicles, who later became one of the

Thirty Tyrants with bribery, but he withholds the full details of a similar charge against the general Nicias, because he admired his character (fr. 41). His desire for peace and for freedom from toil and trouble is illustrated in his description of a Golden Age when 'peace, first of all, was like water—always at hand. The earth brought forth neither fear nor disease, but all the necessities were automatically ready' (fr. 1). The fragment continues with a picture of streams of wine and rivers of soup. He also bids the people refrain from their 'cannibalistic lawsuits' (fr. 2).

Like Cratinus, he did not confine himself to politics. He wrote a play called *The Hesiods* in which he speaks of the nephew of Aeschylus (fr. 14). In another fragment he says that Mnesilochus 'cooks a new play for Euripides while Socrates supplies the dry sticks' (fr. 39). His oath 'by the cabbage' (fr. 27) is reminiscent of Epicharmus, but too much weight cannot be attached to a phrase which may well have been a common Greek joke.

It is possible and convenient to divide Old Comedy into two schools—the lampooning and the urbane—and into two periods—the pre-war and the war; but such classifications are rigid and may dangerously distort the facts. Themes like the Golden Age were shared by all the playwrights; characters like Dionysos, Odysseus, and the Cyclops were repeated; and comic techniques such as parody and mythological burlesques were common. The ancients were conscious only of differences in style and in attitude towards personal invective. They did not recognize any line dividing a comedy of manners from political extravaganza within Old Comedy. Moreover, the comic poets, with remarkable unanimity, directed their attacks against Pericles and his associates—Aspasia, Anaxagoras, and Lampon—against the philosophers, tragic poets, and musicians, with Socrates and Euripides singled out for special mention.

Nor can we discern any real split between the older generation just discussed and the younger. Cratinus and Crates both composed and produced plays in the twenties, and they won victories too, though Aristophanes saucily says their day is done. The plays do not differ in type either, if titles are a clue, for early playwrights wrote comedies entitled *Frogs* and *Birds*, anticipating the works of Aristophanes. Nevertheless, changes can be discerned after 430. Crates and Cratinus were losing their popularity, and four new playwrights began to dominate the stage. Aristophanes, the most famous of all the ancient comic poets, had his first play produced in 427. His bitterest rival, Eupolis, had preceded him by a few years, and Hermippus and Plato *comicus* were active writers throughout the later period.

Athens, too, was changing. All the conflicts which had been dividing the Greek world were intensifying into bitter dissensions. The Spartan-Athenian hostility, never really quiescent, burst into open flame in 431 with the outbreak of the Peloponnesian War, which was fought with only brief respites until the utter defeat of Athens in 404 B.C. Pericles thought this war inevitable and therefore refused to make concessions. He insisted that the Megarian Decrees (a kind of economic sanctions) be not rescinded and, when war began, urged the country people to desert their farms and seek safety within Athenian walls. Since open battle with Spartan armies would have been disastrous for the outnumbered Athenians, he relied upon the navy and invasions of enemy country behind their lines. Whatever military experts may think of this as strategy, it did not win any friends for Pericles. The country gentlemen and farmers did not wish to abandon their estates and farms without a struggle to the devastation of the enemy. Moreover, the sudden increase of population without adequate housing facilities was uncomfortable and dangerous. Plague broke out and thousands died. The people, in anger, turned against Pericles and blamed him for the war and the plague [55].

Charges were brought against Pericles. They were sustained; and he was deposed and fined. His restoration later was succeeded in a few months by his death. Cleon seized the power, a man of shrewd wit and strong character, but a far cry from Pericles. He was the son of a tanner, the first time a man of low birth had been a leader of the Athenians, for Athenian democracy had not hitherto put into practice some of the ideals it extolled. Now, with a democrat by birth as well as conviction in the saddle and with a democratic constitution, the aristocrats lost both power and favour. Party rivalry sharpened into irreconcilable discord [56].

At the same time the new Sophistic movement, which had

been quietly growing in strength, became noisily prominent. Like a vine Sophism spread its tendrils over the whole structure of Greek culture. Scepticism about the gods and myths became alarmingly common among the intellectuals. Protagoras openly proclaimed that he knew nothing of the gods, and spoke the famous dictum, 'Man is the measure of all things' [57]. Hippocrates, a resident of Athens at this time, instituted scientific medicine by supplanting the old superstitious cures and charms with empirical observation. His belief that disease resulted from the encroachment of one of the four elements upon another is a still further sign of the importance of conflict in Greek thought [58].

Educational ideals and practice were also changing. The old classical education of music, poetry, and dancing was being challenged by a new practical education [59]. The aristocrats and wealthy needed defensive weapons to protect themselves from governmental interference. The law courts and the Assembly were now all powerful, and the key to success was oratory. This key was offered for sale by professional teachers called Sophists, a name and profession which fell into disrepute because of charlatans and the adverse publicity of Plato, but was honourable in the fifth century. The early Sophists—Protagoras, Gorgias, Hippias, and Prodicus—were estimable men of good character, intelligence, and ability. They studied rhetoric, government, psychology, language, and grammar, making important contributions to these subjects.

Gorgias and Prodicus are the two Sophists with the greatest influence upon comedy, for quite different reasons. Gorgias was a Sicilian, trained in the school of rhetoric founded by Corax and Tisias in Sicily, when democracy placed new emphasis upon the art of speech. He came to Athens in 427 B.C. to ask her aid, and took the city by storm with his elaborately constructed and embroidered speeches. His Euphuistic style was particularly replete with antithesis. Though he was not so great a philosopher as Protagoras, he was acquainted with the philosophy of Empedocles and accepted his theory of perception. His scepticism is even more far-reaching than that of Protagoras, for he said: 'There is nothing. If there is anything, it can not be known by man. If we did know anything, we could not communicate it' [60].

Prodicus was essentially a grammarian. His best known work is a study of words in which he distinguished between synonyms [61]. Valuable in itself, such nicety of usage could with abuse become verbal quibbling. So Hippolytus could say, 'My tongue swore it, not I' [62]. Prodicus was more famous in antiquity, however, for his allegory, *Heracles at the Crossroads*. The hero dreams that two women approach him. The first promises a primrose path, revealing that her friends call her Happiness but her enemies Vice. The other woman, Virtue, admits that her way is straight and narrow but promises great rewards at the end [63].

The Sophistic movement had strong influence over Greek tragedy; or perhaps it might be truer to say that Euripides was himself one of the leaders of the movement. The *Medea*, produced in 431, illustrates his interest in the intellectual currents of the day. Medea was a woman of passion whose jealousy rose to such a pitch of fury that she was willing to murder her own dearly beloved children for the sole purpose of revenging her husband's desertion. More startling than that is her claim to be *sophê* or *clever*. The citizens are envious of her cleverness, and Creon, the father of her rival and king of Corinth, fears her. Like the contemporary Sophists, Medea is without a city and thus arouses the suspicion naturally felt by all deeply rooted homebodies for the man or woman without a country.

We need only compare Medea to the earlier Antigone of Sophocles to see the differences in the kinds of tragic heroines who interested the audiences of 444 and 431. Antigone was torn between her love for her brother, her obedience to the state, and devotion to the god's commands. Medea has murdered her brother and betrayed her state. Antigone laments that she must die before she has been married and had children, but she expresses no regret that she must leave Haemon, her fiancé. In fact, she says that she would not thus sacrifice her life for a husband or children. Medea is consumed by a sexual passion which has turned to a hatred so bitter that she murders everyone Jason loves. Antigone is a noble, sensitive, courageous woman with strong natural affections. Her tragedy is that she is caught between conflicting loyalties and must choose between a higher allegiance and death or slavery and life. Medea is a barbarian, intellectual, clever, and emotional.

She herself says that the greatest cause of evils for men is the superior strength of the spirit or passion over deliberate resolution. The conflict has become internal.

The Sophistic movement is not easily defined, nor by itself can it account for all the changes in Greece. Innovation and conflict dominated every compartment of life, and Sophistry was perhaps only the intellectual expression of the new trends and rifts. All the old ways and principles were scrutinized, judged, and found wanting. New ways and principles sprang up to take their place, but they could not gain the respect the old had enjoyed, and the result was conflict and scepticism. The constant strife and insecurity bred in turn a violence of unrestrained emotion, clearly reflected in the Melian Dialogue of Thucydides, the speeches of Thrasymachus in the *Republic*, and Euripidean melodramas.

Such was the background against which Aristophanes's comedies were played, the web and woof of which they were constructed. I mean by this not merely that his plays are full of allusions to the Peloponnesian War and other current events or that the characters are often caricatures of contemporary men. These are obvious signs of his keen interest and knowledge of the environment in which he lived, but by themselves might be dismissed as traditional comic material. Far more fundamental a bond between Aristophanes and his age is the structure of his plays, a series of conflicts unified by an emotional and intellectual tension.

The close union of Aristophanes with his environment is so conspicuous that it has diverted attention from his equally close union with the past. Magnes, Cratinus, and Crates represent respectively the three main strands from which comedy was woven: first, the *kômos*, second, the iambic invective in the style of Archilochus, and third, Sicilian debates and mythological burlesques in the style of Epicharmus. To all of these Aristophanes was indebted (though he never acknowledged his debt), and to a host of lyric, elegiac, and narrative poets. He was also thoroughly conversant with Homer, Aeschylus, and other tragic poets, with the historian Herodotus, with philosophers and Sophists.

Yet his knowledge of his literary heritage and of his own world never enslaved his imagination. Aristophanes was neither shackled by his traditions—artistic or religious—nor was he simply a mirror reflecting his environment. He was a genius with an artistic intention and the power and imagination to accomplish his purpose with the material at hand. To discover this intention and to study the dramatic skill and poetic art with which this intention was realized are the tasks of the next three chapters.

NOTES FOR CHAPTER 3

1. Robert J. Bonner, *Aspects of Athenian Democracy* (Sather Classical Lectures, Berkeley, California, 1933), p. 126, comments, 'It can hardly be a coincidence that a popular form of the drama was given official support just after democracy had signalized its growing power by substituting the lot for the ballot in selecting the archons.'

2. *Knights*, 520.

3. Thucydides, I, xcv, xxiii. See also J. B. Bury, *A History of Greece* (3rd ed. by Russell Meiggs, London, 1951), pp. 322-45; *The Cambridge Ancient History*, ed. J. B. Bury, S. A. Cook, F. E. Adcock (Cambridge, 1927), V, 33-97.

4. Our knowledge of Pericles is mainly derived from Thucydides and from Plutarch's *Life of Pericles*. See also Bury, pp. 346 ff., and *CAH*, V, 72-5.

5. Plato, *Phaedrus*, 270a. For ancient sources see *Die Fragmente der Vorsokratiker* (ed. Hermann Diels, 5th ed. by Walther Kranz, Berlin, 1935), II, 5-44. Translations and comment are to be found in Kathleen Freeman, *The Pre-Socratic Philosophers, A Companion to Diels, Fragmente der Vorsokratiker* (Oxford, 1946), pp. 261-74. Plutarch stresses the close relationship between Pericles and Anaxagoras.

6. Plutarch, 154. Cp. John Burnet, *Early Greek Philosophy* (4th ed. London, 1930), chap. 6.

7. *Phaedo*, 97c.

8. John Burnet, *Greek Philosophy, Thales to Plato* (London, 1932), p. 132, n. 1, writes, 'The main point is that Sokrates is represented as hesitating between Ionic doctrine, such as he would learn from Archelaos and Diogenes . . . and Italic doctrines, some of which belong to the school of Empedokles, whilst others are Pythagorean. Sokrates may have learnt the latter directly or indirectly from Philolaos. Empedokles, who took part in the colonization of

Thourioi, probably visited Athens (for we know that Kritias adapted his theory of sensation) and it is not difficult to suppose that Philolaos came there too. Athens is the only place where the Ionic and Italic philosophies could come into sharp conflict like this, and the middle of the fifth century is the only time at which it could happen.'

9. Burnet, *Early Greek Philosophy*, p. 181.

10. Diels-Kranz, I, 276-375; Freeman, pp. 172-204; Burnet, *Early Greek Philosophy*, p. 203.

11. Diels-Kranz, I, 278, quotes Diogenes, VIII, 57, who says that Aristotle in his *Sophist* says that Empedocles was the first to discover rhetoric.

12. Diels-Kranz, frr. 17, 20, 26, 103, 115, 122.

13. Parmenides, fr. 1, is a highly dramatic allegory. Parmenides was borne by horses to the gate of the Two Ways, Day and Night, guarded by Dike. There he is greeted by a goddess who welcomes him. No evil fate has sent him, but *themis* and *dike* (social and legal justice). Famous invincible Truth is contrasted with the Opinions of mortals. For interpretation of this allegory, see Burnet, *Thales to Plato*, pp. 65-6, and Freeman, p. 141.

14. *The Complete Greek Drama* (ed. Whitney J. Oates and Eugene O'Neill, Jr., New York, 1938) is the most convenient collection of translations for English readers. The introductions present the salient facts clearly and accurately.

15. The translation of the *Agamemnon* by Richmond Lattimore in *Greek Plays in Modern Translation* (ed. Dudley Fitts, New York, 1947) is particularly commendable. George Thomson's *Aeschylus and Athens, A Study in the Social Origins of Drama* (London, 1941) and Herbert Weir Smyth's *Aeschylean Tragedy* (Berkeley, California, 1924) make a good combination since they study Aeschylus from different points of view.

16. Herodotus, VI, 21, says that Phrynichus was fined one thousand drachmas. Plutarch, V, *Themistocles*, records the inscription celebrating the victory. *Tragicorum Graecorum Fragmenta* (ed. Augustus Nauck, 2nd ed., Leipzig, 1926), pp. 720-5.

17. T. B. L. Webster, *An Introduction to Sophocles* (Oxford, 1936), gives an excellent account of the poet's life and works.

18. *Ibid.*, chaps. 4 and 5.

19. C. M. Bowra, *Sophoclean Tragedy* (Oxford, 1944), chap. 9.

20. Many books have been written about Euripides, but none

that I have read seems to me to give a full account of this paradoxical and many-sided poet.

21. *Symposium*, 223, where Socrates argues that the tragic poet and comic poet are alike, a clear example of Socrates' delight in proving the truth of a contradiction.

22. Rollin H. Tanner, 'The *Ὀδυσσῆς* of Cratinus and the *Cylops* of Euripides', *Transactions of the American Philological Association*, XLVI (1915), 173-206, traces the indebtedness of both Cratinus and Euripides to Homer and then suggests that Cratinus was parodying the satyr-play in his comedy. Nothing could illustrate better the relationships between epic, tragedy, satyr-play, and comedy than the varied treatments of this episode.

23. (Ed. Gilbert Murray, Oxford, 1902) I, lines 63 ff., 537, 708-9.

24. Sophocles, *The Ichneutae* (ed. Richard Johnson Walker, London, 1919). Cf. William N. Bates, 'The Satyr Dramas of Sophocles', *Classical Studies* (Princeton, 1936), pp. 14-23.

25. Roy C. Flickinger, *The Greek Theater and Its Drama* (3rd ed., Chicago, 1926), p. 201, comments on this Greek trait as follows: 'Within the type there was room for the greatest diversity, but the types did not overlap or borrow much from one another. This practice was a natural outgrowth of the Greek love for schematizing which displayed itself in the formulation and observance of rigid laws in every branch of art and especially in literature; in the field of drama this tendency was strengthened by the festival arrangements.'

26. *Poetics*, 1449a9 ff. Cf. Sir Arthur Pickard-Cambridge, *The Dramatic Festivals of Athens* (Oxford, 1953), pp. 137-53.

27. Sir Arthur W. Pickard-Cambridge, *The Theatre of Dionysus in Athens* (Oxford, 1946), pp. 122-3. Cp. James Turney Allen, *The Greek Theater of the Fifth Century before Christ*, University of California Publications in Classical Philology, VII (1919-1924), 21 ff., and Margarete Bieber, *The History of the Greek and Roman Theater* (Princeton, 1939), chap. 5.

28. Octave Navarre, 'Les Origines et la Structure Technique de la Comédie Ancienne', *Revue des Études Anciennes*, XIII (1911), 245-95, traces to tragedy the origin of prologue, three actors, masks. The part between the parabasis and exodus has been affected by tragedy as the change in the chorus indicates (pp. 271-4).

29. William Ridgeway, 'An Appendix on the Origin of Greek Comedy', *The Dramas and Dramatic Dances of Non-European Races* (Cambridge, 1915), p. 422, says that 'the sudden rise of the Old

Comedy after 460 B.C. was due to the abolition in 462 B.C. of the general powers of censorship vested in the Areopagus, and not to any positive legislation. . . .' This was probably one among many factors contributing to its rise, the wealth of Athens being at least equally important.

30. *Comicorum Atticorum Fragmenta* (ed. Theodore Kock, Leipzig, 1880-88), I, 11-130. A. Körte in *RE*, s.v. 'Kratinos'. Gilbert Norwood, *Greek Comedy* (Boston, 1931), chap. 3, contains texts and translations of the most significant fragments, his own interpretations and those of others, and known and conjectural dates of performances.

31. *Comicorum Graecorum Fragmenta* (ed. George Kaibel, Berlin, 1899), p. 7, quoting from Anon. *de Com.* See Körte, p. 1648.

32. Platonius, Kaibel, p. 6, says that Cratinus was harsh in his invective.

33. *Ibid.*, frr. 10, 95, 198.

34. Aristophanes, *Frogs*, 357, connects Cratinus closely with the Bacchic rites. The Mystae who form the chorus sing that those who do not know the temper of the Muses, or the choruses, or have not celebrated the Bacchic rites of Cratinus with the bull-eating tongue should stand back from the chorus. Amynias is ridiculed as 'an impostor, flatterer, and sycophant' (fr. 212). Callias is mocked for his adultery with a Phocian woman (fr. 333). The effeminacy of Cleisthenes is held up for scorn (fr. 195).

35. Fr. 53. Körte adds a reference to Cleon, not among the fragments published by Kock, derived from the scholia for Lucian, p. 1654. Körte has a complete list of those satirized.

36. Plutarch, *Pericles*, is the source for most of the fragments about Pericles.

37. Max Radin, 'Freedom of Speech in Ancient Athens', *American Journal of Philology*, XLVIII (1927), 220.

38. Plutarch, *Pericles*, 165, 155.

39. *Ibid.*, 169.

40. *Ibid.*, 171.

41. This fragment has evoked much commentary. The text was first published in *The Oxyrhinchus Papyri* (ed. Bernard P. Grenfell and Arthur S. Hunt, London, 1904), IV, 69-72. A. Körte, 'Die Hypothesis zu Kratinos' Dionysalexandros', *Hermes*, XXXIX (1904), 481-98, also published the text with interpretation. He thinks the play was eighth in an alphabetical list and dates it about 430 or 429.

He does not consider the political satire the chief content. W. G. Rutherford, 'The Date of the Dionysalexander', *Classical Review*, XVIII (1904), 440, on the basis of an emendation thinks, 'a sense emerges which implies that when the Dionysalexander was produced the project for the legitimatizing of the younger Pericles was either debating or accomplished. "Turning to the audience they talk with one another on the question of how men may get themselves sons." ' Roy C. Flickinger, 'Certain Numerals in the Greek Dramatic Hypotheses', *Classical Philology*, V (1910), 1-18, argues that the numerals 'were a library device and were assigned the plays represented in the Alexandrian collection according to the date of their production' (p. 16). He dates the play as probably in 445 B.C.

42. Norwood, pp. 118-19, followed by interpretation.

43. Flickinger and Norwood agree in their assignment of the characters; but Norwood, p. 122, believes 'that Cratinus is primarily concerned with a riotous travesty of the legend, and works contemporary satire into the fabric purely as an undertone'; while Flickinger, *Class. Phil.*, V, 9, works out the allegory very closely, concluding, 'In the dénouement Alexander hands over Dionysus to the Achaeans and keeps Helen for himself; in other words, Cratinus advises the people to accept Pericles' plans for the city's adornment, since it is now too late to turn back, but to disavow their author and intrust their administration to safer hands.'

44. For a different interpretation see Edward Capps, 'The Nemesis of the Younger Cratinus', *Harvard Studies in Classical Philology*, XV (1904), 61-75, where he ascribes this comedy to a poet of the Middle Comedy, calling it a 'mythological travesty, incapable of sustaining a satirical allegory such as Bergk imagined' (p. 75).

45. Kaibel, pp. 6-8.

46. *Ibid.*, p. 7.

47. Other interpretations of this passage are given by those who think Epicharmus wrote comedies of manners. So Norwood, pp. 146-7, 'Crates is in this respect the forerunner of Middle and New Comedy, and also in his avoidance of verbal indecency.' Henry W. Prescott, 'The Antecedents of Hellenistic Comedy', *Classical Philology*, XII (1917), 405-25, approaches with caution the theory of a comedy of manners. He writes, p. 412, 'It should, however, be expressly stated that any attempt to reconstruct a comedy of manners from what we know of Epicharmus, Crates, and Pherecrates is bound to result merely in the accumulation of a number of

facts, each weak in itself, and many of them resting upon somewhat dubious hypotheses.'

48. Liddell and Scott, s.v. *ἰδέα*.

49. Another sign of the imitation of Epicharmus is the report by Athenaeus, X, 429a, that Crates introduced drunken men into his comedies. Compare a similar statement about Epicharmus.

50. Anon. *de Com.*, Kaibel, p. 8.

51. *Tyranny*, *Petale* (Leaf-Wreath or the name of a courtesan?), and *The Old Women*.

52. Plato, *Protagoras*, 327d, refers to this play, produced at the Lenaea, and speaks of the misanthropes in the chorus.

53. The *Chiron* is of doubtful authorship, but it must have been similar to his genuine comedies.

54. Norwood, pp. 19-22.

55. Thucydides, II, 21, 59, 65, Cp. *CAH*, V, 193-203.

56. *CAH*, V, 216, 106-10.

57. Diels-Kranz, II, 253-71. Frr. 1, 4. Cp., however, Burnet, *Thales to Plato*, pp. 110-18, in which he says of Protagoras, 'So far from being a revolutionary, he was the champion of traditional morality, not from old-fashioned prejudice, but from a strong belief in the value of social conventions' (p. 117).

58. Hippocrates (ed. and trans. W. H. S. Jones, London, 1923). A good account of Greek medicine has been written by W. R. Halliday, 'Some Notes on the Treatment of Disease in Antiquity', *Greek Life and Thought* (Oxford, 1936), pp. 277-94.

59. B. A. G. Fuller, *History of Greek Philosophy* (New York, 1931), pp. 10 ff.

60. Diels-Kranz, frr. 3, 4. Burnet, *Thales to Plato*, pp. 119-20.

61. Burnet, *Thales to Plato*, p. 118.

62. Euripides, *Hippolytus*, 612.

63. Diels-Kranz, fr. 2.

CHAPTER 4

ARISTOPHANES, THE SERVANT OF DIONYSOS

THE artistic intention of Aristophanes is apparently obvious. He wrote comedies; therefore, ostensibly, he intended to amuse his audience. In this he was successful. What more should or could one expect from a comic dramatist than the ability to evoke laughter? Yet, oddly enough, Aristophanes has rarely been studied as a comic dramatist: his wit has been often acknowledged but seldom fully appreciated, and his dramatic skill has been depreciated by all but a few. Instead, his plays have been mined for historical and sociological data, and he himself has been called a partisan of this or that political party or a patriot above party. Only recently has the need been stressed for a new interpretation of Aristophanes as a writer of comedies and not a political propagandist [1].

Now, perhaps, the pendulum is swinging too far in the other direction. We may need to pause and ask, Was Aristophanes *no more* than a writer of comedies? Did he select his material, considering only its humorous possibilities without regard for any other principle? Was he a jester without conviction, or, if he had convictions, were they private property not publicly displayed? Answering 'Yes' to these questions over-simplifies the problem: Aristophanes was not just a writer of comedies; he was a Greek comic poet.

Aristophanes himself is our best source of information about the intentions of Greek comic poets, though the fact that he was writing amusing plays strews difficulties in the critic's path. A dramatist is at best elusive, and a comic dramatist doubly so. Whatever Aristophanes says may be dismissed as a joke—a joke based on exaggeration, understatement, or contradiction. Or the characters may be speaking in character and not expressing the views of the dramatist at all. Nevertheless, with all due regard for humorous distortion and the dramatic medium, we can perceive Aristophanes's intention, principally because he was an early Greek playwright who possessed an instrument for expressing his views directly to the audience and because he felt no obligation to create or maintain a dramatic illusion. The chorus in the parabases and other odes represents the author, and the speeches of some characters belong openly and definitely to Aristophanes. The aims which he so clearly enunciates in these lyrics and speeches should be dismissed as without foundation *only* if they run counter to Greek literary tradition and to his own practice.

First of all, Aristophanes always spoke of himself and his rivals as poets or *didaskaloi*—the Greek word for teachers, here used in the sense of teachers of the chorus [2]. The Greeks had no word for dramatist or playwright, but only for tragic or comic poets or tragic or comic producers. Aristophanes was above all a poet, and the Dionysiac festival was devoted to poetry—tragic, satyric, comic, and dithyrambic. Usually the poet was also a *didaskalos*: that is, he trained the chorus to sing the music and dance the steps he had composed; he directed the actors; and he supervised the masks, costumes, and staging. By the late fifth century the production of a comedy had become so difficult an art that Aristophanes asked friends to produce three early plays and many later ones (*Knights*, 507-50; *Clouds*, 518-62). It must not be forgotten, however, that Aristophanes often did direct and produce his own comedies and that he had a practical knowledge of the theatre. The skilful way in which he turned to advantage even the limitations of the Greek theatre will be discussed in the next chapter in conjunction with his dramatic skill. His genius as a poet—his diction, imagery, metres, and literary criticism—will be studied in the following chapter. Still one thing eludes: the essence of his comedies or the point from which each radiates.

The dominating idea of all the comedies is Aristophanes's concern for the welfare of the *polis*. This word can not be adequately translated into English, though I shall render it as *city*; for sometimes it refers to a single hill, sometimes to the whole state. It was used familiarly as a shortened form for Acropolis, the centre of Athenian civic and religious life, the site of the theatre and treasury, the hill crowned with temples. In a wider sense, *polis* meant the city of Athens with its Pnyx and agora, walls and harbours, shops and houses, and all the inhabitants—citizens and their families, metics, and slaves.

Finally, since the citizens of Attica were citizens of Athens, the *polis* included the landowners and farmers of the countryside. When Aristophanes said that he taught the city what was just, his claim may have been pretentious, but to an Athenian it would not have seemed trivial [3].

Aristophanes recognized the magnitude of his task and the seriousness of his function as the teacher of the city. In his first extant play, the *Acharnians*, his spokesman says,

> Do not be angry with me, spectators, if I—a beggar—intend to speak to the Athenians about the city, making a comedy. For even a comedy knows what is right. (500.)

And in the parabasis the chorus says that the poet will teach the citizens those things which are just, good, and best (655-9). The vehemence of these protestations may be partially accounted for by the recent charge brought against the poet by Cleon. The demagogue had been seriously offended by the *Babylonians* produced the year before at the City Dionysia, when visitors from the subject islands were in the theatre. Cleon accused Aristophanes of insulting the city. Aristophanes replied through the character of Dicaeopolis (acted by himself)? [4] that he attacked not the city, 'notice that I do not say the city', but 'wretched little counterfeit fellows' (515-19). He pursues the subject in the parabasis, saying that he is worthy of many good things from the city and that he has been the cause of many benefits because he has shown the people how to govern democratically (641-2). Twenty years later Aristophanes said again, 'It is right for the sacred chorus to advise and teach the city what is best' (*Frogs*, 686-7). These words indicate that the claims he made as a young man were a serious declaration of purpose and neither the brash words of an upstart clown nor the angry taunts of a man who has narrowly escaped severe punishment.

Aristophanes expressed his concern for Athens both through the themes of his plays and in lyrics. In almost every play from the beginning to the end of his long career, the saving of the city is a dominant theme [5]. Agoracritus and Trygaeus are hailed as saviours of the city, and Lysistrata and Praxagora try to rescue the city from the mismanagement of the men. The Clouds hope that the affairs of the city will take a turn for the better; the Wasps speak of the many benefits they have bestowed upon the city. Even the *Birds*, although in a backhanded way, demonstrates Aristophanes's concern for Athens. Pisthetaerus and Euelpides, not hating the city but dismayed by the many lawsuits, seek to found an ideal city elsewhere. Aristophanes was keenly aware of the many evils of Athens, but he loved his city and sang her praises in one of his most beautiful lyrics.

> Rain-bearing maidens we come to the fruitful land of Pallas, beholding the lovely country of Cecrops, abundant in good men. Here secret rites are reverenced; here the temple of the initiates flings wide the gates in the holy mysteries. Behold temples for the heavenly gods! Lofty-roofed shrines and statues! The most holy processions of the blessed and the well-crowned sacrifices and festivities of the gods in every season! And with the returning spring Bacchic joy, the exciting contests of melodious choruses, and the strong deep music of the flutes. (*Clouds*, 299-313.)

And again in a fragment,

> Oh dear city of Cecrops, autochthonous Attica!
> Hail glistening plain, most fertile of good land. (Fr. 110.)

Athens needed, according to Aristophanes, not only saving but also purifying. He calls himself *alexikakos* and *kathartes*, the averter of evil and purifier of the country (*Wasps*, 1043). Both words are pregnant with religious meaning. The worship of Apollo *alexikakos* had been recently introduced into Athens at the time of the plague, for Apollo was the god of healing as well as of prophecy and poetry [6]. The cry, *alalalai ie paion*, sacred to Apollo, rings through many choruses. He is also invoked in a hymn addressed to the three gods to whom Aristophanes was most devoted—Apollo, Athene, and Dionysos.

> Speak to me Phoebus, Master, Delian who dwells on the high-crowned Cynthian rock. And the blessed one who lives in the golden home of Ephesus honored by Lydian maidens. And our native goddess, the aegis-bearing guardian of the city, Athene. And he, possessing the Parnassian rock, who shines forth with the Delphian Bacchae, revelling Dionysos. (*Clouds*, 595 ff.)

Of these three gods, Dionysos was Aristophanes's favourite. This is, of course, to be expected. Dionysos was the patron god of the drama. The comedies were part of his cult and an outgrowth of his ritual. The god himself was escorted to the theatre at the beginning of the festival, and his priest had the seat of honour in the front row. Nor is there any evidence that these were merely obsolete conventions without true religious significance. Aristophanes was not only aware of the meaning of Dionysos; he worshipped him [7].

Almost all the aspects and rituals of Dionysiac cult are represented in the comedies. The Rural Dionysia is celebrated by Dicaeopolis in the *Acharnians*, with the god invoked as Phales (263 ff.). In the *Frogs* the Mystae call him Iacchus, link him with Demeter, and stress his love of the chorus (340 ff.). The chorus of the *Thesmophoriazusae* sing of the 'ivy wearing Bacchus', son of Semele, who haunts the wooded mountain sides (985 ff.). The revelling Dionysos of Delphi is celebrated in the ode from the *Clouds* quoted above. Reminiscences of Dionysos Lysios are to be found in the references to Lysimaches and in the name Lysistrata. The priest of Dionysos sends for Dicaeopolis to attend the Feast of the Cups, and the many marriages which end the plays may well reflect the influence of the sacred marriage between Dionysos and the Queen of Athens.

Dionysos was also the hero of Aristophanes's most popular and successful play, the *Frogs*. It was appropriate for the patron god of drama to seek a great tragic poet when the deaths of Sophocles and Euripides had left on earth only inferior dramatists, and it was equally appropriate that he should be the judge of the contest between Aeschylus and Euripides. Everyone concedes this, but the religious sincerity of Aristophanes has been questioned [8]. Was not Aristophanes blasphemous when he presented Dionysos as a craven fool? How could any religious man portray his god acting in such ignoble ways? To-day, it would be impossible, but the Greek anthropomorphic religion admitted freely the vices and weaknesses of the gods so long as their essential attributes were unquestioned. Dionysos had been cowardly in the *Iliad*, and his love of wine and women was revered and not depreciated. As the god of comedy he aroused laughter; as the god of tragedy he aroused pity and terror. Is not this dual role natural for the god of drama and the god of wine?

Two themes with religious bearing run through the plays.

They are reconciliation and release. Reconciliation is personified by the chorus in the *Acharnians* (989) and appears as a beautiful maiden at the end of the *Lysistrata.* In these two plays particularly, and in many others, the reconciliation of opposites is a leading idea. Hermes in the *Peace* is delighted when the Greek cities are reconciled (541); Poseidon leads an embassy in the *Birds* to gain accord with Pisthetaerus (1577, 1532); and Bdelycleon hopes that he and his father may agree without recourse to blows (*Wasps*, 472).

The need of releasing or freeing the city of evils and ills is even more significant, although the idea of release is not personified. Dicaeopolis, himself released from war and evils (*Acharnians*, 201), prays to Phales, comrade of Bacchus, to free the people from battles and troubles (267-70). Trygaeus seeks beloved peace in order that all the Greeks may be liberated from battles and troubles (*Peace*, 293-4). Chremylus restores the sight of Wealth so that just men may be released from a chilly and uncomfortable life (*Plutus*, 115, 263).

In four other plays the chief characters are suffering from a disease or madness for which either they or their relatives are looking for relief. So Pheidippides is sick with horse fever, a disease which has driven his father into debt and necessitates his seeking an escape (*Clouds*, 74, 243). Pheidippides is cured by Socrates, but unfortunately the cure is as disastrous as the disease. The theme of the *Wasps* is similar. In this play it is the father who is sick, and the son desperately seeking a cure (71, 503). Bdelycleon has tried to reason with his father; then to purify him; and after that to make a Corybant of him. When those rites were unsuccessful, he took his father to Aegina and the temple of Asclepius, again without success. Bdelycleon says that he wishes only to release him from his 'early-prowling base-informing, sad-litigious plaguey ways'. Later he remarks, 'It is hard even for a clever opinion and one greater than those found in comedies to cure a disease long ago bred in the city' (650-1). Euelpides says that he and his friend are leaving Athens because they are sick of troubles and long for a quiet city (*Birds*, 31), and Dionysos goes in search of Euripides because he is maddened with desire for his tragedies (*Frogs*, 59, 66). The chorus of women in the *Lysistrata* pray to Athene to save the city from war and madness (342).

Directly and indirectly, through choruses, speeches, characters, and plots, in all the comedies Aristophanes plays the variations of a single theme. Save the state! Avert evil, free the city of war and troubles, of sickness and madness, and clothe it anew in the glistening garments of the Marathon-fighters. Aristophanes thus combined the functions of teacher, prophet, priest, and doctor into the single aim of the poet.

In so doing he was no more than continuing the traditional functions of the poet, as he himself clearly recognized. He tells how the very earliest poets, Orpheus and Mousaeus, had conferred many benefits upon mankind: the first by teaching men sacred rites and the need of refraining from murder, the second by teaching cures of diseases and the interpretation of oracles. Hesiod instructed men in the working of the land and the seasons of the year; Homer taught men virtue and the arts of war (*Frogs*, 1030 ff.). Euripides in the *Frogs* says that the function of the poet is to make men better citizens (1009), and the Poet in the *Birds* tells Pisthetaerus, 'We are all teachers, nimbly serving the Muses according to Homer' (912).

The whole history of Greek poetry supports the claims of Aristophanes. Hesiod was clearly both a didactic and religious poet. The elegiac poets frequently sang advice to their native cities, urging the citizens to defend their countries and to adopt just laws. Solon, in particular, the first Athenian poet, had been passionately devoted to Athens and her welfare. The iambic poets, too, had a religious function, the expunging of evil by ridicule.

If Aristophanes's artistic intention is so clearly in accord with that of other Greek poets, why then does he insist upon his right to advise the city? He seems, in fact, sometimes to apologize for being serious and at other times to boast of his originality. A large part of his claim of originality must be assigned to poetic conceit, comic exaggeration, and the strong Greek competitive spirit. The Greeks spoke well of themselves in a way foreign to us. Pindar is a good example of this trait. Moreover, the comedies were being exhibited in a competition, and Aristophanes naturally was eager to win the prize. Praising his own wisdom, usefulness, and cleverness might sway the judges to vote in his favour.

Comedy had from the beginning been amusing, and the amusing as Aristotle recognized is likely to be dismissed as insignificant. The other comic poets may not have been fully aware of their ancient prerogatives as poets; they may have merely seized upon the humorous possibilities of iambic ritual scurrility and exploited them. We tread upon uncertain ground here, for few fragments remain of Aristophanes's rivals, and he is not a completely reliable witness when a prize is at stake. Nevertheless, there does seem to be some truth in his claims to have developed more fully than his competitors the intellectual and political aspects of comedy. He attacked Cleon while the other poets contented themselves with the weaker Hyperbolus, and he continued his attacks in the face of dangerous threats from Cleon (*Clouds*, 518 ff.; *Wasps*, 1015 ff.). He persisted in urging the Athenians to make peace throughout the Peloponnesian War.

Aristophanes scorns the low tricks used by other comic poets, the red-tipped leather phallus at which the boys laughed, the jokes about bald men, the *kordax* (an indecent dance), the old man striking another with a staff, torches, and cries of '*iou, iou!*' (*Clouds*, 537 ff.). He regarded with disfavour characters in rags fighting lice, Heracles eating and complaining of hunger, and stale dialogue between slaves (*Wasps*, 58 ff.). On occasion he himself made use of these farcical devices with the exception of the *kordax*, nowhere certainly danced in his comedies. The phallus played a prominent part in the *Lysistrata*; he jokes about his own baldness (*Peace*, 765-774); Strepsiades beats off his creditors; Cleon cries out '*iou, iou!*' when the Sausage-seller strikes him (*Knights*, 451); Heracles is hungry in the *Frogs*; two slaves open the *Wasps* and the *Peace*. The hackneyed can be turned to fresh use, as the opening of the *Frogs* testifies, where Dionysos forbids Xanthias to repeat hackneyed jokes, or the opening of the *Knights*, where Nicias and Demosthenes are the 'slaves' of the People. Aristophanes's claim—'I contrive skilfully, introducing new ideas'—is not an empty boast (*Clouds*, 547).

What distinguishes Aristophanes from his contemporaries, so far as I can judge from the limited evidence, is his full consciousness of his purpose in life, of the serious function of comedy in civic life, and the breadth and depth of his interpretations. He did not ridicule private men and women (he never mentioned by name an Athenian woman), but only public men, men whose lives, habits, ideas affected the body politic [9]. He saw beyond individuals to their principles and effects and tackled with courage and persistence the real issues of his day.

THE IDEAL OF ARISTOPHANES

Aristophanes is unusual among satirists because he presented what he liked as vividly as what he disliked. He preached the Dionysiac way of life, a life of joy and comfort, of personal modesty and reverence for the gods, of just dealings among men, civic responsibility without meddlesomeness, and as the great prerequisite for all this—peace. This inclusive programme extended all the way from 'international' accord through 'national' prosperity and social ethics to individual morals and religion. Despite the breadth of Aristophanes's view, the whole ideal is consistent and, if put into practice, would have insured the happiness of all.

The love of and longing for peace which permeate the comedies can only be appreciated when we recall the sombre times in which they were written. Aristophanes had little first hand knowledge of peace. The incidents foreshadowing the Peloponnesian War began in 435 when Aristophanes was a youth of fifteen or sixteen. Three years later the Megarian Decrees (economic sanctions imposed by Athens on Megara which almost ruined the tiny state) were promulgated. Pericles thought the war with Sparta inevitable and refused to make the concessions which alone could have postponed, if not prevented, war entirely. War broke out in 431, when Aristophanes was about twenty years old, continued until the Peace of Nicias in 421, was renewed in 413, and ended in the utter defeat of Athens in 404. The most productive years of Aristophanes's life were thus spent in the shadow of war.

No record of his military service has come down to us, though probably Aristophanes participated in some of the campaigns. However, even if he did not stir from Attica, he could see clearly for himself the ravages of war. The yearly invasions of the Spartans left a ruined countryside of burned houses and uprooted vineyards. The country people were driven from ancestral homes into a crowded city. Plague broke out and civic life was disrupted. In the second war the disastrous Sicilian expedition and other costly battles took a large toll of Athenian manhood. The difference in effects of the two wars is clearly reflected in the comedies. The early plays are concerned with the problems of rescuing the farms; the later ones with the need of restoring the men to their homes.

The policy of Pericles had been to rely upon the navy and foreign trade, leaving the country to the enemy. This was possible because Athens was changing from an agricultural to an industrial economy in which manufactured exports could pay for imported food. A mild war might stimulate industry and trade; at any rate the seaways and free trade with the colonies must be protected. Aristophanes urged the maintenance of the older system, believing that prosperity was based on the cultivation of the land, which in turn necessitated peace [10]. Aristophanes says in a fragment, 'Rich Peace and a little team of oxen, if ever an end of war should come, I shall dig and hoe and then—having bathed—I shall eat shining bread and new wine and cabbage' (fr. 109). Cultivation he calls the sister and daughter of Peace, dear to all men (fr. 294).

The *Acharnians* and *Peace* are full expressions of this essential connection between peace and prosperity. Dicaeopolis makes a private treaty with Sparta and sets up a market for the buying of agricultural products from Megara and Boeotia. Trygaeus (his very name signifies his occupation as a vineyard worker) brings back to earth Opora and Theoria with Peace. Opora is the fruits of the fields and Theoria is public festivals. The latter smells of fruit, entertainment, Dionysiac frolics, flutes, tragedies, the songs of Sophocles, dithyrambs, and the words of Euripides (*Peace*, 529 ff.).

Private bliss as well as public wealth springs from peace. The bridegroom in the *Acharnians* asks Dicaeopolis for a little of his treaty. The women too want peace: the married women so that their husbands will stay at home; the mothers so that their sons will not be killed; the young women so that they can have a chance to marry while the fresh bloom of youth is still upon them. Family life, sexual delight, joy, comfort, poetry and the arts all depend upon the attainment and preservation of peace.

Yet with all his passionate longing for peace, Aristophanes

does not prefer peace at any price or condone cowardice. He praises often those who fight in defence of their country, particularly those veterans of the Persian wars who fought at Marathon against the Persian hordes and saved Athens from foreign domination. The Acharnians, Knights, and Wasps all boast of their achievements as young soldiers, boasts no doubt frequently heard among Athenians of the older generation. Though they speak in character, Aristophanes plainly sympathizes with them. Moreover, Aeschylus in the *Frogs* claims as his contribution to Athenian welfare that he has made men more warlike through his tragedies.

Peace could be achieved, Aristophanes thought in 411 B.C., if the Athenian people would elect and support good officials, relinquish their anger, try to see the Spartan point of view, and compromise (*Lysistrata*, 574-86). The Spartans had several times suggested peace, but the Athenians, then in a strong position, repulsed the offers. They were ready for a truce only when necessity compelled them to capitulate. Thus in the *Lysistrata* Spartans and Athenians are brought together by force to talk directly to each other, yielding a point here and a point there. At the banquet the wine and food calm their tempers and dispel their suspicions so that at the end, united in common Greek fellowship, they sing the praises of both Sparta and Athens.

International peace (*eirene*) has a counterpart in national concord or *hesychia*. Another Greek word, *apragmosyne*, denotes a similar concept—the absence of troublesome affairs. Aristophanes wished and hoped for a city in which people quietly minded their own business, earned a decent living and interfered with no one. At the same time he thought the people (*demos*) should be the real and not the nominal rulers of the state. They should come promptly to the Assembly and vote intelligently (*Knights*, 1340 ff.). Euelpides describes the ideal city thus:

> Where the greatest troubles would be these: some one of my friends would come early to my door saying, 'By Olympian Zeus, come to my house, you and your children, having washed early, for I intend to hold a marriage feast. And don't do anything else; but if you won't come, don't come to me then when I am in ill circumstance. (*Birds*, 128 ff.)

The Birds promise the Athenians, their children and their children's children, 'a wealthy and healthy, happy, peaceful life, full of youth, laughter, choruses, festivals, and the milk of birds' (*Birds*, 729-33).

This desire for freedom from troubles was not an escape from responsibility. Euelpides founded another city; he did not retire to a cave. Moreover, the private citizens praised by Aristophanes were extremely active in affairs of state. He speaks highly of the heroes of the Persian Wars—Aristides, Miltiades, and Themistocles (*Knights*, 812 ff.). He revered Thucydides, son of Melesias, a conservative statesman who had been superseded by Pericles, and he mentions with respect the general Myronides, and the naval officer, Phormion [11]. Nicias and Demosthenes of his own day he defended as the real victors at Pylos, defrauded by Cleon of the just recognition of their victory. In general, he approved of citizens who were 'well-born, modest, manly, just, "beautiful-and-good", nourished in the palaestra, choral dancing, and the arts' (*Frogs*, 727 ff.).

His preference, so clearly expressed, has given rise to the notion that he was an aristocrat [12]. He was, in the sense that he wanted the best to govern, but he was at the same time a democrat who wished the *demos* to rule. The paradox is resolved only when the *demos* and the *aristoi*, the people and the best, are one. The best evidence for this statement is the *Knights*, the comedy in which the deluded, doddering Demos is rejuvenated. He reappears in ancient costume, wearing the cicada, and taking to himself a beautiful maiden named Treaties. When Aristophanes told the audience that he fought in their behalf, he spoke to the Athenian people and not to a special clique.

This Dionysiac way of life was not restricted to men. The chorus of women in the *Lysistrata* describe their maidenhood as follows:

> When I was seven years old, I carried a basket containing secret objects; then, when I was ten, I ground the wheat for our Founder; next I wore the yellow robe as bearer at the Brauronian festival for Artemis; and when I became a lovely maiden, I carried a chain of figs and a sacred basket on my head at the festivals of Bacchus, Demeter, and Athene. (641-7.)

The religious duties of Athenian women were many, and some festivals were entirely theirs—the Thesmophoria, for instance, to which no man was admitted. The private life of women, so long as war did not interfere, would consist of early marriage and then many domestic duties. The weaving of clothes, a long process beginning with the preparation of the wool, occupied a large part of their time and energies. The good management of the home was desirable, if not always the accomplished fact that Praxagora and Lysistrata claimed for Athenian women.

The ideal life for men is even more clearly etched. Just Argument describes the fine life of a young man.

> But shining and blooming you will spend your days in physical exercise,
> Not mouthing coarse jests in the market-place as the young men do now
> Nor being dragged into court about some greedy, pettifogging, knavish lawsuit,
> But you will go down into the Academy and run beneath the sacred olives
> With some temperate youth of your own age, garlanded with the white reed,
> And smelling with honeysuckle and the life of ease and the white poplar shedding its leaves,
> Rejoicing in the spring season when the plane tree whispers to the elm. (*Clouds*, 1002-8.)

As he grows older, he should earn a temperate living at honest work. Aristophanes shows no scorn for merchants, craftsmen, or farmers; in fact, through the mouth of Poverty, he recognizes the necessity for workers as the bases of life [13]. On the other hand, he objects to any pursuit which monopolizes the time and attention of men, whether it be war, lawsuits, education, or horses. The happy man is the one who can accept the invitation of the priest of Dionysos.

> Hasten, for you have been keeping the dinner waiting. Everything else is ready: the couches, tables, cushions, mattresses, wreathes, perfume, dessert, the wenches, the cakes, cookies, sesame cakes, wafers, and the beautiful dancing girls, and the delight of Harmodius. (*Acharnians*, 1088-93.)

The old men should be cared for by their sons in appropriate ways with barley-soup to guzzle, a soft cloak, and a young girl (*Wasps*, 736).

Men and women will find happiness if they enjoy the good things of life, indulge in no excesses, and wrong no one. A balanced, intelligent, comfortable way of life, but contingent upon international peace and national harmony.

THE SATIRE OF ARISTOPHANES

The reverse of this ideal picture is even more sharply drawn. The comic poet could naturally portray ugliness, vice, and stupidity with greater humorous effect than beauty, virtue, or intelligence. As a result, we find in the comedies not only the counterparts of the virtues—War for Peace, Unjust Argument for Just Argument—but also a swarm of contemporaries and lesser characters pilloried for the amusement and instruction of the audience.

War is presented in the *Peace* as a dreadful giant, chopping the Greek states into mincemeat. His servant is Kudoimos or the Hubbub which accompanies war. His instruments are the Athenian pestle (Cleon) and the Spartan mortar (Brasidas). Cleon, constantly attacked in the plays, was particularly abhorrent to Aristophanes because he urged the people not to accept Spartan offers of peace and stirred up Athenian anger and hatred against the Spartans. For similar reasons Aristophanes disapproved of Pericles, and twice he tried to thrust the blame for the Peloponnesian War upon the high-handed policy of Pericles, his devotion to Aspasia, and his fear (*Acharnians*, 523 ff.; *Peace*, 605).

In addition to these individuals, groups of citizens favoured the continuance of war. The munitions makers, of course, profited by war and wished to sustain the market for shields, helmets, and spears. The military men, too, could earn their livelihood and practise their skill only during a war, and the informers had a bigger scope for their nefarious activities when trade restrictions made traffic with the enemy treasonous. Otherwise estimable people thought the war should be continued until Sparta had been completely defeated because they were angry at the destruction of the countryside and at the deceitfulness of their enemy. Aristophanes denounced the warmongers and war profiteers, and tried to convince the sincerely angry Athenians of their errors in judgment, but he never condoned cowardice. Cleisthenes is repeatedly scorned for throwing away his shield.

Democratic government of the Athenian kind, in which each citizen had direct voting power in the Assembly, was not at its best in the troublesome times of war in defence of an empire. One demagogue after another came to the fore, each one worse than his predecessor. Pericles had been a great man. He was succeeded by a leather-worker, Cleon, strong and shrewd but brutal. After his death Hyperbolus seized power and then Cleophon, neither good statesmen though not so dangerous as Cleon because they were weaker. Two revolutions engineered by the oligarchs upset the democracy—the Revolution of the Four Hundred in 411 and of the Thirty in 404.

Throughout his career Aristophanes struggled against this usurpation of power by demagogues and oligarchs. He held up for ridicule the gullibility of Demos and its susceptibility to flattery. The people needed only to be told that Athens was shining and violet-crowned, and they would grant the orator anything he wished (*Knights*, 1329). They needed only to be thrown a few obols for attending the Assembly or judging the lawsuits, and they would ignore the huge resources being squandered by their apparent benefactors (*Wasps*, 682 ff.). It was Aristophanes's desire to awaken the people to a real knowledge of their power and to expose the devices with which the demagogues were disguising their evil ways.

Another disease in the body politic was the abuse of the judicial system. The panel of judges might run to as many as one thousand, and ten courts might sit in one day. The judges earned three obols a day, just enough for a bare livelihood, but attractive to old men who could not earn a living elsewhere. The pleas of the defendants gave the men a sense of power they would not otherwise have known. Aristophanes satirizes their vindictiveness in the *Wasps*, at the same time that he ascribes their failings to delusion rather than innate malevolence and sympathizes with their poverty.

For the sycophants he has no sympathy whatsoever. They prowled through the streets looking for some breach of law in order that they might denounce the culprit and win a share of his fine if he were convicted. The system originally was democratic because it assumed that every citizen was responsible for law and order, but it was easily abused. In many plays these sycophants are caught and driven from the stage with execration. The litigiousness of the Athenians, their restless eagerness to try a new scheme, and their optimism that somehow they would muddle through, and that the gods would rescue them from harm are heartily condemned by Aristophanes.

Just as distasteful to him were all the pretenders and boasters, the idle babblers, the irreverent, and unjust. He denounces the Sophists and their students as word-quibblers who care little about either truth or morality so long as they can win an argument. They have dethroned Zeus and the ancient anthropomorphic gods and deified instead the natural forces of Air and Whirlpool. The charges levelled against Socrates at his trial are also hurled by Aristophanes in the *Clouds*: he is a corrupter of youth, an atheist, and a believer in strange gods. Euripides is even more offensive.

The atheistical teachers and physical scientists were not the only enemies of religion. The votaries of religion were themselves corrupt. The priests were greedy opportunists. Beggars wandered around the country trying to sell oracles, reciting verses supposed to have been delivered from the god through Bakis. Other false prophets smelled out sacrifices and demanded the right to read the omens from the entrails in order that they might have a good dinner.

Lowest of all on the scale were the *pharmakoi*, those wretches of known vice and filth from whose ranks a human sacrifice was made each year. Stratton, Ariphrades, Cleisthenes were three of the worst among many named by Aristophanes. Tolerant as he was of many weaknesses, he unceasingly flays dirt, cowardice, effeminacy, lasciviousness, and unmentionable vices.

Hardly a prominent individual or group escaped the satirist's sting. Even Sophocles, so universally admired and often praised by Aristophanes, was accused of avarice. His victims ranged from high to low, from Pericles to the swinish Theogenes, from the general Lamachus to the effeminate fop Amynias. The Athenian women, though not singled out by name for reproach, were portrayed as excessively fond of the pleasures of bed and bottle [14].

THE PROFESSION OF THE COMIC POET

To interpret Aristophanes simply as a wit or as a playwright or as a political propagandist misses the point and consequently the value of his work. He looked upon the life of his day, as a Greek poet would, with a compound of purposes for which modern civilization offers no analogies. Either to overestimate or underestimate his seriousness is equally fallacious; for he can neither be accepted as a reliable source of historical data nor dismissed as a buffoon. The function of the Greek comic poet was the product of over a century's growth, slowly evolving with the increasing importance of the theatre and the changing needs of the people. The maintenance of this inheritance and the privileges accorded the profession were really the first concern of the poet.

This professional loyalty goes far to explain the essential conservatism which is so prominent in his comedies and so seemingly incompatible with his gay mockery. Comic poetry, as he knew it, could only flourish in a peaceful, prosperous city governed by intelligent and literate people who wished to preserve religious festivals, to grant the comic poet full freedom of speech, to bear willingly the expense of producing plays with splendour, and to appreciate the most subtle witticisms and literary allusions.

The demagogues infringed on these rights by trying to suppress those who spoke boldly. The degenerating taste of the spectators led them to prefer vulgar characters and cheap tricks to the clever dishes Aristophanes served them. The Sophists, most outrageous of all, tried to take the place of the poets. They offered advice and expected to be paid for it. They also undermined the influence of the comic poets by denying their religious sanctions and setting up success in law and politics as the goal of life.

The fragments of the other comic poets confirm this interpretation of Aristophanes. So far as we can tell from the limited remains, all the poets of Greek Old Comedy had similar aims and similar objects of attack. The far-fetched supposition that they were all party hacks for an oligarchical clique is not necessary to explain these similarities. They practised the same profession, a profession so closely linked with the state, religion, and literary tradition that the diversity of aims found in our contemporary theatre is not comparable.

Eupolis was Aristophanes's chief rival [15]. For him too the welfare of the city came first:

> Oh city, city, how fortunate you are rather than how well you plan! (Fr. 205.)
>
> Oh best city of all, upon which Cleon looks, how happy you were formerly and now will be. It is necessary that first of all freedom of speech should be given to all. (Frr. 290-1.)

He speaks of someone who has brought pollution into the city, and of Cleon, who has distressed the city in many ways. Again he says that many things come to be in a long time by a change from troubles.

He stood for many of the same ideas that Aristophanes did, and attacked the same men. He disliked babblers, Socrates, Protagoras, and other Sophists. The dignity, too, of the profession was being lowered by the meanness of the choregus, the unseemly jokes, the Megarian and stale comedy, the childish tricks which the audience enjoyed. Even the more sophisticated members of the audience are accused of turning away from native Athenians to listen to foreign poets.

The same names crop up throughout the fragments of Old Comedy. The demagogues lead—Cleon, Hyperbolus, and Cleophon—the last two receiving the doubtful honour of being the titles of comedies. Other prominent citizens satirized include Antiphon, Nicias, and Peisander. The Sophists are second, with Socrates in the lead and Protagoras, Prodicus, and Chaerephon not far behind. Euripides is frequently ridiculed; Sophocles often praised. The human dregs, *katharmata*, are ones we have met before: Theogenes, Morsimus, Sthenelus, and Melanthius.

Though the comic poets united in attacking the men and trends dangerous to their profession, they were by no means a harmonious group. Their jealousy was stimulated by the highly competitive system of production. Only eight comedies were produced each year—three at the City Dionysia and five at the Lenaea—and only two could win the first prize. Moreover, the authors were not hampered by any modern ideas of professional ethics. Aristophanes speaks condescendingly of his older rivals Magnes, Crates, and Cratinus, and slightingly of the others. He accuses them of plagiarism, cowardice, vulgarity, and stupidity. They in turn mocked his bald head, his preoccupation with Euripides, his large statue of Peace.

The Greek comic poets were a jealous group—jealous of each other, jealous for their privileges and prerogatives, and jealous for the glory of Athens. They wished to see her honour unstained by foreign domination or native corruption; they bent every effort to maintain the splendour they imagined had invested the city in earlier days. But they were struggling against the full force of progress or degeneration according to one's point of view. Athens was defeated by Sparta and never regained her imperial power. Agriculture gave way to commerce and industry. The old state religion sank in importance as new foreign religions, atheism, science, and philosophy gained in influence. The fourth-century philosophers Plato and Aristotle would have banished the scurrilous poets of Old Comedy as corrupters of youth if comedy had not changed by their time. The iambic ritual of personal satire, fantasy, and licence gave way to a new kind of comedy. Everything the old comic poets had fought for was dead.

NOTES FOR CHAPTER 4

1. A complete bibliography of Aristophanic criticism is beyond the scope of this book; a few typical examples will have to suffice. Werner Jaeger, *Paideia* (trans. from the 2nd German ed. by Gilbert Highet, Oxford, 1939), I, 362: 'Comedy was the censorship of Athens. That is what makes Aristophanes' wit so deadly serious despite its mask of outrageous laughter.' David Grene, 'The Comic Technique of Aristophanes', *Hermathena*, L (1937), 88: 'First and foremost the Attic Comedian is a propagandist and only secondly a playwright.' Edward Capps, 'Comedy', *Greek Literature* (New York, 1912), p. 140: 'Aristophanes no doubt does pose as a reformer, as a censor of morals, as a sage adviser, and as a benefactor of the people. It is the pose habitual to the satirist, a part of his stock in trade. As for the moral effect of the ribald jokes and obscene buffoonery of our Athenian reformer, the less said the better.' A. W. Gomme, 'Aristophanes and Politics', *Classical Review*, LII (1938), 97, complains because scholars have regarded Aristophanes 'as primarily a politician: a man with a policy to advocate, opinions

to defend, who wants to see certain things done—in this sense a *practical* man'. They 'do not think of him as a dramatist', and give only lip service to him as a comic poet. Gomme believes that 'impartiality is a desirable quality for most of us; for an artist it is essential—or rather a positive sympathy, for impartiality is but a negative quality. . . . All drama represents a conflict of some kind; but there will be little success for the writer who can only take one side' (p. 102). A moderate position is maintained by John Williams White, Introduction to the English Version, Maurice Croiset, *Aristophanes and the Political Parties at Athens* (London, 1909), p. xiv; 'This extreme conception of the function of Greek comedy as chiefly censorial and monitory has been modified. . . . On the other hand the mistaken disposition, recently manifested, to regard Aristophanes simply as a jester and to deny that he had any other purpose than to provoke laughter is an extreme, though natural, reaction.' William Meredith Hugill, *Panhellenism in Aristophanes* (Chicago, 1936), takes a sound stand in his Preface.

2. Victor Ehrenberg, *The People of Aristophanes* (Oxford, 1943), p. 17, says, 'The poet was the *chorodidaskalos*, the teacher and trainer of the chorus (*A.* 628f.); the "comic poet" was the "comedy teacher" (*P.* 734, 737), and in this quality the true servant of the Muses (*B.* 912f.), just like the "tragedy teacher" (*Th.* 88). This means that he himself wrote the words and rehearsed the music and the dancing of the chorus.'

3. The word *polis* was used by Aristophanes more than one hundred and twenty-five times according to the concordance. In some contexts the city and the theatre are equated, as Ehrenberg points out, p. 26. Agoracritus, *Knights*, 1316 f., says, 'It is fitting to speak fairly, to shut one's mouth and refrain from bearing witness and to close up the law courts in which this city rejoices so that the spectators may sing a song of triumph at their new good fortunes.' Ehrenberg, p. 242, states this point succinctly: 'The chief aim, therefore, of all the political attacks in comedy is in essence unpolitical, the securing of a clean public life.' Mitchell Carroll, 'The Athens of Aristophanes', *Studies in Honor of Basil L. Gildersleeve* (Baltimore, 1902), pp. 241-52, cites all the references to the mountains, demes, wells, gates, harbours, buildings, and statues, a convincing demonstration of Aristophanes's love and knowledge of Attica and Athens.

4. Cyril Bailey, 'Who Played "Dicaeopolis"?' *Greek Poetry and Life* (Oxford, 1936), pp. 231-40, answers 'Aristophanes'. He points out how rarely the first person is used even in the parabasis and how naturally Dicaeopolis speaks of himself as a comic poet. He suggests

that the name means 'a just city' and compares Aristophanes's use of the word with Pindar's Pythian Ode, VIII, 31, in which Pindar addresses Aegina. 'Is not *Δικαιόπολις*, the famous Pindaric epithet, besides its primary meaning, intended to suggest the "Aeginetan", just as a character called *'Ιοστέφανος* would inevitably be an Athenian? And if it is the "Aeginetan", then it is Aristophanes; the hero's name was a clue to his actor' (p. 238).

5. *Knights*, 149; *Wasps*, 650-1; *Clouds*, 576; *Peace*, 914, 1035; *Birds*, 36; *Lysistrata*, 498; *Frogs*, 1030; *Ecclesiazusae*, 105-9.

6. Walter Addison Jayne, *The Healing Gods of Ancient Civilization* (New Haven, 1925), pp. 309 ff. L. R. Farnell, *The Cults of the Greek States* (Oxford, 1909), V, 133, says, 'It is only indeed at Athens that a Dionysos *'Ιατρός* is attested on fair evidence. . . . .'

7. See particularly the choral ode in the *Clouds*, 595-606.

8. The religious views of Aristophanes are a controversial subject. The following opinions are representative of the two opposing modern interpretations. Roy C. Flickinger, *The Greek Theater and Its Drama* (4th ed. Chicago, 1936), p. 127, writes, 'Furthermore, the Sicilian mime seems to have been unassociated with religious worship, and perhaps this fact has a share in explaining the irreverent, almost atheistic, tendency which Attic comedy manifested. Though it was part of divine worship, it treated the divinities with the utmost disrespect. Even Dionysus himself, the patron deity of the festivals, is represented in Aristophanes's *Frogs* as cowardly, lecherous, and foolish, beaten with many stripes before the eyes of his worshippers.' A. W. Verrall, *Euripides the Rationalist* (Cambridge, 1895), pp. 82-3, says in contrast: 'To our habitual feelings it is somewhat odd to see Aristophanes, while in the very act of exhibiting in postures of farce or harlequinade the patron-god of the sacred theatre, idol and leader of the deepest and tenderest mysteries, turn round to vilify the innovators who dared to depreciate the accepted deities in comparison with their own inventions. But it is constantly assumed by the comedian, that no confusion was possible between his attitude in this relation and that of such a man as Euripides; it is assumed that his own ridicule was in the popular sense religious, and that of Euripides in the like sense irreligious, the two forms not merely different but antagonistic.'

Various explanations for the puzzling religious beliefs of Aristophanes have been offered. Jules Girard, 'La Religion dans Aristophane', *Revue des Deux Mondes*, XXVIII (1878), 589-615, and XXX (1878), 391-417, stresses the significance of the popular religion and the state cult. Otto Moessner, *Die Mythologie in der dorischen und altattischen Komödie* (Erlangen, 1907), agrees, pointing out in addition the intimacy of human beings with human gods and the freedom which sprang from a lack of priests and holy documents (pp. 22-3). Comparison is frequently made between Athenian and medieval religious customs. The analogy is based upon the similarity of saints to gods and the unquestioning belief of the faithful which prevents their fault-finding or playfulness from becoming irreverent. As Basil L. Gildersleeve wrote, 'Orthodoxy covered a multitude of sins then as it does now.' *Selections from the Brief Mention* (ed. C. W. E. Miller, Baltimore, 1930), p. 226.

It is important to remember that the majority of Athenians were superstitious and intolerant, that if they had considered the comedies of Aristophanes impious threats to the religious foundation of the state they would never have permitted them to be performed. Evidence for this may be found in the ambiguity of the tragedies of Euripides, the exile of Anaxagoras, the execution of Socrates, the fear aroused by the mutilation of the Hermae on the eve of the sailing for Sicily, and the harm done Alcibiades by the rumour that he had held a mock celebration of the mysteries.

9. La Rue Van Hook, 'Crime and Criminals in the Plays of Aristophanes', *Classical Journal*, XXIII (1927-28), 282.

10. Ehrenberg, chap. 3.

11. *Acharnians*, 703 ff.; *Lysistrata*, 801 ff.

12. This is the theory of A. Couat, *Aristophane et l'Ancienne Comédie Attique* (Paris, 1889). He supports his argument by pointing out that the dramatists were of humble origin and had no visible means of support aside from the prizes and that production depended on the archons who chose the plays and the choreguses who paid for the costumes and training of the poets. For rebuttal, see Croiset, p. 15, n. 1. The main difficulty lies in the lack of tangible evidence linking Aristophanes with a specific party or individual aristocrats.

13. *Plutus*, 510 ff. Ehrenberg, p. 239.

14. Herman W. Haley, 'The Social and Dramatic Position of Women in Aristophanes', *Harvard Studies in Classical Philology*, I (1890), 159-86, while making allowances for comic effect, thinks that the popular opinion of women is exemplified in the comedies. He adds to their faults coarse language, deception, and superstition.

15. For Eupolis see Kock, I, 258-369; G. Kaibel in *RE*, s.v. 'Eupolis'; and Gilbert Norwood, *Greek Comedy* (London, 1931), pp. 178-201.

CHAPTER 5

ARISTOPHANES, COMIC DRAMATIST

Aristophanes was faced with a double problem: he had to convey his ideas to his audience both dramatically and amusingly. The difficulty lay in the fact that the simplest and most direct method of communicating ideas is also the least dramatic and inclined to be the least amusing. He could speak to the spectators through one or more characters, plainly stating the opinions he held, but such barefaced teaching was in ill accord with a comedy and not at all dramatic. He thus would risk losing the attention of the audience, and both his teachings and his comedy would fail. The other two methods of expressing ideas—allegory and example—while more dramatic and potentially more humorous, may be ambiguous. Aristophanes solved the dilemma by using all three methods, heightening the dramatic effect by every possible means and leavening the seriousness of his beliefs with wit and farce.

EXPOSITION

The Greek dramatist found it easier to speak directly to his audience than a modern playwright does because he possessed in the chorus an instrument for that very purpose. The chorus was, and always had been (so far as we know), an integral element of comedy; in its early days the leader of the phallic chorus improvised the insults he hurled at the spectators, and later, when the poet was no longer the leader of the chorus, the chorus still continued to express the poet's thoughts. This was true not alone of the comic chorus. Greek choral poetry had the same intimate personal character as lyric poetry. Alcman and Pindar testify clearly to this.

The ancient function of the chorus is most clearly to be observed in the parabasis. The parabasis is a highly complex choral ode with distinctive metrical form embedded in the centre of the comedy. The actors leave the stage; the chorus remove some garments which might hamper them in the dance and begin to sing. A brief introduction is followed by the parabasis proper in anapaestic measure finished by a *pnigos*, a few lines supposed to be recited in one breath. A complete parabasis concludes with an ode, an epirrhema, antode, and antepirrhema, each part balancing the other in form and thought. The parabasis proper belongs particularly to the poet. There Aristophanes tells the audience about his life and art. He states his political beliefs, casts aspersions upon his rivals, rebukes the spectators for their lack of appreciation, and in general says freely whatever he has in mind. Occasionally in the epirrhemas he also speaks of himself, but more usually the chorus return to their own character.

The members of the comic chorus assumed a character of their own, unlike the phallic chorus but similar to the *kômos*. Traces of the *kômos* can be seen in the wasps, frogs, and birds which formed the choruses in fifth-century comedies, continuing the earlier animal disguises. In character, the chorus often expressed opinions directly contrary to Aristophanes's own, e.g. the angry Acharnians, the Wasps with their love of law-suits, the Clouds who aid and abet Socrates. However, the chorus is usually won over to the poet's cause by the parabasis and from then on fulfils the poet's purpose by exposing vices or encouraging the protagonist.

The effect of this large non-dramatic element would not have been unpalatable in the Greek theatre. Music and dancing accompanied the words, satisfying eye and ear. The ideas were also phrased with cunning. Moreover, the parabasis and the odes followed hilarious scenes full of action, and thus offered points of rest. The central position of the parabasis was psychologically best not only for the playwright but also for the spectator [1]. Prologues and epilogues are likely to find the audience restless and inattentive, busy either settling down or hurrying away. On the other hand, the audience welcomes a breathing space in the middle of the comedy, a complete change of tone and pace, which relaxes the tension aroused by the first part and enhances the enjoyment of the last. The unity of the play is preserved by the character of the chorus. The objection that the parabasis breaks the dramatic illusion is an anachronism. For the fifth-century dramatist actors were speaking and acting either as characters in a drama or as his spokesmen. It was late in the history of comedy before the idea developed that a dramatist creates an illusion of reality which momentarily leads the spectators to respond to actors as if they were in reality human beings [2].

Actors were also pressed into duty as the poet's spokesmen, a reminiscence undoubtedly of the days when the poet and actor were one. Both Aeschylus and Crates had begun their careers as actors, and the tradition that Aristophanes himself acted the part of Dicaeopolis is not unlikely [3]. Dicaeopolis, of all the characters, is most closely associated with Aristophanes; for one of his early speeches plainly states ideas which tally with ones elsewhere stressed by the poet. Xanthias, the slave of the *Wasps*, also speaks directly to the audience in the name of the poet (54 f.).

Many other characters assist the poet by non-dramatic exposition. First of all, after an opening full of action, one steps forward and explains to the audience the main idea of the play, the preceding circumstances, and the present situation. Demosthenes, Euelpides, Praxagora and others are helpful in this way. Secondly, some characters champion the poet's cause without losing their identity. Lysistrata and Trygaeus develop fully their theses as their own and fight for them in their way, but the audience could clearly perceive that Aristophanes shared their desire for peace.

The danger of boring the audience with long speeches is lessened by emphasizing the personality of the character and enlivening the exposition by jokes and puns. The speeches, like the choral odes, are made more dramatic by their relationships to the action. Sometimes they follow lively scenes; sometimes they are delivered in highly exciting circumstances. So Dicaeopolis speaks with his head on a block awaiting execution; Trygaeus is mounting his beetle, preparatory for his assault upon heaven, Praxagora is rehearsing her speech to be delivered in the Assembly.

ALLEGORY

The most inherently dramatic method of conveying ideas is allegory, since allegory is, by definition, the visible presentation of invisible ideas [4]. Both concepts and their relationships may be externalized into characters and action. War, accompanied by Uproar, imprisons Peace. The People unite with Peace Treaties. Trusty Companion marries Sovereignty. Such combinations of personifications and allegorical action make coherent networks of ideas.

That nine of the eleven extant comedies are either completely or partially allegorical may seem incredible. False allegorical interpretations in which all sorts of obscure allusions are read into lucid passages have cast a blight upon allegorical interpretation. Moreover, the very dullness of so many allegories makes it seem impossible that the bright gaiety of Greek comedy could have any relationship at all to a moralizing tract. Aristophanes has refuted our easy contempt for allegory by proving that it may be amusing as well as dramatic.

The comedies are full of vividly conceived abstractions. War is a huge, blustering giant, living in a cave with only his servant, Uproar. Peace is a beautiful, silent woman. Wealth is a god, but blind. His power and his good intentions are thwarted by his inability to see whether a man is good or evil. Because he has been deceived so often, he has grown suspicious of all men, however tempting their promises. Men have either bound him in a dark cellar or robbed him of everything and sent him empty away. Poverty is portrayed as a hideous hag, dressed in ragged clothes. She reminds Blepsidemus of a tragic Fury. Demos, the People, is a crusty old man who dotes on the flattery and subservience of others, but allows himself to be hoodwinked by their deceit [5].

The allegorical significance of some of the comedies may escape the reader's attention because so many of the abstractions are mutes. In the theatre, of course, the presence of the characters would speak for itself, especially since they are portrayed as beautiful maidens. The six mute women are Peace (a statue), Plenty, Festival Time, Sovereignty, Reconciliation, and Peace Treaties. The parts of the last five were probably acted by slave women, chosen for their beauty. Despite their silence, they serve many purposes. They complete the action by marrying the hero; they enforce the point by personifying an ideal and uniting with another abstraction; they are a source of laughter through the ribaldry they evoke;

and they satisfy the spectators' desire to look at beautiful girls.

The characters in an allegory need not be confined to abstractions. Types are also allegorical because they represent a class of people rather than a single person. The great majority of the characters in Old Comedy are types—named and unnamed. The heroes of all but the *Thesmophoriazusae*, *Frogs*, and *Plutus* are types: Dicaeopolis, Agoracritus, Strepsiades, and Pheidippides, Bdelycleon and Philocleon, Trygaeus, Euelpides and Pisthetaerus, Lysistrata, and Praxagora. Their names indicate the class of people or qualities they represent, and their actions exemplify their natures. Dicaeopolis, the Just Citizen or City, longs for peace. Agoracritus is the Choice of the Market-place. Strepsiades twists and turns in his efforts to escape repaying his debts. Bdelycleon hates Cleon, and therefore tries to thwart the influence he wields over the jurymen, while his father loves Cleon because he caters to the old men. Euelpides hopefully sets out to find another city with Pisthetaerus, his trusty companion. Lysistrata dissolves war, and Praxagora transacts business in the market-place.

Type characters are sometimes confused with stock characters or suspected of pallid dullness. Neither criticism of Aristophanes's characters seems to me justified. The types are presented as lively, full-blooded human beings with individual personalities. Even characters who represent closely allied ideas or types are sharply differentiated; Dicaeopolis and Trygaeus both seek peace, but in far different ways. Dicaeopolis is concerned with justice and the city and uses legal means to achieve his aims. He despatches a private messenger to Sparta who returns with three sample treaties. The thirty-year treaty tastes of ambrosia and nectar, and therefore he accepts it. His later trading in his private market is legal, since he is no longer at war with Sparta. Trygaeus is a man of the soil, but well versed in the myths and a visionary. A beetle to carry him to heaven like Bellerophon on Pegasus, the rescue of Peace from War's cave by farmers from all the Greek states, and a sacrifice to Peace accord well with his personality.

Many other examples could be cited, but one more should suffice. The two women protagonists—Lysistrata and Praxagora—are intelligent, strong-willed women who wish to save the state from the mismanagement of the men. The militant

Lysistrata storms the citadel, defends it against attack, restrains her accomplices by force, and finally defeats the men by the very violence she deplores. Praxagora resorts to trickery, dressing herself and friends in their husband's clothes, and seizing power by a decree passed in the Assembly by the women.

Aristophanes delineated his chief characters with care and precision, but many of the minor characters he left unnamed. They were no more than the types they represent: they play a part in the unfolding of the idea and in developing the action; they give us a glimpse of ordinary Athenian life; but they are not interesting in and for themselves. The heralds and messengers are useful to announce coming events and report off-stage action. More important are the public officials—the ambassadors, magistrates, inspectors, and policemen. The many sycophants differ little from one another. Priests and poets, dealers in oracles and decrees, makers of crests, armour, and sickles, and farmers jostle one another. The comedies even include the following odd assortment: a landlady, a woman who sells bread, a parricide, a friend of a bridegroom, and a just man.

Fables are another branch of allegory of which Aristophanes made use though not extensively. He reveals here the influence both of the *kômos* and Aesop's fables. Aesop was a favourite among the Athenians as the references to him in the comedies show, but his fables were not dramatized. The scene of the trial of the dog Labes for stealing a cheese shows a trace of the fable which disguised political comment behind animal masks. In the *Wasps* Labes is a pun for Laches, a general. The Wasps and Clouds are also allegorical: the Wasps represent irritable old men with stings, the Clouds airy nothings.

EXAMPLE

Aristophanes has so vividly portrayed his allegorical characters that they shade off into realistic individuals. It is, therefore, often difficult to distinguish between allegory and example—the third method of dramatic teaching. The burning of the house of Socrates may be interpreted in either way. It symbolizes the destruction of his ideas, and it also warns

Socrates and the other Sophists what may befall them at the hands of an angry populace. Scenes showing the consequences of peace, prosperity, or communism may also be designed to exemplify what may happen if certain principles are put into action.

The same ambiguity clouds the interpretation of the many historical characters who participate in the action. They are as numerous and important as the abstractions, consisting of Cleon, Socrates, Lamachus, Demosthenes, Nicias, Euripides, Aeschylus, Agathon, Meton, Cephisophon, Chaerephon, Cinesias, a kinsman of Euripides usually called Mnesilochus, Cleisthenes, and the sons of Lamachus and Cleonymus. This varied group, ranging from generals and demagogues to poets and Sophists, had this in common—all were very much in the public eye, except for the sons of Lamachus and Cleonymus, who are introduced as chips from well-known paternal blocks. Are these characters portraits of men so clearly drawn that recognition was instantaneous, or, if not portraits, recognizable caricatures? Or have the characters been so distorted that only a faint resemblance to the real person is left, and the name the only clue for an identity which otherwise might now be unknown? Criticism has veered between these two extremes, one critic emphasizing the historicity of the characters, another their generality [6]. The truth probably lies in accepting the paradox that they were both individuals and abstractions.

That the characters were reasonable caricatures of historical men seems probable, notwithstanding the scanty knowledge we have about some of them. Lamachus, we know, was an active general [7]. He was brave but undistinguished. Nicias was hesitant and superstitious [8]; Demosthenes bolder in strategy and tactics [9]. Cleon was a shrewd man with an eye to his own advantage and power over the Assembly based upon oratorical skill and insight into the tempers and emotions of the people [10]. The history of Thucydides is our best source of information about these public men, and that tallies with the characters as they appear on the stage. Socrates is the most controversial character; but Socrates seems to have had no doubt that he was the butt of the *Clouds*, no matter how grossly misrepresented, or that the Athenians recognized his identity [11].

Foibles were, of course, exaggerated and qualities ascribed to the victim which he probably never had. Lamachus may not have been a braggart, nor Cleon so coarse and despicable. Certainly, Demosthenes and Nicias were only metaphorically slaves of the People. These men were characters in a comedy and, as such, were caricatured to exploit to the full their humorous possibilities. These distortions, however, do not alter the essential likeness between the man and his theatrical counterpart, nor did the men resent their appearances (so far as we can tell), with the exceptions of Cleon and Socrates. Some of the men are defended—Nicias and Demosthenes, for example—and others are praised. Aristophanes could not help admiring the cleverness of Euripides, at the same time that he feared his influence [12]. He commented on the braveness of Lamachus (*Frogs*, 1039-40) after his death, and shows his regret that Agathon had gone to Macedonia (*Frogs*, 85).

Cleon he quite evidently detested. Even when the man was dead, he could not refrain from attack although he himself said it was wrong to speak ill of the dead (*Peace*, 270, 313, 648). Cleon was too strong a man to allow Aristophanes to insult him unchecked. Twice he brought suit against the comic poet, and the second time Aristophanes only succeeded in escaping serious punishment by playing the ape, as he himself admits (*Acharnians*, 377 f., and *Clouds*, 518 f.). On the other hand, the *Symposium* of Plato, if acceptable as historical evidence, shows Aristophanes on both good and intimate terms with Agathon and Socrates, celebrating the victory of Agathon and discussing philosophical problems with Socrates. One wonders how Aristophanes felt if he heard Socrates in his defence of his life accuse Aristophanes of contributing to the rancour which was about to cause his death. Did perhaps the execution of Socrates make him cease portraying individuals, realizing that what was designed for fun in one generation might prove fatal in the next?

These men were more than historical characters distorted for comic effect; they exemplified and embodied concepts [13]. Cleon is the epitome of hateful Demagoguery, Socrates of Sophistry, Aeschylus of the Old Tragedy, Euripides of the New, and Lamachus of War. By their double natures the characters accomplished two ends. Their lively colourful personalities were dramatic and comic; the concepts they embodied harmonized with the other allegorical characters and the plot. The device was brilliant, but at the same time the ambiguity is a source of confusion. Socrates especially suffered. As Sophistry, he was accused of practices which the historical Socrates himself condemned—the taking of fees, for instance, and making the worse cause appear the better. The ideas were too complex to be accurately equated with an individual. The virulence with which Aristophanes assailed dangerous ideas was added to personal satire to make a double-edged sword.

Not all the characters serve an intellectual purpose. Some are realistic, fictional, or mythical. They lend an air of verisimilitude, contribute to the fun, or keep the plot moving. Hades would not be complete without Pluto, Aeacus, and the boatman Charon, nor Heaven without Hermes, Poseidon, Iris, Heracles, and doubtfully the barbarian god, Triballus. In the later plays more and more real men and women with common Athenian names take the chief parts. The *Ecclesiazusae* includes in its list of *dramatis personae* Blepyrus, Chremes, two men, three old women, a young woman, and a young man. The chief characters of the *Plutus* aside from the god are Chremylus, Blepsidemus, and the slave Carion. The trend toward realism can clearly be perceived in these fourth-century plays. Realistic touches in the earlier plays firmly anchor the comedies in fifth-century Athens. The wife of Dicaeopolis watches the Rural Dionysia from the window, while their daughter carries the sacrificial basket. The son of one of the Wasps carries the lantern for his father and asks for a fig. The little daughters of the Megarian prefer to be sold as pigs rather than die of starvation, and the children of Trygaeus beg their father not to fly away on the beetle. The slaves, grumbling at their tasks, were undoubtedly familiar sights in Athens.

Aristophanes solved the problem of communicating ideas through comedy as satisfactorily as possible. He used every means of expression—direct exposition, allegory, and realistic example—without letting the action lag nor the humour fade. Only in the *Knights* does his feeling against Cleon and his policy dangerously imperil the fun. In all the comedies, however, the characters naturally lack the emotional depth and psychological complexity of Greek tragedy or epic. Their motivations are simple and clear; their emotional responses limited. Fear, disgust, anger, joy, sexual desire, hope and sympathy about exhaust the emotional range, and these emotions are often short-lived. Fear is quickly followed by self-confidence, anger appeased, and hope fulfilled. The lives of the characters are viewed for only a moment; they have little or no past and no future. We catch a glimpse of the young Strepsiades marrying a city wife and caring for his infant Pheidippides, but the lives of the other characters are empty blanks on each side of the play, and even within the comedies they do not lead normal, realistic lives. The result is a lack of substantiality which undermines the most vividly drawn characters.

On the other hand, it must be said in Aristophanes's favour that no other Greek poet portrayed as wide a range of character or surpassed him in perception and sympathy. He delineated gods, heroes, clouds, human beings, animals, and insects. Poseidon and puppies are outlined with equal skill, and so are ideals and vices, abstract arguments and pert little lantern boys, contemporary individuals and types, honest men and scoundrels. No age escaped his touch. We find in his comedies old men and women, middle-aged men and women, youths and maidens, boys and girls. Megarians, Spartans, Boeotians, Scythians and barbarians as well as native Athenians take speaking parts. Finally, almost every class of society is represented: soldiers, merchants, manufacturers, farmers, government officials, priests, poets, landladies, flute girls, students, slaves, servants, demagogues, aristocrats, moneylenders—almost everyone, in fact, except sailors and the very wealthy [14]. Aristophanes compensated for his lack of height and depth with a breadth of view unsurpassed in the history of the drama.

DRAMATIC STRUCTURE

So extraordinary a group of characters could never act together in the conventional realistic-romantic comedy we are familiar with in the works of Menander, Terence, or Shakespeare. We are so familiar with this conventional comedy, in fact, that we tend to treat it as a standard form and measure other forms as deviations from the norm. This holds true especially of the plot structure. Aristotle described the comedy of his day with its complex plot of complication and solution, the kind of plot we also know best. Old Greek Comedy did not have this structure. The scenes are not held together in a mesh of circumstances; the characters are not entangled with each other in difficulties from which they must extricate themselves. As a result, all plot has been denied to Old Comedies; the scenes are said to be merely jumbled together without inherent connections; the structure to be loose; the plays formless [15].

Aristotle holds the clue for the plot structure of Old Comedy, when he describes another basic kind—the single plot. In the single plot the scenes are connected like beads on a string and not interlaced. The crisis of the play may not contain a reversal of fortune or a recognition. The foundation of the structure is quite simply conflict, the basis of all drama, but here not multiplied in the complications of the later comedy. The antagonists are introduced and prepare for trouble; they contend with one another; one is victorious, or the two are reconciled; and finally the consequences of victory are revealed. Strife, decision, and consequences—these are the basic ingredients of Old Comedy.

This single plot of conflict is admirably suited for the expression of ideas and for the motley crew of characters Aristophanes used. It is allegorically significant, inherently dramatic, and potentially comic. In almost every play a clash of ideas is dramatized into a conflict of characters. In the *Acharnians*, *Peace*, and *Lysistrata*, peace and war are at odds; in the *Clouds*, the old education fights the new; in the *Wasps*, two ways of life are opposed; demagoguery contends with democracy in the *Knights*; old tragedy against the new in the *Frogs*; wealth against poverty in the *Plutus*.

The conflicts of the other three plays are not so clear-cut. The women are pitted against Euripides in the *Thesmophoriazusae*; but the idea at stake—the portrayal of women in the tragedies versus their real nature—is only the stepping-off point for the fun that follows. In the *Ecclesiazusae* a case might be made for a conflict between private property and communism, but this conflict does not dominate the action. Finally, two cities are contrasted in the *Birds*, but the major struggle in the comedy is between the birds and the gods.

Although the structure of strife, decision, and consequences is uniform, the plots are not stereotyped. Varied emphasis and development of the parts of the structure combined with varied characters prevent monotony. Dicaeopolis in the *Acharnians* is opposed by the Assembly, the Acharnians, and Lamachus. He circumvents the Assembly, appeases the Acharnians, and triumphs over Lamachus. The consequences of his victories are fully shown. The *Knights* is built of a series of contests between Agoracritus and Cleon, with Agoracritus always the victor, and the results of victory are presented in a single final scene. The *Clouds* is composed of a wide variety of opponents: Strepsiades against debtors, Socrates, and his son Pheidippides, and Just Argument against Unjust Argument. The *Wasps* and *Peace* are similar; for in both the preparation and argument of the protagonists are almost equally balanced by the consequences. On the other hand, the *Lysistrata* and *Thesmophoriazusae* are chiefly a series of conflicts with minor results. In the *Ecclesiazusae* the major struggle takes place off-stage, and the consequences of the victory achieved there fill the rest of the play. The *Birds* has a double plot, for the first conflict and victory result in new conflicts and a second victory. The *Plutus* shows the changing plot structure which was to end eventually in the New Comedy. The single contests are beginning to give way to purpose and accomplishment, though traces of the older structure are still apparent in the scene with Poverty and the later episodes.

One grave charge, almost universally held against Aristophanes, is that many of the scenes are so loosely connected that their order might be transposed without damage to the sense. This is particularly true of the scenes following the parabasis, where the consequences of the previous action are frequently shown. But did Aristophanes intend that one scene should develop into another? Or is development the only legitimate relationship between scenes? Are not the scenes rather balanced and contrasted so that the whole forms a pattern? The *Acharnians* is a good example of pattern. Dicaeopolis goes to celebrate the Rural Dionysia while Amphitheus flees the pursuing Acharnians. Later a Megarian comes to trade with Dicaeopolis, but they are interrupted by a sycophant. This scene is balanced by the next in which a Boeotian is hindered from trading by an inspector of markets. Between the balance of these two scenes and the contrasts of the last two, a series of three scenes is interposed. These scenes contain the men who interrupt the sacrifice, asking Dicaeopolis for a little of his peace; the servant of Lamachus and the farmer are refused, but the friend of the bride is granted a share. Then heralds announce to Lamachus that he must go to war and to Dicaeopolis that he is invited to attend the feast of the cups. A stichomythy follows between Lamachus and Dicaeopolis as they prepare for their contrasted journeys. After a choral ode the two return, one wounded and one joyously inebriated. The final scene is another contrast between the general and the just citizen.

The other plays also are built from parallel and contrasted scenes, with an occasional group of three or four to vary the rhythm. The *Peace* is a beautifully balanced play. Peace with two satellites is contrasted with War and his single servant. One craftsman of the instrument of peace—a sickle-maker—comes to give thanks to Trygaeus, but five manufacturers of arms follow after him. Finally, the pair of children, the sons of Lamachus and Cleonymus, enter singing songs characteristic of belligerence and cowardice. Examples could be multiplied if one wished to study each play, but these illustrations should be sufficient to prove the point. The single plot and patterned scenes combine easily into a comedy organized by ideas.

Two weak points in this type of construction are the dangers that the plays will not be unified and that they will be static. Both dangers are obviated by dramatic preparation, hints given to the audience of events to come and foreshadowing of later scenes. Amphitheus arouses the pursuit of the Acharnians and prepares us for their anger against Dicaeopolis. Dicaeopolis speaks of the miserable plight of the Megarians and the interference of sycophants early in the play, and the Acharnians call for Lamachus to aid them against Dicaeopolis. In the *Knights* Agoracritus asks who will come to his aid, and Demosthenes foretells the arrival of the Knights. The Clouds warn Strepsiades that he may regret the education his son will receive from Socrates, a warning that is later fulfilled. Philocleon himself tells his son that drinking leads to lawsuits, a prophecy Bdelycleon learns to his cost. The kinsman of Euripides exacts a promise from him to come to the rescue if harm should befall him. The rehearsal scene of the *Ecclesiazusae* takes the place of the off-stage action. By this foreshadowing the plays are made at once both more dynamic and more unified.

The translation of ideas into drama is facilitated by allegorical action—action which both develops the idea and carries forward the plot. This allegorical action is one of the most distinctive parts of Old Comedy. Sometimes it affords the theme for the whole play, as in the *Plutus*, where the restoration of sight to Wealth is the idea motivating the action. In other plays minor scenes are allegorical; the weighing of words on a scale, the pounding of cities into mincemeat, the tasting of treaties. In five comedies allegorical sacrifices, rejuvenations, and marriages play prominent parts [16].

The sacrifice of thanksgiving was a common Athenian ritual reproduced on the stage as the normal consequent of victory. Trygaeus sacrifices to Peace and Pisthetaerus to the Birds—his new gods. Both sacrifices are interrupted by men who have profited from the victory and wish to join in praising the gods and by intruders who have lost their livelihood through the defeat of the antagonist and who wish to stop the sacrifice. So the sickle-maker and the munitions-makers have reason to be interested in the sacrifice to Peace; the priests of the Olympian gods and the dithyrambic poets in the sacrifice to the new bird gods. The greedy men who lurk near sacrifices in order to eat a share of the subsequent feast are satirized for comic effect.

The rejuvenation of the old men, Demos and Philocleon, is symbolized by their new costumes. Demos appears in the shining garments of the Persian Wars with a cicada on his shoulder. The People are thus restored to the simplicity and glory of those great days in which the Athenians saved Greece from the barbarians. Philocleon, in contrast, must shed his threadbare cloak for a thick wool chlaina and his old shoes for Laconian slippers. He now looks like a fashionable aristocrat of leisure.

Three plays end with 'marriages', the heroes uniting, not always in lawful wedlock, with beautiful maidens. These marriages are not the usual weddings which end romantic comedy, the culmination of all the trials and complications which have kept the young hero and heroine apart. These heroines are silent—a rare phenomenon in comedy—and the heroes are sometimes married men. The fact that the brides are without exception abstractions indicates to my mind that these marriages are allegorical, visible signs of the invisible union of Trusty Companion with Sovereignty, the People with Treaties, the Vineyard with Fruitfulness.

The symbolic union was well known in Athens, since every year Dionysos 'married' the king archon's wife, a marriage symbolizing the close relationship between the god and the city. This was, moreover, a central theme in Aristophanes's philosophy, if we may accept Plato's *Symposium* as trustworthy. In the *Symposium* Aristophanes contributes as his share of the discussion a myth of the origins of love which explains human restlessness as the constant search for a mate, and human bliss as the discovery of the mate and union. Sexual desire and satisfaction symbolize all human craving and joy [17].

THE THEATRE AND THE AUDIENCE

Aristophanes several times describes the difficulties of theatrical production to extenuate his custom of asking friends to produce his comedies (*Knights*, 507-50; *Clouds*, 518-62; *Wasps*, 1015 ff.). In Greece the comic poet was expected to train the actors and chorus and to supervise the staging, a custom which began in the days when poet and actor were one and the production of a play a simple matter. By the end of the fifth century, five actors were playing as many as twenty-four parts and extra mutes were hired; the costumes were elaborate; the masks many and varied; the mechanical devices complicated [18]. The spectators also were a problem. They demanded originality, and they pitched their standards high; yet at the same time the gulf between the clever and the mob widened. Aristophanes tackled and solved the problems arising from theatrical conditions and from the nature of his audience by his thorough knowledge of his craft and by his dramatic genius.

The Greek theatre lacked many conveniences. No programmes were distributed, which meant that the audience had no way of knowing in advance the time, place, or characters of the opening scene. The sun provided the only light, and that of course remained constant. The time of day at the beginning of the play or changing time within could not be indicated by darkening or brightening the stage. The setting, too, was indefinite. The same building had to serve as a cave, a temple, or a house. A few symbolic movable properties may have been used—an altar, a Herm by the front door, a tree, or a bush. Our knowledge of this aspect of the Greek theatre is very limited. Some indications of the place were probably given the spectators, but certainly the sets were neither realistic nor elaborate. Finally, the theatre had no curtain, so that all entrances and exits had to be made openly. The actors had to come forward at the beginning and take up their positions; the stage had to be cleared at the end.

There were compensations for the lack of programme, curtain, artificial lighting, and realistic sets. The theatre was itself beautifully situated. The spectator, sitting on the slope of the Acropolis, could raise his eyes from orchestra and scene-building to the temple of Dionysos and beyond to the purple mountain Hymettos. The sun was bright and the atmosphere clear, so that the spectators could see well despite their distance from the actors. More important, the acoustics were perfect; the audience could hear every word clearly. This was essential, for the simplicity of the theatre thrust the whole burden of dramatic exposition upon the speeches of the characters. But the audiences knew no other theatre, and they accepted the conventions of their theatre with the same ease of familiarity with which we accept the rising curtain, the three-walled rooms, and the simulated dawn.

A clever dramatist could turn to good account the seeming disadvantages of his theatre. The place of action might be almost anywhere, and the scene could be changed swiftly within a play. Thus we find characters starting from an Athenian house, descending to Hades or ascending to Heaven, crossing a lake or flying through the air. Houses were improbably juxtaposed, with the result that Strepsiades could knock at the door of the Thinking Shop, and the action could proceed quickly, shifting from the house of Socrates to that of Strepsiades without pause. Flexibility and variety of setting were great advantages for a comic poet, giving him a chance for imaginative scope and dramatic effect [19].

Aristophanes possessed remarkable powers for writing dramatic exposition. An opening monologue might seem dull, but in Aristophanes's hands it was lively as well as instructive. Dicaeopolis waits impatiently for the Assembly to open, grumbling about his discomforts and complaining of the tardiness of the citizens. We grasp at once from this speech where he is and why and what kind of a man he is. Strepsiades tosses on his bed, bemoaning the wildness of his son and his debts. Praxagora addresses her lamp in mock tragic fashion as she waits for her accomplices. In all three monologues the characters are waiting, thus creating a sense of anticipation; yet all are waiting for something different. The idea of the play is suggested, the circumstances outlined, the character established, and the audience amused.

A dialogue between slaves opens three comedies, but again the similarity of the introductions is not apparent. The slaves of the *Knights* are Nicias and Demosthenes, and they are in deathly fear—not of their master but of a fellow slave who has become their master's favourite. One tiptoes into the house to steal an oracle, and the whispering atmosphere of terror is maintained until the entrance of Cleon brings the scene to a climax. The slaves of the *Wasps* are engaged in preventing the escape of Philocleon. He burrows in the walls like a mouse, goes up the chimney disguised as smoke, and clings to the belly of a donkey like Odysseus. Meanwhile his son and the slaves rush from door to window, frantically guarding the persistent old man. The slaves of the *Peace* are busy with the loathsome task of feeding dung to a beetle. In all three scenes, after the excitement of the opening action has caught the attention of the spectators, a long speech is inserted, explaining more fully and directly the meaning of the situation so that no one will fail to grasp it. Demosthenes and a slave in the *Peace* speak in character, but Xanthias in the *Wasps* speaks for Aristophanes. These three scenes are undoubtedly the most dramatic and amusing of all the introductions.

The first scenes of the *Birds*, *Frogs*, and *Thesmophoriazusae* are alike because the two main characters are journeying together. Through their dialogue they convey to the audience who they are, where they are going, and what their mission is. Euelpides and Pisthetaerus seek the land of the birds, carrying a crow with them as a guide. After many jokes about 'going to the crows', an expression similar to our 'going to the dogs', Euelpides turns to the audience and clarifies his reasons for wishing to leave Athens. In the *Frogs* the slave of Dionysos complains of his burden and questions the god until Dionysos reveals his destination and purpose. Similarly, Mnesilochus questions Euripides in the *Thesmophoriazusae* as they go to the house of Agathon.

The exposition within the plays is handled with equal skill. The characters are usually identified by name either before or after their entrances [20]. Costume and mask were sometimes used, but Aristophanes reinforced the characterization by the names. The characters prepare the audience for the place of the next scene by announcing their intentions [21]. Frequently they say that they are going to another house, and then they knock at the door, calling for the man to whom they wish to speak. Dicaeopolis says he is going to celebrate the Rural Dionysia; Dionysos looks first for Heracles and then Charon; Euripides seeks Agathon and then despatches Mnesilochus to the Thesmophoria. Once the play has started, each new character is prepared for in advance. Clarity is gained, although perhaps some element of surprise is lost.

The chorus of twenty-four, usually present on the stage after its entrance, would seem like a dramatic impediment; actually it was highly useful [22]. During the choral odes any amount of time could elapse from a few minutes to three or four days. The unities of time and place meant nothing to the early Greek comic poet. The chorus freed the dramatist from the limitations of time and space instead of restricting him. The chorus helped, too, throughout the play by naming new characters and commenting on the action. Their presence was particularly helpful because they could entertain the spectators with singing and dancing, a pleasant contrast to the comic scenes of action and repartee, while important events were happening off-stage. In reverse, the chorus occasionally was busy off-stage while the actors amused the audience.

The chorus of women in the *Ecclesiazusae* depart to the Assembly and win the important victory there. Similarly, while some women take the oath from Lysistrata, another group has captured the Acropolis. The birds build a wall around their new city; Lamachus is wounded in the wars; Dicaeopolis wins the Feast of the Cups; Philocleon attends a banquet; in fact, every play has some important scene reported but not presented to the audience. The perspective of the play is thus deepened. Scenes which could never have been acted are nevertheless vividly projected, and the comic results of the off-stage action can be presented.

The entrances and exits of the characters are always adequately motivated and often highly dramatic. The entrances of the chorus were varied and frequently spectacular. The angry Acharnians come in furious pursuit, searching for Dicaeopolis. The Knights ride proudly to the rescue of Agoracritus. The Clouds drift in from the mountains, singing some of the most beautiful lyrics in the comedies. The Wasps pick their way carefully through the darkness and the mud; the Farmers of the *Peace* gather in response to the call of Trygaeus for help. The Birds, too, are called, and enter one by one beginning their full choral song only after all are in the orchestra [23]. The chorus of the *Lysistrata* is divided into old men and women. The old men enter first with logs, intending to burn the women out of the Acropolis. The old women come with water to quench the fire. Nowhere does the genius of Aristophanes shine more brilliantly than in his handling of the chorus.

The Greek theatre was limited in the effects which could be produced by mechanical contrivances. A machine was available which could hoist an actor in the air, making possible the ride of Trygaeus on his beetle and the basket swinging in the air for Socrates. The exact nature of the 'eccyclema'' is puzzling [24]. In the *Acharnians* (408-9) Dicaeopolis calls to Euripides and asks him to let himself be 'rolled out', and Euripides finally agrees. In the *Thesmophoriazusae* (96, 265) Euripides says Agathon is being rolled out, and later Agathon says, 'Let someone roll me within as quickly as possible.' The ambiguity of these references has led to controversy. Was a couch rolled in and out from the scene-building or a portion of the wall rolled back to show an interior? Probably the tragic poets were rolled out on couches as part of Aristophanes's satire of their character.

The precise details of the production of a Greek comedy are beyond our power now to recall, because we know too little about the appearance of the scene building, the costumes, the masks, the style of acting, and the dances of the chorus. But there can be no doubt of the splendour of the total effect. Beauty was combined with the grotesque to delight and amuse. Picture, for example, Socrates aloft in his basket lost in contemplation of the sky, while below pale scholars stare upon the ground. Then Strepsiades comes knocking at the door, shouting and cavorting, a startling contrast to the choral entry of the slow drifting Clouds. The picture was an unforgettable one, as Socrates himself ruefully acknowledged in his *Apology*.

When Aristophanes spoke directly to the audience, he was addressing almost the entire body of citizens [25]. The admission fee was small; and later, when some citizens were too poor to pay even a few obols, the state paid for them. The Lenaea in January-February was a private Athenian festival, not because of any law but because few Greeks cared to travel in the season of wintry storms. But in the spring leading citizens of the subject cities were in Athens with the allotment they paid for naval protection. They came to the City Dionysia, and strangers from all over Greece gathered for the renowned festival. These audiences were truly representative of the Greek people since they included the wealthy, middle class, and poor, the educated and uneducated, the business men, craftsmen, professional men, farmers, sailors, and soldiers. They all saw the same plays at the same performances, and they all could express their opinions with equal force both through applause and through the five judges selected by lot from the citizens.

Were women, children, and slaves also present? The evidence seems to support the affirmative [26]. Women and children were not usually excluded from Greek festivals, particularly public ones. Some jokes of Aristophanes would suggest their presence. For example, he says that the phallus was worn to make boys laugh (*Clouds*, 538-9). On the other hand, the chorus in the *Birds* remarks that an adulterer with wings could fly to his victim's home and make love to his wife while her husband was in the theatre (793-6). Clearly, some women stayed at home. If the audience included women, children, and slaves, the poet's task was a hard one, since he had to please a wide range of interest and taste; if he succeeded, his plays might retain the wider appeal they had once achieved.

The dramatic success of Aristophanes depended fundamentally upon his clear perception and clever manipulation of primary dramatic themes, not only the basic conflict but also the variations afforded by the search, the trial, the seizing of hostages, the escape, and the rescue. Some of these themes and situations had already proved their worth in tragedies so that the comic burlesque was doubly amusing. Thus Telephus in the tragedy of Euripides had seized a child in order to ensure fair trial for himself; in the *Thesmophoriazusae* Mnesilochus snatches the 'child' of an Athenian woman to save himself only to discover that it is a bottle of wine! Later, in the same play, Euripides tries to rescue Mnesilochus by appearing as Menelaus and then as Perseus in burlesque of his *Helena* and *Andromeda*.

Little has been directly said so far of the humour of the comedies, although much has been implied. The seriousness of most studies of comedy is generally felt to be a flaw, and yet the attempt to point out the humour is likely to destroy it utterly. Once the shock of surprise is over, the flavour is lost. Nevertheless, a few memorable scenes survive repetition and guidebook direction. For me the scene of the corpse in the *Frogs* is always funny. Dionysos wants him to carry his bundle for him to the underworld. The corpse demands two drachmae for the job; Dionysos offers him nine obols. The corpse says, 'May I live again.'

Some of the scenes which would be amusing in the theatre slip by with little notice when one is reading the play. The changes of costume must have been hilarious in performance. For example, Dicaeopolis believes that he can plead for his life more effectively if he is dressed like a tragic hero in a Euripidean tragedy—in rags. He, therefore, goes to the house of Euripides to borrow the clothes of a beggar from the tragic poet's ample supply. Euripides in the *Thesmophoriazusae* shaves Mnesilochus and arrays him in women's clothes so that he can spy upon the women at the Thesmophoria. After the parabasis of the *Birds*, Pisthetaerus and Euelpides emerge from a cave covered with feathers and perhaps wearing bird masks to indicate their new allegiance.

Not all the humorous scenes are clever. Vulgar and indecent farce is mixed inextricably with the highest comedy. Nor can all the indecency be excused on the ground of Dionysiac ribaldry. A good proportion of the indecency was as indecent in fifth-century Athens as it is to-day—the defecation on the stage of Blepyrus for example. The only basic difference between the ancient audience and modern audiences is that Greeks who wanted to see comedies went in a body to one theatre and saw the comedies chosen for them by state officials as part of a religious festival, whereas modern men and women who wish to see comedies choose the ones which appeal to their taste from the selection offered them by producers engaged in the theatrical business to a greater or lesser extent for the sake of the profits. To-day, for the most part, those who like low comedy can find it in one playhouse; those who like high comedy can find it in another. The audience of fifth-century Athens was varied, and Aristophanes offered a varied fare to please every palate—the coarsest buffoonery for some, the most delicate and subtle lyrics for another. As he himself said, 'The wise will remember and judge me by my wisdom; the jokesters by my jests' (*Ecclesiazusae*, 1175).

NOTES FOR CHAPTER 5

1. The central position of the parabasis has been ably defended by Philip Whaley Harsh, 'The Position of the Parabasis in the Plays of Aristophanes, *Transactions of the American Philological Association*, LXV (1934), 178-97.

2. Henry Lloyd Stow has treated fully the subject in *The Violation of the Dramatic Illusion in the Comedies of Aristophanes* (Chicago, 1936). He points out that the audience was drawn into the play by the actors and the chorus (p. 5).

3. Cyril Bailey, 'Who Played "Dicaeopolis"?' *Greek Poetry and Life* (Oxford, 1936), pp. 231-40, has made a very convincing case for Aristophanes.

4. Similarly Werner Jaeger writes in *Paideia* (2nd ed. trans. Gilbert Highet, Oxford, 1939), p. 364, 'He put this unholy alliance on the stage by means of a fantastic allegory—not a bloodless set of symbols as allegories usually are, but a visible embodiment of an invisible fact.' Cp. S. H. Butcher, *Aristotle's Theory of Poetry and Fine Art* (London, 1932), p. 381: 'His imagination works by giving embodi-

ment to what is abstract. His love of bold personification is in part inherited from his predecessors on the Attic stage: Cratinus had introduced Laws (*Νόμοι*) and Riches (*Πλοῦτοι*) as his choruses. But Aristophanes goes farther; he seems to think through materialized ideas. He personifies the Just and the Unjust Logic, and brings them before us as lawcourt disputants; he incarnates a metaphor such as the philosopher "in the clouds", the jurymen with waspish temper, mankind with their airy hopes.'

5. Only the two Arguments in the *Clouds* are undifferentiated by appearance, but our text is corrupt. In the performance they may have been dressed in the Old and New fashion to fit their ideas.

6. The chief attack on the historicity of the characters has stemmed from the attempt to fit them into stock moulds. F. M. Cornford, *The Origin of Attic Comedy* (London, 1914), believes that there was a fixed set of masks originating in a ritual drama. These included an Old Man, Young Man, Old Woman, Young Woman, Alazon or Impostor, Eiron or Buffoon. Among the different kinds of Impostors are the Miles Gloriosus, the Learned Doctor, the Cook, and the Parasite. According to this theory Aristophanes began writing the *Frogs* with the idea that a Buffoon should go to Hades to bring back a Learned Doctor and instead returned with a Miles Gloriosus. Aeschylus and Euripides are merely names attached to the stock characters who bear no other resemblance—not even grotesque exaggeration—to the tragic poets (chap. viii). Butcher emphasizes their generality, 'The same bent of mind leads him to give a concrete form to the forces and tendencies of the age, and to embody them in actual persons' (p. 381). Roy C. Flickinger, *The Greek Theater and Its Drama* (3rd ed., Chicago, 1926), pp. 212-13, believes that realistic masks were used and implicitly accepts the historicity of the characters. 'In Old Comedy contemporaneous personages were often introduced, and we are told that their masks were true enough to life for their identity to be recognizable before the actors had uttered a word.'

7. Thucydides, iv, 75; v, 19, 24; vi, 49, 101. Plutarch, *Life of Alcibiades*, xviii, xxi.

8. Thucydides, v, 16; Plutarch, *Life of Nicias*, iii.

9. Thucydides, iii, 95.

10. Thucydides, iv, 36, 39. Cp. *Cambridge Ancient History* (ed. J. B. Bury, S. A. Cook, and F. E. Adcock, New York, 1927), V, 102, 236, 215; Aristotle, *Constitution of Athens* (ed. John E. Sandys, London 1912), xxviii.

11. After a thorough study of all the evidence A. E. Taylor, *Varia*

Socratica, First Series (Oxford, 1911), p. 141, writes, 'We have thus every reason to suppose that the picture of Socrates in the *Clouds* is a careful and elaborate piece of art, a distortion into the grotesque of a figure with which both the poet and the audience upon whom the success or failure of his comedy depended were familiarly acquainted.'

12. Evidence is found throughout the comedies, but particularly in the *Frogs*.

13. David Grene, 'The Comic Technique of Aristophanes', *Hermathena*, L (1937), 87-125, presents much the same idea. He writes, pp. 89-90, 'For instance, the attack on Socrates is directed against the whole idea of the domination of human life by a philosophical principle, the subjection of simple emotions and simple human pleasures to the spirit of intellectual analysis. His satire on Cleon is not so much against Cleon personally, but against the vital principle of democracy—of the rule of the people by the people for the people, even when those who rule are intellectually incapable. His satire against Euripides is inspired by a dislike of the entire intellectual movement at whose head the poet stood, and against the new technique in poetry.'

14. Aristophanes was sympathetic to the sailors. For the evidence, see A. W. Gomme, 'Aristophanes and Politics', *Classical Review*, LII (1938), 107.

15. This charge of formlessness is levelled particularly at the scenes following the parabasis. Even those who are sensitive to the basic conflict have not applied this principle to the structure of the whole comedy. So Butcher writes, pp. 381-2, 'A play of Aristophanes is a dramatized debate, an *ἀγών*, in which the persons represent opposing principles; for in form the piece is always combative, though the fight may be but a mock fight. These principles are brought into collision and worked out to their most irrational conclusions, little regard being paid to the coherence of the parts and still less to propriety of character.'

16. Cornford has interpreted the sacrifices, rejuvenations, and marriages as canonical parts of a plot formula derived from an early ritual. A. W. Pickard-Cambridge, *Dithyramb, Tragedy and Comedy* (Oxford, 1927), has discussed Cornford's theory in Appendix B, pp. 329-49. My own interest lies in the dramatic effectiveness of the action rather than in its origin.

17. This myth is reminiscent of Empedocles, frr. 60-6.

18. A number of excellent books on the Greek theatre is available. Flickinger has been cited above. The two most recent books

of Pickard-Cambridge are very helpful indeed for those who can read Greek: *The Theatre of Dionysus in Athens* (Oxford, 1946) and *The Dramatic Festivals of Athens* (Oxford, 1953). I have also used and liked Margarete Bieber, *The History of the Greek and Roman Theater* (Princeton, 1939), and James Turney Allen, *The Greek Theater of the Fifth Century Before Christ* (University of California Publications in Classical Philology, VII, 1919-1924).

19. Flickinger, chap. v.

20. David Martin Key, *The Introduction of Characters by Name in Greek and Roman Comedy* (Chicago, 1923), has discovered that 'In the eleven plays of Aristophanes, 86 characters are named. Over one half, 51, are named within 10 lines before or 10 lines after entry' (p. 15). The unnamed characters are either so unimportant or so important that names are not necessary—e.g. Cleon, who is called the Paphlagonian or Leather-tanner.

21. Kathryn S. Bennett, *The Motivation of Exits in Greek and Latin Comedy* (Ann Arbor, Michigan, 1932).

22. Flickinger, chap. vi.

23. W. E. Blake, 'The Aristophanic Bird Chorus—A Riddle', *American Journal of Philology*, LXIV (1943), 87-91, discusses the special problem raised by this chorus and concludes that it was composed of twenty-eight members.

24. Pickard-Cambridge has collected and analysed the evidence in *The Theatre of Dionysus*, pp. 100-22.

25. The composition of the audience is discussed by Flickinger, p. 120 f. and 215-20, and Pickard-Cambridge, *The Dramatic Festivals*, pp. 268-85.

26. B. B. Rogers, *The Ecclesiazusae* (London, 1902), pp. xxix-xxxiv, argues that women were not present in the theatre. Flickinger, p. 121, and Pickard-Cambridge, *The Dramatic Festivals*, p. 268, believe women were present.

CHAPTER 6

ARISTOPHANES, COMIC POET

THE functions of the comic poet as they developed in Athens and as Aristophanes interpreted them were threefold: one, to reconcile man to his world; two, to save the city; and three, to release man from troubles. The reconciliation of man could be accomplished by revealing to him the beauty of nature and the joys of simple, peaceful living. This reconciliation was essentially a religious experience fostered by the gods. The saving of the city was the responsibility of every citizen in the democracy, but the poet had a particular duty to persuade and convince the people of the best course to take because the poet had the ear and the attention of the same people who sat one day in the theatre, another in the Assembly. Moreover, the personal interests of the dramatists were at stake. The dramatic festival was under the aegis of the city and depended for its artistic splendour upon the prosperity of the city. Above all, the people oppressed by war, lawsuits, and poverty turned to the comic poet for a release from these troubles which he could effect by inducing them into the self-abandonment of laughter.

While these may be the basic functions of the Greek comic poet, the obvious one is the delight of audiences through words which are poetic, dramatic, and comical. It is the ability of Aristophanes to cause this delight which to my mind constitutes his genius. It is this which raised him above Eupolis and Cratinus in his own day and has preserved his plays to our day. We do not share his religion, nor can we see his plays performed as he intended, but we can read eleven of his comedies. The art of the comic poet is extremely rare in the history of literature because it is not only very difficult but verges on the paradoxical. We expect of poetry that it be rhythmical and imaginative; we expect of dramatic dialogue that it be relevant to character and situation; we expect of witty prose that it first surprise us in some way and then satisfy us with its aptness.

To fulfil all these expectations is indeed an art. The purpose of this chapter is the analysis and evaluation of this art [1].

Aristophanes was fortunate, first of all, in having a chorus. Dramatic dialogue is necessarily limited in its possibilities even when soliloquies are acceptable conventions. The chorus, however, is designed to add the arts of dance and music to poetry and thus accent the rhythmic patterns of the verse. It increases the imaginative range because it may represent the non-human world of clouds, birds, and animals. It also may sing out of character in the person of the dramatist and thus add the scope of lyric poetry to the dramatic. This function of the chorus is especially fulfilled in the parabasis, where the chorus, having put aside its costume in order to dance more freely, speaks directly to the audience. The parabasis also usually includes two odes, frequently invocations of the gods.

These odes and other hymns to the gods are the best starting-point for a study of Aristophanes's poetry because they illustrate perfectly his sense of rhythm and image, of dramatic relevance and comic twist. A wide variety of gods is invoked, each one appropriate to the occasion. Dicaeopolis naturally calls upon Phales, a cultic attribute of Dionysos, when he celebrates the Rural Dionysia. The Knights properly invoke Poseidon, god of horses and ships, and Athene, patron goddess of Athens. The Mystae invoke Iacchus; the Clouds the gods of heaven, sea, air, and sun; the women in the *Thesmophoriazusae* Artemis and Hera. The hymeneal is sung at the end of the *Birds* and *Peace* in honour of the marriages of the heroes. The concluding ode of the *Lysistrata* enforces the point of the play. The Athenian half of the chorus in its rejoicing at peace calls upon the Graces, Artemis, and Peace, ending with the victory refrain of the paean. The Laconian half also sings of the Bacchic dance, but the main burden of its refrain is the honour of 'Asana', the Doric pronunciation of Athana. Thus does Aristophanes try to impress upon his Athenian audience the realization that Athenians and Laconians worship the same gods though they may pronounce their names differently. If only these two warring peoples would recognize their common humanity and their common religion, they might learn to live in peace with each other.

The tone of the odes varies with the god invoked and with

the character of the singer, and with the varied tone goes a varied source of delight. The invocation of Phales is obviously comic on a bucolic plane. It starts with respectable epithets,

> Phales, comrade of Bacchus
> Drinking-companion, night-wanderer

and then surprises by finishing the line with 'adulterer, lover of boys' (*Acharnians*, 263-79). The rest of the ode combines a plea for help in making peace and gaining release from troubles and wars and also in 'rifling the vineyard' of Thratta, maid of Strymodorus, when he catches her stealing wood.

In contrast, the invocation of Poseidon by the Knights is apparently dignified with many polysyllabic words and a repeated *k*-sound to suggest the repeated beat of the hooves of horses. Even here, however, the unexpected word gives the ode a witty turn without diminution of the essentially religious worship due to the god of horse and ship.

> Master of Horses, Poseidon,
> The sound of the brazen-hoofed horses
> And their neighing pleases you,
> The dark-prowed ships
> The triremes with hireling crews
> The crowd of youths distinguishing themselves
> On their yoked chariots
> By being very unlucky.
> Come hither to our chorus, god of the golden trident,
> Guardian of dolphins, worshipped at Sunium
> And at Geraestus, son of Cronos,
> Most dear to Phormio
> And above all the other gods
> To the Athenians. (*Knights*, 551-64.)

The translation of an ode is a baffling experience. One has no way of conveying in English the force of the second line, *chalkokroton hippon ktupos*, or the surprise of the adjective for ships—*kuanemboloi*, a 'poetic' word found outside of Aristophanes only in the *Electra* of Euripides—and *misthophoroi*, with its political implications of mercenaries and not Athenian sailors on board. Similarly, the youths in the chariot race are described by two participles—*lamprunomenos*—which has the implication of splendour followed by the surprise of *barudaimonountos*, 'of very bad luck'.

The first ode of the *Clouds* has a graceful lilt:

> High ruler of the gods
> Zeus the king, I shall
> Call first to our chorus.
> And the mighty treasurer of the trident
> The angry heaver-upper of earth and briny sea
> And our own father, the giver of glory,
> Aither, most blessed life-nurturer of all.
> And finally the keeper of horses,
> Who pours down on the earth
> The brilliant rays
> A great spirit among gods
> And among mortals. (*Clouds*, 563-74.)

Many of the words are also used by the tragic poets, but 'heaver-upper' is a comic word, a translation of *mochleuten*, the Greek word for 'lever'. The image of Poseidon using a lever to cause an earthquake is a comic one.

Even when Aristophanes would seem to have the least opportunity for originality—the marriage hymn with its conventional refrain—he differentiates between the rustic chorus of the *Peace* singing in honour of the vineyard keeper and the Birds singing in honour of their new king and queen. So the half chorus of the *Peace* asks, 'What shall we do to the bride?' and the other half replies, 'We shall *reap* the harvest.' ('Trugesomen' is a pun on the name of Trygaeus.) The chorus of Birds makes no references to the sexual act in its invocation of Hera, goddess of marriage, of the Fates, and of Eros. Their hymeneal is fit for a queen.

The song of the Mystae in the *Frogs* (316-459) is to my mind the finest of Aristophanes's religious odes. It is too long to quote here, but the reader desirous of studying Aristophanes's poetry further would do well to read this ode with close attention. It is full of the Dionysiac spirit of joy, of night revelry, of dancing, torches, meadow, and mountain. The chorus promises Demeter to say many laughable things and many serious.

The full contribution of these hymns to the comedies can hardly be appreciated unless one compares them with the fourth-century comedies—the *Ecclesiazusae* and *Plutus*. The first play has no hymns; the second has the word *choros* written in where the odes were sung. With the loss of the hymns the plays have lost the joy of Dionysos, the faith that gaiety has divine sanction. The comic world has lost a dimension and now is flat and circumscribed. The gods no longer join the chorus. The god the fourth century worshipped was Wealth, and he was blind.

These fourth-century comedies have lost touch also with the natural world. One has only to compare Aristophanes's treatment of sex in the *Peace* or *Lysistrata* with that in the *Ecclesiazusae* to see with sadness how natural sexual desire has been distorted. In the *Peace*, sexual relations are part of agricultural fertility rites. We breathe country air where the generative process of plant, animal, and man is a constant source of wonder and comment because it is the source of life. In the *Lysistrata* the emphasis is upon marital relations. It is not women the men want so much as *their* wives. But in the *Ecclesiazusae* the tables have been reversed, and the sight of old women fighting over a young man is unnatural and displeasing. Moreover, the fight has no overtones of political significance, unlike the marriage of a vineyard keeper with the fruits of the earth or the forcing of enemies to peace by the women. The consequence is clearly to be discerned in the poetry. The love duet of the *Ecclesiazusae*, 952-68, is no more than a conventional song of physical attraction, lacking both emotional appeal and gusto.

In the fifth-century comedies the natural world of cloud and bird and insect and the country life of farmer and vineyard worker is depicted with sensitivity and skill. Aristophanes is without doubt one of the greatest poets of nature in Western literature. He had an ear for the country. Witness the croak of the frog—brekekekex koax koax—and the trill of the birds—

> torotorotorotorotix
> kikkabau kikkabau.
> torotorotorotorolililix. (*Birds*, 260-3.)

But this imitative skill is only the beginning. Aristophanes knew the haunts of frog and bird. The frogs dwell in marshes, and when the festival of Dionysos in the Marshes is held, they *iachesamen*, 'sound forth', a pun on the cult name for Dionysos, Iacchus. The *Birds* is full of references to the names and habits of dozens of birds. For example, lines 302-4 consist entirey of eighteen names of birds, six to a line. Their invocation to the Muse of the woods (737-51) is a delicate and lovely ode, a combination of images of vale and wooded mountain and sweet-smelling song. The description of the building of the wall by cranes and herons and woodpeckers shows clearly Aristophanes's keen eye for the size and shape of beak and wing. One of the most beautiful lyrics is the opening song of the Clouds as they rise from the ocean and float up the wooded mountain slopes.

Aristophanes was a realistic lover of the country. Birds can dirty a new white tunic; frogs can croak when the flutes play; clouds can rain. Country life is not an idyll of carefree indolence. The sturdy Acharnians invoke their Muse, as strong and virile as flaming fire (665-75). The picture of their life that follows suggests in a few words a country kitchen—the sizzling of fish over the charcoal fire, fanned by the bellows to a hot flame, the mixing up of a Thasian sauce for the fish, the kneading of dough. (The fishsauce—*liparampuka*—is a parody of Pindar's 'with shiny fillet', *Nemean* VII, 22). In other plays Aristophanes shows the same realistic understanding that the farmer and his wife work hard for their living—digging, planting, pruning, and harvesting—and the rewards are only the warmth of the fire and a simple meal of beans and figs, perhaps a bird or two and a rabbit (*Peace*, 1127-90).

Again, the best way of realizing the poetic values of these pictures of natural and country life is to compare a play like the *Acharnians*, *Clouds*, or *Peace* with one of the fourth-century comedies. The *Plutus*, for example, has a pastoral duet (290-321), but it is a pastoral in the conventionalized form which later blossomed under the sophisticated touch of Theocritus. Carion pretends to be the Cyclops; the chorus pretends to be the followers of Odysseus. The pastoral is a game; the serious work is the getting of Wealth.

The poetry of earth is never dead. The poetry of the divine is undying also even if the gods change, for the worship of superhuman powers inspires the poet to breathe into his poetry emotional fervour which moves us even though we no longer share his worship. But to save the city in witty poetry is indeed a challenge to a poet. Such a task seems undramatic, unpoetical, and too serious for either laughter or delight. Aristophanes solved the problem at the foundation: he built his early comedies on metaphors, thus providing a basis for many imaginative effects. Consider, for example, the *Wasps*. Aristophanes starts with the image of some of the old Athenian men as wasps. Like wasps they are indigenous; they stung the Persian invader with their lances and drove him from their shores though he tried to smoke them out; they swarm in groups; they are quick-tempered and readily sting their opponents; but at least they have earned a pension from the state, unlike the drones who live upon the state without ever having done anything to deserve that living. The visual image in the theatre of the men dressed like wasps is in accord with the verbal image; the image is witty because we are first surprised by the juxtaposition of insect and man and then amused by the likeness of things supposedly unlike. At the same time Aristophanes himself is waspish, stinging the Athenians into awareness of the political dangers of the power wielded by the jurymen. Another example of the way Aristophanes develops an image is to be found in the *Lysistrata*. If women are rulers of the state, they will rule in accordance with their own terms. Thus Lysistrata describes her political programme in terms of washing, carding, spinning, and weaving wool (574-86).

These images continue to amuse us although the point may be obscured by time and its pertinence lost through changing conditions. The images are memorable even where their meaning is not. We remember the image of a tragic poet constructing tragedies as a carpenter does a house, cities pounded to pieces between mortar and pestle, poetic diction weighed in scales, a philosopher who worships airy nothings. How can one save the city? Why, all the farmers can unite and work together for peace. And the result is the rhythmic cry of the chorus as they pull Peace from her cave and the odes of welcome they sing to her. Or, a tragic poet can teach the people the way of salvation. And the result is the god of the drama rowing over the marshes to Hades to the tune of the frogs and being greeted by those initiated in his mysteries.

Another source of amusement is the writing in verse of material commonly heard in prose. To the Greek audience the speeches in comedy with their parodies of speeches in the Assembly and law courts must have been doubly amusing in metrical form. Aristophanes uses every available rhetorical device to hold the attention of the audience and to thrust home the points. Mnesilochus takes the women by surprise, defending Euripides by saying that Euripides has understated the case. The real crimes of the women are much worse than any Euripides has presented (*Thesmophoriazusae*, 466 f.). Dicaeopolis does not try to defend the Spartans. He hates them and the destruction they have caused. His attack is aimed at the causes of the war, trying by ridiculing their insignificance to undermine the importance of the war (*Acharnians*, 496 f.). Agoracritus does not try to defeat Cleon by being better than he but by being worse, and Pheidippides is willing not only to prove that it is right to beat one's father but also to beat one's mother (*Clouds*, 1443).

These bold offensive defensives in speeches and debates follow the pattern of contemporary speeches [2]. The divisions of introduction, conclusion, and separate arguments are clearly marked. The main point is emphasized throughout. Arguments based upon justice and probability are bolstered by examples drawn from history and everyday life. Appeals are made to the emotions of the spectators—to their pride in the victory of Marathon, to their love of Athens and Attica, to their veneration of old people, and desire for power. And always an unexpected pun, a ribald figure of speech, a new word, or a thrust at some unpopular Athenian keep the speech in proper tune with the comedy.

The speech of Dicaeopolis is a prime example of Aristophanes's artistry (*Acharnians*, 496-556). We listen, in effect, to four men speaking on four different planes: a man pleads for his life; a just city argues for peace; a mock-Telephus defends himself with his head on a block; and Aristophanes defends the stand he took in a previous play. Thus we are aware throughout the speech of the intensity of the situation, of the political implications, of the parody of Euripides, and of the emotional and intellectual integrity of the poet. Dicaeopolis begins by addressing the spectators; they are the true judges, not the Acharnian chorus. He asks them not to be angry if he speaks about the city even though he is a beggar (a parody of the *Telephus*) and a maker of a comedy (switch back to Aristophanes). Even a comedy knows what is just—*dikaia* (switch to the character, Dicaeopolis). As Aristophanes, he replies to the criticism of Cleon, who had accused him of speaking evilly of Athens in the *Babylonians*, a comedy performed at the City Dionysia when allies from the tribute-paying cities were in the audience. Since the *Acharnians* is being performed at the winter festival of the Lenaea, Aristophanes is speaking only to citizens and metics. He next, as Dicaeopolis, agrees with the Acharnians that the Lacedaemonians are hateful. He wishes Poseidon would shake down their houses over their heads because they have cut down his vineyard. His defence rests on two arguments: first, that the causes of the war are trivial; and, second, that the Lacedaemonians are doing only what the Athenians would do in a similar situation. The end of the speech is a lightning reversal to the *Telephus*, and a summary, 'there is no sense in us'.

The range of Aristophanes's verbal ingenuity is illustrated by the following list. He puns frequently on the name of Dicaeopolis. He coins a word—*methusokottaboi*, 'drunk-with-cottabus playing'—to describe the youths who stole a harlot from Megara. He borrows from cock-fighting a term, 'to be excited from eating garlic' and applies it to the Megarians, who were notorious for their garlic consumption. He blames the war not on Laconians nor 'the city' nor even on men but on the diminutive of men, 'manikins', and applies five epithets to them, three with the repeated prefix of *para*—meaning aside or wrong. He uses diminutives and lists again in speaking of the sycophants, who benefit from the embargo of Megarian goods. He uses alliteration, e.g. three out of the four words in line 548 contain 'st'. He repeats key words from line to line—*trugodia* in 499 and 500, *dikaia* in 500-501. Two metaphors are particularly conspicuous. At the winter festival, when storms kept the allies home on their islands, the audience has been 'winnowed of chaff'; the metics, who dwelt in Attica but were not Athenian citizens, are as close to the citizens as husks to grains. Pericles is an Olympian who 'lightnings', thunders, and throws Hellas into a ferment. If the Laconians had stolen a Seriphian puppy (Seriphos is a small Aegean island), then the city would have been full of the uproar of soldiers, of an outcry about the fitting out of the triremes, of payments, of gilding the statues of Pallas, and of packing knapsacks with food. Farewell parties ended with 'crowns, anchovies, flute-girls, and black eyes'.

One way a Greek comic poet thought he could save his city was through purifying it of vice and folly. The epithets mentioned above are mild compared to the scurrilous language Aristophanes can use. Just how poetic and witty invective can be is to some extent a matter of tradition and taste. Aristophanes was in the iambic tradition of the ritual flaying of the scapegoat. Demagogues of every country and time gain ascendancy partly through their ability to fling mud at their opponents and make it stick. And seeing the profit gained from mud-flinging, some opponents will wipe the mud off and fling it back. If Cleon calls Aristophanes 'un-Athenian', can we wonder that Aristophanes calls Cleon 'a knave, a troubler of the cavalry, a tax-collector, a gully, and rapacious Charybdis'? (*Knights*, 247-8). Much of the invective is too local in allusion to retain its original flavour and force. If Aristophanes were alive to-day to pit his comic vocabulary against those who can think of nothing more devastating than 'parlour pink', his rich, varied, extensive vocabulary of abuse with its freshly minted compounds and its unexpected metaphors might satisfy one function of a poet—to express our feelings better than we can. Name-calling is not polite nor Christian, but it is a release from tension, and, if it is done well, it is an art whatever our opinion of the ethics or manners involved.

The release from tension can be accomplished in many ways which do not include abuse. Surprise is the most effective method of provoking laughter. Aristophanes's favourite method of surprising the audience is by introducing words from varied levels of diction [3]. If we start with what we can call 'standard Greek', the expected diction of an average middle-class Athenian, we find six deviations from this norm. The most obvious deviation is the Doric dialect. Boeotians, Megarians, and Lacedaemonians are frequent characters in the comedies, partly of course because they have a role to play but partly also no doubt because of the amusement caused by their pronunciations of Greek. The foreigner trying to speak one's native tongue is a second source of amusement exemplified in these comedies by Pseudartabas in the *Acharnians*.

Laughter on a childish level is caused by hearing words not

used in polite society, a third deviation. Aristophanes time after time shocks the audience by introducing vulgar and indecent words into both dialogue and chorus. He had inherited from the Ionian iambic poets—Archilochus and Hipponax—a large comic vocabulary for parts of the body and natural processes not mentioned in tragedy and lyric. Aristophanes invented additions to this vocabulary through compounds and metaphorical neologisms. The word *chasko*, 'to gape', must have been particularly amusing to the Greeks since it appears so frequently. A fourth group of words consists of colloquialisms and slang expressions which contribute liveliness to the dialogue.

The fifth and sixth deviations from standard Greek are technical terms and poetic words. Aristophanes draws upon the crafts of building, butchery and leather-working, the household chores of cooking, weaving, and caring for woollens and babies, the raising and selling of vegetables, the professions of soldier and sailor, the processes of the law, the jargon of the horsey set, of sportsmen, hunters, and fishers. Often the reduction of problems of state to the terms of everyday activity is a matter not only of comic understatement or comic surprise but an honest effort to see from a fresh point of view and on a smaller scale problems which seem insoluble because of our emotions.

Aristophanes's use of 'poetic' words is a subject for a chapter all its own. Sometimes an isolated grandiloquent word suddenly pops up in surprising context, amusing us by its inappropriateness. Sometimes the word is sufficiently unusual to recall to the intelligent audience the original context of lyric or tragedy and thus enrich the whole scene by its suggestiveness. The parodies throughout all the comedies form in themselves a golden vein of wit for the cultivated. Even with the help of the scholiasts, many of these parodies are probably lost, with the consequent loss of poetic overtones. Even so, enough are recognizable to provide us with evidence that the critical theories of Aristophanes, propounded in the *Frogs*, were constantly in his mind from his young manhood. He believed that tragic diction becomes comic diction when it is bombastic, turgid, or flat, and through his parodies Aristophanes writes a running critical comment on Greek tragedy, adding to the immediate amusement of surprise the more permanent pleasure of recognition. Aristophanes also surprises us by slight tamperings with the form of a poetic word. Sometimes he compounds it with another tragic word or with a word from another level of diction. Sometimes he changes a letter or two and thus renders the word ridiculous.

One way to illustrate these levels is by examining the history of each word in a list. Lists were traditional comic devices often employed by Aristophanes, and the fun resided in incongruous juxtapositions as well as in accumulative force. Amphitheus describes the Acharnians as 'hard, old men, tough, unyielding, belligerent, and sturdy' (180-1). Such a translation totally obscures the wit of Aristophanes because the metaphors are untranslated. The word for 'hard' was applied by Theophrastus to charcoal; Aristophanes no doubt had this use in mind when he chose the adjective since the Acharnians were famous for their charcoal. In fact, Dicaeopolis seizes a basket of charcoal as a hostage as if it were their child. The word for 'tough' meant 'made of oak', used first by Aristophanes in its metaphorical meaning. 'Unyielding' is mainly found in Homer and Aeschylus. 'Belligerent' is a translation for 'Marathon fighters', first found in Aristophanes though it may have been a popular word. 'Sturdy' is similar to the word for 'tough'. 'made of maple wood'. This word is found outside Aristophanes in a fragment of Cratinus of uncertain date, but not metaphorically. The Acharnians thus have a kind of natural and patriotic strength which renders them at once formidable and admirable.

By the time the double meanings of such metaphors or of puns are explained to the reader, the surprise and pleasure both have been sacrificed. Aristophanes plays with words constantly, but his play becomes tedious if reported at length. The names of Euripides and Socrates, for instance, are turned into verbs; and Gela, a famous Sicilian city, couples with an imaginary Catagela. Much of the humour is buffoonery. A character makes a serious appeal or speech while a buffoon comments on it. For example, the disciple of Socrates shows Strepsiades a map.

DISCIPLE. Euboea, as you see, stretches very far.
STREPSIADES. I know. It was stretched on the rack by us and Pericles. (*Clouds*, 212-3.)

Later Strepsiades plagues Socrates by his failure to grasp the technical meanings of metre and dactyl. The *Frogs* is full of this buffoonery, with Dionysos often the buffoon. Later in the comedy Aeschylus reduces Euripides to despair by finishing his line with the refrain 'and found his oil-flask gone', a refrain which fits the metre and completes the sense in a ridiculous fashion. One whole scene turns on a pun, the double meanings of *choiros*—'pig' and 'female organs'. A Megarian, starving because of the economic embargo of Athens, has put his daughters in a sack and brought them to the market of Dicaeopolis, hoping that he can sell his 'pigs' in a poke.

The means by which Aristophanes fulfilled the threefold functions of a Greek comic poet have been discussed. His success in fulfilling them can be judged by at least two standards: the prizes he won in his own day and the qualities which have endured to our own day. The Greek judges could compare his comedies with those of Eupolis, Cratinus, and others. They saw and heard the comedies as they were expected to. Thus they could judge originality and pertinence to contemporary culture as we never can. Aristophanes won the first prize for the *Acharnians*, *Knights*, and *Frogs*, the second prize for the *Wasps*, *Peace*, and *Birds*, and the third prize for the *Clouds*. No records exist for the success of the *Lysistrata*, *Thesmophoriazusae*, *Ecclesiazusae*, and *Plutus*. The lasting qualities of Aristophanes's art are, in my opinion, his brilliance of image, a delicate but firm control over motion, and an intelligent and articulate critical theory.

The quality of brilliance has already been amply illustrated. Only the descriptions of scenes off-stage need be added. Here the very limitations of the Greek stage gave Aristophanes the opportunity to practise the art of verbal play. The report of the Assembly in the *Ecclesiazusae*, for instance, is amusing because the point of view is shifted. We have seen the women preparing for their *coup d'état* and then departing, confident in their masculine disguise. Later, Chremes returns from the Assembly and tells Blepyrus, husband of the ring-leader, about the great crowd of men who had come early to the Assembly, the greatest crowd ever seen there, all white like shoemakers. Neocleides, the blind man and Evaeon, a pauper, spoke concerning the city. They were followed by a handsome young man, who said that the city should be turned over to the women. Then the great multitude of shoemakers roared and cried out while the men from the country murmured loudly. The speech of Praxagora is summarized with comment and prompting from Blepyrus. The city was delivered to the women. 'This alone seemed never yet to have been done in the city' (456).

Several amusing banquet scenes are reported. Thus we hear of the uncouth behaviour of Philocleon, who skipped and leaped around like a donkey full of parched barley, insulted all the other guests, joked in a rustic fashion, and staggered home drunk, striking everyone on the way. Strepsiades reports that his son, Pheidippides, fresh from the school of Socrates, refuses to sing a song by Simonides, saying that it was old-fashioned to play the cithara and sing while drinking, like women grinding barley. Moreover, he thought Simonides a bad poet and Aeschylus full of empty noise and unpolished, bombastic, craggy words. Instead, he wished to recite the verses of Euripides about incestuous love. This poetic controversy was followed by a scuffle in which Strepsiades claims that Pheidippides leapt upon him, crushed, pulverized, and pressed him hard.

The images are clear, exact in detail, memorable, and suggestive. When we remember the comedies of Aristophanes, we remember the beauty of the clouds, the 'oaken' Acharnians, Philocleon making an ass of himself, the supercilious young convert to modern literature, the horses rowing over the sea to Corinth, the oil-flask of Euripides, and many another image created by the poet and visible only in the mind's eye and not the spectator's. Often the verbal image we hear in the dialogue and the scene in the theatre work together to produce either comic incongruity or emphasis, but even without the theatrical image we can find constant delight in the verbal images of Aristophanes.

The qualities of the motion in the comedies can be discussed with only an approximation to accuracy because the music which accompanied so much of the poetry is lost to us and because our knowledge of Greek metrics is limited. Greek metrics is a controversial subject which can be dealt with satisfactorily only by specialists in the field. However, the recognition of our deficiencies need not deter us entirely from commenting on one of Aristophanes's most precious gifts.

What first strikes the ear, I think, is the variety of motion to be found in the comedies. We hear the repeated thud of the march, the gallop of the horse, the graceful float, the quick angry give and take of an argument, the lighter rejoinders of banter, the hurried steps hither and thither of a search, swift flight, the intricate rhythms of the dance, the long, hard pull of the rope. These impressions are admittedly subjective, but the methods used to produce these impressions can be analysed. The methods include the division of the line among the speakers the weight of the line, the length of the line, and the metre.

Many lines by one speaker have so slow a motion that Aristophanes usually has another speaker break in at intervals with a question or comment. For arguments, stichomythy may be used, particularly if the passage is a parody of tragedy. Most rapid of all is the division of the line into halves. Consider lines 247-327 of the *Acharnians*, for example. Dicaeopolis enters making arrangements for his celebration of the Rural Dionysia and then singing an invocation to Phales, 32 lines. The chorus cries out,

> This is he, this.
> Hit, hit, hit, hit,
> Strike, strike the wretch.
> Not hit? Not hit?

There follows an interchange of a line each between Dicaeopolis and the Acharnians, then three lines by the chorus, one by Dicaeopolis, one by the chorus, one by Dicaeopolis, and three by the chorus. A new section starts with twenty lines of argument, two lines for each contestant. Then, as the argument gains in heat, the next three lines are broken in half between the speakers, a staccato rhythm which ends in the continuation by Dicaeopolis of his speech for two more lines.

The speed of the motion is also determined by the weight of the line, i.e. the preponderance of verbs or of nouns and adjectives in a line or passage. The repeated verbs of the chorus quoted above are one extreme while the many epithets of reverence in the invocations of the gods are at the other extreme. In between we find Aristophanes altering the rhythms of long speeches by his distribution of the parts of speech. Somewhat related to this device is the number of words to a line, varying from the extreme of many short words to three or four long ones. (The longest word in the Greek language—the hundred and sixty-nine letter invention of Aristophanes which concludes the *Ecclesiazusae*—is a *tour de force* and in my opinion neither very funny nor clever.)

The principal determinant of the speed of the motion is the length of the line and the metre of the foot. In this respect again Aristophanes shows himself master of varied forms. He may break out of metre entirely with an exclamation 'phooey!' or the squeak of piglets, 'koi koi'. The line may be only two feet long; it may be six. The iambic measure was the common one, coming nearest to daily speech, as Aristotle said (*Poetics*, 1449a25). By reversing the normal rhythm by the use of the trochee, Aristophanes gains force and liveliness. The dactylic hexameter was sparingly used because its association with epic, oracle, and religious ceremony made it effective mainly for parody. The long roll of the anapaestic tetrameter was a rhythm particularly pleasing to Aristophanes and continues to be to the modern reader.

One danger of discussing qualities of poetry one by one is that the relationships between qualities may be overlooked. Motion and diction are not two separate qualities. Their intimate connections have been so clearly and succinctly stated by Mr Richards that I am going to quote his statement in full.

> About Aristophanes the all-important fact to bear in mind is that there are usually four or five different levels upon which various parts of a comedy are composed, four or five different strata below or above one another. Of these strata the common iambic trimeters are the lowest. Probably iambics were not the earliest comic metre, but in our comedies they may be called the standard or normal metre more than any other. The players speak iambic trimeters when there is no particular reason for their speaking something else. In this standard or normal metre the diction is in an ordinary way almost entirely that of actual life and the poetical vocabulary above described has no natural place. At a level distinctly higher come trochaic tetrameters, a metre of more movement and excitement, as we know from tragedy also; and into them sparingly but unmistakably, are admitted words a little above common speech, not used in the

ordinary course of things and seldom or never—except for special reasons presently to be stated—allowed to appear in iambic senarii. There are two or three other forms of verse which go more or less with trochaic tetrameters, such as iambic tetrameters, and dimeters both iambic and trochaic. It is very hard to draw a line between these four species as regards the vocabulary allowed. They are all freer than iambic senarii, and perhaps the dimeters are the freest, for they have a touch of the lyrical about them. A very well-marked interval separates from any and all of these the anapaestic measures, mainly tetrameter, but sometimes dimeter, of which Aristophanes is so fond that the commonest and finest of them was called after him. 'The rise and long roll' of the ordinary anapaestic verse raises it a long way above the rhythm and general effect of prose, and its poetical character in this respect is matched by a corresponding liberty in the matter of diction, restricted however within a few limits by no means wide. We find very many words, and a few forms of words, in anapaests that would be out of place in any inferior metre. Finally, as our highest stratum of verse, we have the lyrics, varying infinitely among themselves in subject and language, character and elevation, some still humorous and common, some purely poetical. We may say of them as a class that they admit the diction of poetry in considerable though varying degrees, and of a few, especially those religious or semi-religious in character, that they admit it almost as much as the lyrics of tragedy. [4]

Metre and meaning are related in another way. Mr White points out:

> It is instructive to observe that the half of the celebrated debate in the *Ranae* conducted by Aeschylus (1006 ff.) is in anapaestic rhythm, that conducted by Euripides (907 ff.) in iambic. The contrast between the Good Young Man and the Bad Young Man is similarly marked in the *Nubes* (961 ff., 1036 ff.), and it is not without significance that Aristophanes in his *Equites*, designing to out-Cleon Cleon, has his famous blackguard in the second debate carry on in iambic tetrameters the argument which Cleon has begun in anapaests (Eq. 763 ff., 843 ff.). [5]

The metres of the comedies were not always determined by the meaning or emotion the poet wished to convey. Two parts of the comedies—the parabasis and the agon—had conventional metres assigned to the separate parts. The individual poet was free to depart from the convention if he wished, but he necessarily wrote with the convention in mind. The norm for a parabasis consisted of a commation in anapaests, the parabasis proper in anapaestic tetrameters, a pnigos in anapaestic hypermeter, an ode with a metre chosen by the poet, an epirrhema in trochaic tetrameter, an antode in the metre of the ode, and an antepirrhema in trochaic tetrameter.

The parabasis of the *Knights*, 498-610, is a good illustration of a 'normal' parabasis. The commation is a transitional passage from the action of the comedy to the song of the chorus. The chorus expresses to the departing Sausage-seller its hopes for his victorious return. Then it turns to the audience, saying, 'And you turn your attention to us, to our anapaests, you who have had experience with the Muse of every kind.' In the anapaests the chorus speaks for Aristophanes, explaining his hesitation about producing his comedies in his own name, citing the experiences of older comic poets and the difficulties of production. The anapaests end with a bid for victory in the Lenaean festival, the last sentence flowing over into the pnigos. This section was so called, the Scholiast says, because the chorus was supposed to recite it in one breath, and the word means *choke*. The ode is an invocation of Poseidon, god of horses and ships. The term epirrhema means 'the words following after' the parabasis. In the epirrhema of the *Knights*, the chorus reverts to character, praising the great deeds of their fathers. The antode is an invocation of Athene. The antepirrhema is a praise of horses, an amusing fantasy of their leaping into the ships and rowing to Corinth, crying as they row 'hippapai' a parody of the boatsman's cry of 'rhuppapai'. The pervading theme of the parabasis is 'victory'—victory for the Sausage-seller, victory for the poet, victory of the knights of old, victory of the knights of the present, victory of the horses. The return of the Sausage-seller as Victorious-in-the-Council is thus prepared for by the parabasis even though we laugh at the obvious falsehood of the Chorus when the leader greets the Sausage-seller with the reassurance that the chorus has been out of its mind with anxiety during his absence.

The rhythmic beauty of the parabasis consists in the delicate balance between variety and repetition. Ode and antode, epirrhema and antepirrhema, provide symmetry while the irregular rhythms of the odes are a pleasing contrast to the regularity of trochaic tetrameter. The length and rise of the anapaests are pleasing contrasts to the shortness and fall of the trochees.

The metres of the agon are not so strongly marked nor the separate parts so sharply differentiated as they are in the parabasis [6]. The simplest scheme divides it into an ode, a call to action, an epirrhema, antode, a pnigos, and a sphragis or seal. The structure of the agon is thus similar to that of the parabasis, despite its difference in purpose. First, the chorus usually sings an ode and calls the contestants into the arena. The antagonist opens the fray in the first epirrhema. Then the chorus comments on his arguments and encourages or taunts the protagonist to reply. He does so in the antepirrhema. The epirrhemata are often concluded with a pnigos. The decision of the contest is presented in the sphragis. In the excitement of the battle between the characters some parts of the agon are lost and others duplicated. The metres of the odes and epirrhemata change from play to play; only the call to action is the same in all agons—either anapaestic or iambic tetrameter.

The parabasis and the agon with their formal metrical structure accentuate the structure of the whole play. They emphasize the role of the chorus as spokesman for the dramatist and the significance of the contest in the plot. The recurring metrical contrast and symmetry heighten Aristophanes's theme of conflict and reconciliation. Yet strong as these conventions were, they had no binding force [7]. The poet was free to vary the metres and to omit or duplicate parts. Only four complete and normal parabases are extant, those of the *Acharnians*, *Knights*, *Wasps*, and *Birds*. The last two plays, the *Ecclesiazusae* and *Plutus*, have no parabasis, the *Frogs* and *Lysistrata* no anapaests, the *Peace* no epirrhemata, and the *Thesmophoriazusae* neither odes nor epirrhema. Moreover, the same metres are not invariably used. The commation of the *Birds* is not anapaestic, and even more surprising, the parabasis proper of the *Clouds* is Eupolidean.

The movement of Aristophanes's poetry has freedom and originality, control and balance. The rhythm of each chorus as it enters is distinctive. Within the play contestant answers contestant, half-chorus answers half-chorus. The parabasis, which might seem to stop the action of the comedy, actually spans with dance and song the time required for off-stage action. The audience is active indeed, watching the movements of the dance, listening to the music, thinking about the poetry, and if any one has imagination to spare, imagining what is happening to Dicaeopolis, to the Sausage-seller, to Strepsiades or to any of the heroes who have gone into danger.

The third quality which I value particularly in Aristophanes is his intelligent and articulate critical theory. He was one of the best-read and most cultivated men of his generation, if not of all Greek civilization. If we can judge from his allusions, quotations, and parodies, we find him familiar with almost all Greek poetry and prose of the past and his own day. He evidently knew the epics of Homer, Hesiod, and the Cycle, the lyrics of Alcaeus, Anacreon, Pindar, Simonides, Ibycus, and Stesichorus [8]. Perhaps he also knew the choruses of Alcman and the elegiacs of Theognis, though the evidence for them is less certain [9]. He surely was acquainted with Solon's verses, and with the iambics of Archilochus and Hipponax [10].

The whole history of the theatre was well known to him. He must have attended the theatre assiduously from boyhood with an observant eye and ear. The *Telephus* of Euripides, produced when Aristophanes was about eleven years old, seems to have impressed him very much, for he returned to it often in his comedies. Earlier plays must have been published, for he refers to Thespis, Phrynichus, and Aeschylus, who were of an earlier generation [11]. Sophocles, Euripides, and Agathon he knew personally, and also a host of minor tragic poets: Xenocles, Theognis, Meletus, Sannyrion, Morsimus, and Melanthius [12]. How much he knew of Epicharmus, the first comic poet, is problematical. He never refers to him by name nor clearly alludes to him, but some comic devices and characters are reminiscent of the Sicilian's [13]. Since Plato knew him so well, it is at least likely that Aristophanes too had read his sketches, but withheld acknowledgment in typical Greek fashion. The other comic poets were, of course, his rivals for the affections and prizes of the Athenians and were observed with a keen and jealous eye. Magnes, Cratinus, Crates, Eupolis, Phrynichus, and Pherecrates, the most important of the comic poets, are all mentioned by Aristophanes.

Prose was in its adolescence during the fifth century, just

emerging into full maturity during the lifetime of Aristophanes. He knew only popular legends of Thales, the early sixth-century Ionian philosopher, and the popular fables of Aesop were doubtless still being circulated in oral form [14]. How much he read of contemporary prose—speeches, history, handbooks—it is very hard for us now to say. He mentions Gorgias and Prodicus, and he was familiar with the work of Herodotus, probably through listening to the men speaking or reading their own works [15]. Similarly, the new ideas of the Sophists and the devices first promulgated by the Sicilian rhetoricians, Corax and Tisias, were current topics of conversation among intellectual Athenians and among the characters of Euripidean tragedy [16]. Tricks of rhetoric were being used daily in the Assembly and law-courts and could be picked up there by an alert listener.

The difficulty of tracing the exact source for some of Aristophanes's ideas is well illustrated by the *Ecclesiazusae* [17]. Two of the central ideas of Plato's *Republic* are presented for ridicule in this play: the communism of goods and community of women. Yet the *Republic* was not published until many years after the *Ecclesiazusae*. Were these ideas prevalent in Athens early in the fourth century? Had Plato published an early edition of the *Republic*? Did Plato borrow the ideas of some philosopher whose works are no longer extant? No definite answer can now be proved; all we can safely say is that Aristophanes discovered what was new whether it was published in books, spoken in the Assembly, produced in the theatre, recited in the market-place, or discussed at private banquets.

He looked at old and new alike from one point of view and judged literature by one set of standards. First of all, he believed that poets are morally responsible human beings who are not absolved from contributing to the welfare of society by their profession. They are the teachers of the city whether or not they wish to be. Since they are responsible for the effect of their poetry on the spirits of men, they should be aware of the kind of society they wish to live in and try to achieve it. All poets share in this responsibility. The tragic poet cannot excuse himself on the ground that he is simply dramatizing a myth; nor the dithyrambic poet on the ground that he is simply writing a song; nor the comic poet on the ground that he is only joking. In the *Frogs*, Euripides says and Aeschylus agrees that one of the reasons a poet is admirable is that he makes men better citizens. Sound moral advice in itself does not constitute art. The true artist is clever: he is original but not fantastic; he combines a sense of proportion and decorum with vigour and realism.

The tragedies of Sophocles come the closest perhaps of all works of Greek literature to fulfilling the qualifications stated above, though Aristophanes honours early poets like Simonides. Aristophanes vigorously attacks bombast, frigidity, meaningless trifles, obscurity, and triteness wherever he found them. In the *Frogs* the tragedies of Aeschylus are criticized for as many faults as those of Euripides. Dionysos, after a careful weighing of the evidence, chooses Aeschylus simply because he pleases, not because his tragedies can be said objectively to be better than those of Euripides. The attitude of Aristophanes toward Euripides is a complicated one. He was obviously fascinated by Euripides, for only someone who had studied the tragedies with minute care could have parodied so many of them so frequently. The fascination was part attraction and part repulsion. Like other Athenians he was attracted by the originality of Euripides and his technical skill. No mute figures stood idle in the tragedies of Euripides as they did in those by Aeschylus. His diction was clear and simple, unmarred by the unintelligible words, metaphors, or constructions which Aeschylus used. But he was repelled by the religious and ethical scepticism which undermined traditional standards of conduct without providing another foundation.

The role of literary criticism in the comedies indicates clearly Aristophanes's belief in the importance of poetry and its pervasiveness in life. The comedies of the fifth century are full of literary criticism stated either directly or indirectly. The chorus is the main vehicle for this criticism and the parabases our main source, but criticism is to be found in all parts of the comedy and by many speakers. Dicaeopolis goes to Euripides to borrow rags, satirizing the many beggars Euripides portrays. The education of Philocleon in the *Wasps* and of Pheidippides in the *Clouds* is largely concerned with their taste in poetry. The melodramatic rescues of Euripides are burlesqued in the *Thesmophoriazusae*; and the *Frogs*, of course, is devoted to literary criticism. In addition, speech after speech contains a sudden reference to a poet, usually a contemporary poet whose works no longer survive.

While Aristophanes's critical theories are intelligent and articulate, his practice is consistent with them only up to a point. He said that his comedies were designed to make men better, and he strove to be clever, to be original, to be skilful in exposition, and to be true to the form of comedy. He was, however, torn by the conflict which he could not resolve in terms of principles. The judge of literature may be a very god of knowledge, experience, and impartiality, but his final criterion is pleasure. So the Greek judges, like Dionysos, weighed the comedies at each festival, and sometimes Aristophanes pleased them and sometimes he did not. Aristophanes wanted passionately to win the first prize, and he frequently asks the spectators to roar their approval and help him to victory. He tries to retain his integrity in the face of the pressure for victory, and he draws the line at throwing the audience nuts, but as the decades rolled on the Old Comedy began giving way to the Middle Comedy. Conservative as Aristophanes was in his politics, religion, art, and ethics, his originality was a stronger trait than his admiration for the past. His last comedies herald the new even as his first preserved the old.

When all is said, perhaps this ability of Aristophanes to please is the true mark of his genius. Dionysos, faced with the choice between Aeschylus and Euripides, says candidly, 'I shall choose the one my soul wishes' (*Frogs*, 1468). We can talk of the brilliant imagery of Aristophanes's poetry, of the gay and varied rhythms, of subtle symmetry and bold contrast, of his intelligence, wide learning, and critical acumen, his sound and sensible values, but in the end the ultimate question is, Does his poetry please? This is a question each reader must answer for himself.

NOTES FOR CHAPTER 6

1. The few works I have found helpful will be cited in their proper place. The beginner can find little to help him develop an appreciation of Aristophanes's poetry. Scholars have written about the

metrics of comic poetry but very little about its qualities. For an introduction to the nature of comic poetry I recommend 'Wit and High Seriousness', chap. 2 in *Modern Poetry and the Tradition* by Cleanth Brooks (Chapel Hill, North Carolina, 1939). Mr Brooks says, for example, 'One is even tempted to indulge in the following paradox: namely, that wit, far from being a playful aspect of the mind, is the most serious aspect, and that the only poetry which possesses high seriousness in the deepest sense is the poetry of wit' (p. 38).

2. Charles T. Murphy, 'Aristophanes and the Art of Rhetoric', *Harvard Studies in Classical Philology*, XLIX (1938), 69-113. He writes, p. 81, 'there are fifteen speeches in the eleven plays worth investigating from the rhetorical point of view, varying in length from 23 lines to well over a 100'. These fifteen are carefully analyzed. Cp. August Burckhardt, *Spuren der athenischen Volksrede in der alten Komödie* (Basel, 1924).

3. Herbert Richards, 'The Diction of Aristophanes', *Aristophanes and Others* (London, 1909), pp. 116-59.

4. *Ibid.*, pp. 119-20.

5. John Williams White, *The Verse of Greek Comedy* (London, 1912), p. 368-9.

6. Paul Mazon, *Essai sur la Composition des Comédies d'Aristophane* (Paris, 1904), p. 12. A more detailed division is presented by Milton W. Humphreys, 'The Agon of the Old Comedy', *American Journal of Philology*, VIII (1887), 179-206.

7. White comments on this: 'Some of these divisions have canonical form and most of them show canonical use of rhythm, but Aristophanes is bound by neither. He varies and changes, shifting his rhythms to secure special effects and subordinating form to the better development of the action, often weaving division imperceptibly into division, but always in such fashion that the fundamental structure and limits of the divisions are discoverable. He is always flexible, he has complete mastery of his materials, and the development of his theme never suffers from slavish adherence to convention' (p. 314). Cp. A. W. Pickard-Cambridge, *Dithyramb*, *Tragedy and Comedy* (Oxford, 1927), p. 293.

8. The subject of Aristophanes's literary criticism has been thoroughly discussed by J. W. H. Atkins, *Literary Criticism in Antiquity* (Methuen, 1952), I, 22-32. Aristophanes either mentions the name or parodies the poetry of the following authors:

Homer: *Clouds*, 1056; *Peace*, 1089-90; *Birds*, 575, 685; *Lysistrata*, 520.

Hesiod; *Peace*, 754; *Plutus*, 36-9.
Cycle; *Peace*, 1271; *Lysistrata*, 155.
Alcaeus: *Knights*, 1251-2; *Thesmophoriazusae*, 159.
Anacreon: *Thesmophoriazusae*, 161; *Plutus*, 1002.
Pindar: *Knights*, 1264-5; *Birds*, 926, 939; *Acharnians*, 637.
Simonides: *Knights*, 406; *Clouds*, 1356; *Birds*, 919.
Ibycus: *Thesmophoriazusae*, 159.
Stesichorus: *Peace*, 775.

This list is suggestive only, not a complete record of all mentions of the authors.

9. *Birds*, 251, may possibly be influenced by Alcman. *Acharnians*, 1134-5, may be a parody of Theognis.

10. Solon: *Clouds*, 1187; *Birds*, 1660.
Archilochus: *Acharnians*, 120; *Peace*, 1297; *Lysistrata*, 1257.
Hipponax, *Frogs*: 661.

11. Thespis: *Wasps*, 1479.
Phrynichus: *Birds*, 749; *Lysistrata*, 805.

12. Xenocles: *Clouds*, 1264-5; *Thesmophoriazusae*, 169.
Theognis: *Acharnians*, 11, 140; *Thesmophoriazusae*, 170.
Meletus: *Frogs*, 1302.
Sannyrion: fr. 149.
Morsimus: *Knights*, 401; *Peace*, 801; *Frogs*, 151.
Melanthius: *Peace*, 802, 1009; *Birds*, 151.

13. Epicharmus: *Wasps*, 1253; *Plutus*, 564: fr. 5.

14. Thales: *Clouds*, 180; *Birds*, 1009.
Aesop: *Peace*, 129; *Birds*, 471; *Lysistrata*, 695.

15. Gorgias: *Wasps*, 421.
Prodicus: *Clouds*, 361; *Birds*, 692; fr. 490.
Herodotus: *Acharnians*, 524; *Knights*, 84; *Birds*, 552; *Lysistrata*, 191.

16. Murphy, p. 71 ff.

17. The problem is fully discussed by James Adam, *The Republic of Plato* (Cambridge, 1902), I, 345-55.

CHAPTER 7

ATHENIAN MIDDLE COMEDY: 404 TO 338 B.C.

GREEK comedy of the middle fourth century B.C. has received very little attention even from classical scholars. Dismissed as dull and trivial by the literary historians [1], it has produced only one issue of controversy: i.e. whether or not it deserves the title of Middle to distinguish it from the Old Comedy of the fifth century and Aristophanes on the one hand and the New Comedy of the Alexandrian age and Menander on the other [2]. Theoretically, one would suppose that knowledge of fourth-century comedy would be important and interesting to every student of Greek history, philosophy, and literature. If the comedies of Aristophanes and Menander tell us of contemporary attitudes toward contemporary events and people, the major political and social conflicts, and the topics of daily conversation and jest, one might reasonably expect that Middle Comedy would be a similar treasury of information about the period between the Peloponnesian War and the Macedonian conquest.

Comedy and philosophy were closely linked in the late fifth and the late fourth century. Aristophanes and Socrates, Menander and Theophrastus, though diverse in relationship were nevertheless friendly. Comedy has preserved philosophic beliefs, though Socrates is distorted in the comic mirror of Aristophanes. Popular opinions about philosophic questions—ethics, aesthetics, science, and religion—are also to be found in Old and New Comedy. One might hope, then, to find in Middle Comedy the impression Plato made upon his contemporaries and some of the conflicting opinions of his day.

A literary critic, aware of the striking difference between Old and New Comedy, naturally turns to the intervening period to find the explanation. In the Old Comedy the chorus was the distinctive element which gave form and tone to the whole. Dressed in the fanciful costumes of wasps, birds, clouds, and so forth, it participated actively in the dramatic conflicts, danced in the interludes of action, sang lyrics of natural beauty or of obscene and satiric jesting, spoke in the parabasis directly to the audience for the poet, giving the audience advice about the management of the city and defending the poet's life and art. It was a satiric, political, literary, fantastic, allegorical, witty, farcical, ribald, and operatic comedy. One hundred years later the chorus was only a vestige, a band of revellers who sang between the acts, with no dramatic or poetic significance. Comedy had become a portrayal of life or rather of certain conventional aspects of life: the young couple in love, the obstacles, the happy ending. Intrigue and seduction, the exposure of infants and the discovery of their identity through tokens, were the main elements in the plot, and the family relationships of father and children, husband and wife, master and slave were the generators of dramatic emotion. With comedy undergoing a complete transformation within seventy-five years, one naturally wonders about the comedies produced during this period of radical innovations. Did Middle Comedy have distinctive characteristics of its own, or was it merely transitional, loosely strung together conglomerations of vestiges from the Old and abortive anticipations of the New without anything essentially Middle?

Since Middle Comedy is potentially a significant body of literature, it is unfortunate that so little of it has survived. Only two complete comedies of the period are extant, the *Ecclesiazusae* and *Plutus* by Aristophanes. They are valuable signposts, pointing toward a new *genre* of comedy; but they were written by a genius of the Old Comedy. We know the names of forty authors, and the titles of over six hundred plays [3]. More than a thousand fragments have been preserved, varying in length from one word to several hundred. About three-quarters of these fragments are quotations, selected by Athenaeus to illustrate his book *The Deipnosophists*, and thus are concerned with food, drink, cooks, courtesans, hosts, and parasites. About one-fifth are aphorisms from the *Florilegia* of Stobaeus. A few references to philosophers were preserved by Diogenes Laertius. The rest are mainly single words or short phrases collected by Pollux, Photius, Suidas, and other late lexicographers.

The bias of the selection reduces the value of these fragments. They may well tell us more of Athenaeus and Stobaeus than of the nature of fourth-century comedy or fourth-century ideas and attitudes. On the other hand, that Athenaeus and Stobaeus found so much in the Middle Comedy to quote is itself indicative. For instance, of the five hundred and seventy-eight fragments preserved from the lost plays of Aristophanes, only one-fifth were quoted by Athenaeus and only six fragments came from Stobaeus. Two of the six are about peace, very similar in phrasing and tone to Aristophanes's extant play, *Peace*. Two New Comedy dramatists—Diphilus and Philemon—are represented by fragments almost equally divided between Athenaeus and Stobaeus. Athenaeus, then, drew most heavily from the Middle Comedy; Stobaeus very few from the Old, some from the Middle, and many from the New.

Much of what is essential for the study of comedy—plot, comic techniques and episodes, the portrayal of character—is missing in these fragments. Furthermore, without the context, there is the ever-present danger of attributing to all characters the ideas of one and attributing to the dramatists the ideas of the characters. The interpretations which follow are no more than hypotheses based on partial evidence; they make no claim of certitude.

One basic difference between Old and Middle Comedy may be traced to the playwrights. Aristophanes addressed the spectators boldly as a fellow citizen (although some connection with Aegina led to charges that he was not a native-born Athenian), and his contemporary poets were all Athenians [4]. In the fourth century the two most prolific dramatists, Antiphanes and Alexis—were foreigners, and so were two lesser ones, Anaxandrides and Anaxilas. Antiphanes was said to have been born in Thessaly or Chios; Anaxandrides came from Rhodes or Colophon; Anaxilas has a Dorian name; and Alexis was a naturalized Athenian from the colony of Thurii [5]. Antiphanes and Alexis settled down in Athens and were given citizenship, but they could hardly have felt free to criticize Athenians as the poets of Old Comedy had, nor could they expect the audience to be interested in their ideas and lives. Not a single fragment survives filled with the love of Athens and concern for her welfare which are so marked in Old Comedy. Athens, indeed, is rarely mentioned and then usually in reference to food. Antiphanes, for example, praises

Attica for the honey, bread, figs, and above all the water (K. 179).

Perhaps to their foreign birth may be ascribed their lack of knowledge of or interest in comic and poetic tradition. They make no reference to their predecessors and very little to any poets other than Euripides. The spectators too must have lacked an interest in their heritage. It is not only that the chorus and parabasis have dwindled, that Dionysiac worship is ignored, that Ionic poetry is almost entirely unnoticed; but the very vocabulary of Old Comedy has been superseded. Since humour has a natural tendency to be contemporaneous, the process of breaking the continuity with the past was a quick one.

The dramatists as personalities have none of the individuality of the earlier poets. Aristophanes has characterized vividly for us the roaring Cratinus, dainty Crates, and piping Magnes (*Knights*, 520 ff.); but no one has done that for the fourth-century dramatists. The fragments are almost entirely devoid of individuality, so devoid that many are duplicated or attributed to several authors. The dramatists almost never speak in the first person, and later commentaries add little to our knowledge of these men. The one significant fragment and the one biographical note refer to the professional and not personal lives of Antiphanes and Anaxandrides.

Antiphanes envies the tragic poet because his stories are known to the audience (K. 191). The tragic poet has only to mention one word—Oedipus—and then everybody knows everything: his father Laius, his mother Jocasta, his daughters, his sons, what he suffered, what had been done. The story of Alcmaeon was similarly well known. At the end of the play the *deus ex machina* can extricate the characters and the poet from any complications otherwise insoluble. 'But these things are not possible for us; it is necessary to invent everything: new names, antecedent action, present action, the catastrophe, the introduction. If a Chremes or Pheidon should omit any of these, he would be hissed off the stage; but Peleus or Teucros could do it.' Aristophanes would have agreed that a comic poet's work was hard, but he was thinking of the training of the chorus, not of constructing plots (*Knights*, 516). He prides himself on his invention, but the invention of new forms

(*Clouds*, 547). The fourth-century emphasis on plot was noted by the anonymous writer on comedy who says that the poets of Middle Comedy did not undertake 'poetic form', but that they worked hard on their plots [6].

It had always been customary for poets to revise unsuccessful plays. Traces remain of another *Peace*, *Thesmophoriazusae*, *Clouds*, and *Plutus* by Aristophanes; and other dramatists also practised this economy. Only Anaxandrides apparently was too proud and resentful when he lost a victory to use the plays again, but gave them to the censor to be destroyed (Athen., IX, 374a, b). For that reason few of his fragments remain except from the victorious plays.

The little we know of the fourth-century dramatists all points in the same direction: they were professional playwrights who wrote comedies for the diversion of the Greek world. Their professional attitude shows in their remarkable productivity. Over eight hundred titles have survived. Essentially dramatists and not poets, they concentrated their attention on fictitious characters and their actions, not intruding with non-dramatic speeches or songs. They neither addressed the audience nor expressed themselves, but began working toward a dramatic illusion in which audience and playwright are by convention non-existent. Their only aim was the diversion of the audience; they had no desire to cure through laughter, to teach, to delight the soul [7]. And they wrote for a new audience, no longer composed almost entirely of Athenian citizens and allies, but increasingly of young men from all over the Greek world who came to the schools of Plato and Isocrates, and older men who came for business with manufacturers, merchants, and bankers.

This new class of men, whose power was based on wealth and not family and that wealth on money and not land, altered the structure of Athenian society. The change may clearly be traced in the plays of Aristophanes. In his early plays he has faith in the power of the small Attic farmers and the knights. The lines of conflict are drawn between them and the adherents of Cleon and other demagogues [8]. His references to the poor in the fifth century are few in number and always in connection with political alignments. Agoracritus, the Sausage-seller, says that the wealthy fear Cleon and the poor are terrified of him

(*Knights*, 224). The poverty of the jurymen in the *Wasps* is the cause of their seeking office and the result of Cleon's policy to keep them under control by keeping them poor.

In contrast, the two parties of the fourth century are economic [9]. 'It seems best to the poor, but not to the wealthy and the farmers', says Praxagora (*Ecclesiazusae*, 197-8). She denounces the new payment for attending the Assembly, and she places the responsibility for the wretched plight of Athens squarely in the hands of the people. 'For, taking in wages the public money, you each individually consider what you may gain, but the commonwealth rolls like Aesimus' (205 ff.). The remedy is 'one common livelihood for all and this alike'. (590). The result will be that one will not be wealthy while another is poor, nor one farm a large section of land and another not have enough land for a grave, nor one own many slaves and another not even possess an attendant.

The *Plutus* picks up the theme of economic justice, but with a variation. The problem of money is not merely the inequality of its distribution but the unfairness with which the wicked are rewarded and the good sent empty away. If Wealth is a god, then the cause for injustice must be his blindness and the solution the restoration of his sight. Poverty (not Beggardom) pleads that she is the source of skill and wisdom and thus ultimately responsible for the good things of life; but the men refuse to consider her case and drive her from their sight. Wealth is crowned king. A hungry priest is told that Zeus has come to the feast in honour of the new sovereign.

Wealth was, indeed, sovereign in the fourth century, if the witness of the comedies is to be trusted. 'What is his race?' asks A in the *Thebans* by Alexis. 'Wealthy', replies B. 'Everybody says they are the best race. No one ever sees poor people of good family'. (K. 90.) In the *Treasure* by Anaxandrides, a character takes issue with the old drinking song which praised health, beauty, and wealth. Wealth, he says, should be second, because beauty starved is ugly (K. 17). Wealth is too uncertain to be treasured for itself alone; it is the good things of life which money buys that are the ultimate satisfaction (Alexis, K. 281). A character in the *Wine-drinker* by Philetaerus illustrates this idea vividly: 'Those mortals who live poorly though possessing abundant livelihood, I say they are fools;

for when you die you may not eat an eel nor is a wedding-cake baked among the dead' (K. 13).

The market is a wonderful place for the well-to-do, but miserable for the poor (Timocles, K. 11). Fish from the Black Sea, wine from Thasos, eels from Boeotia, cheese from Sicily, honey, olives, and fresh green vegetables from Attic farms, loaves of white bread and sesame cakes—a paradise for the man with silver coins in his pocket. Although in a description of one feast over ninety kinds of edibles are listed, the epicure's delight was in quality rather than quantity (Anaxandrides, K. 41). 'The scarce is everywhere the fine and dear,' says a character in the *Boeotian Woman* by Antiphanes (K. 58); and another fragment states, 'Joy is not in the excessive but in the expensive'(Alexis, K. 254). True pleasure lies in moderation; 'One should be neither over-stuffed nor empty but pleasantly self-contained' (Alexis, K. 216).

The taste for delicacy was catered to by professional cooks hired for each banquet. 'I wish to take two cooks, the very cleverest I can find in the city; for I expect for dinner a Thessalian, not an Athenian who is uncritical from hunger. Whatever is necessary for each of them shall be provided' (Alexis, K. 213). A cook was not, however, a hireling; he was an artist. A mere scullery-maid is not to be compared with a chef any more than a mere general with a true leader. Anyone may set a table, cut up spices, boil, and tend a fire; a true culinary artist knows the place, the season, the guest, and he personally buys the fish (Dionysius, K. 2). The art of cooking is similar to the art of painting (Anaxandrides, K. 33). Pleasure depends on the proper functioning of artist, material, and recipient. The guest, like the observer of art, must do his part in achieving the fullest pleasure: he must be prompt; for, if he is too early or too late, he deprives the craft of its pleasure (Alexis, K. 149). Chefs resemble artists in temperament. They have their pupils, and they write cook books which outstrip Homer in popularity (Philetaerus, K. 15: Alexis, K. 135).

With the dinner went wine, savoured not only for its taste but praised for its benefits. 'The man who takes wine as his general leads daring to the forefront of good council,' according to Antiphanes. 'Rising up at night he obtains what he wishes' (K. 18). 'No lover of drink is an evil man. The double-mothered Bromius does not like the wretched nor the uneducated life' (Alexis, 283-4). Drinking to excess was scorned, like eating to excess. 'Much wine does much harm' (Alexis, K. 82) and 'The constant drinker is negligent, but the slow drinker is very thoughtful' (Antiphanes, K. 271). One fragment gives a lesson in drinking, cup by cup.

> Mix three bowls only for the men of good judgment. One is for health, which they drink first, the second for love and pleasure, the third for sleep, which the clever drink and then go home. The fourth does not belong to us but to pride, the fifth to shouting, the sixth revelry, the seventh a black-eye, the eighth a witness for a law-suit, the ninth anger, the tenth madness which makes one strike out. Much can be poured into one small jug which easily trips up the heels of those who drink it. (Eubulus, K. 94.)

The pleasure of the second cup might be games of music or both. The cottabus was a favourite. One fragment contains a dialogue in which one character is trying to teach another how the game is played (Antiphanes, K. 55). Flute girls are listed with wine, fish, and perfume as natural accompaniments of banquets. At the elaborate feast described by Anaxandrides, famous musicians were hired to play the flute and the lyre, and to sing (Anaxandrides, K. 41). Amateur playing is suggested as a pleasure: 'Unite, youth, the music of the flute and the lyre with our sportive play; whenever anyone harmonizes well with those in concord with his nature, then the greatest joy will be discovered' (Ephippus, K. 7).

Love is coupled with pleasure as the benefit from the second cup, but that love is not always light and blithesome is a favourite theme of the dramatists. They questioned particularly the wings which the painters portrayed on the god Eros. Eubulus says that the artists know how to draw nothing but swallows, being ignorant of the god's nature. 'For he is not light nor is it easy for anyone to be cured of the disease he brings but very hard indeed' (K. 41). Alexis says that the wise know lovers are winged but not Love (K. 20). Love is neither male nor female, god nor man, worse nor better. 'The daring of man, the cowardice of woman, the folly of madness, the reason of sanity, the violence of the beast, the toil of the tireless, the distinction of a daemon' (K. 245). There is but one cure for the disease of love—a courtesan (Alexis, K. 279).

Courtesans were endlessly fascinating to the fourth-century dramatists. They named their plays *Neottis*, *Melitta*, *Malthace*, *Aischra*, the names of courtesans with a double meaning—young chick, honey, soft, shameful. Lais, the most notorious of all, was attacked by Epicrates in his *Antilais*. 'This Lais is idle and a tippler, doing nothing all day but drinking and eating' (K. 3). Indeed, little good is spoken of the *hetaerae* in the surviving fragments. That they prefer old wine but young men is a frequent charge (Alexis, K. 282; Eubulus, K. 124-5). What is more, they employ all kinds of tricks to make themselves taller or shorter. They blacken their eyebrows and rouge their cheeks (Alexis, K. 98). The attraction of the repulsive is neatly summarized by Antiphanes, 'An *hetaera* is a convenience for the man who maintains her; he rejoices, possessing a great evil in his home' (K. 2).

Life is a carnival, enjoyed to the fullest by the man who laughs the most and drinks and loves and dines (Alexis, K. 219). But 'life' is also a mere word, a fair name for the baseness of human fate.

> I tell you this, although I cannot say whether anyone will say that I judge well or ill. I know from observation that everything human is completely mad. We, the living, have the chance of a leave of absence, as if we had been released from death and darkness to go to a carnival, into amusements and into this light upon which we look. He who laughs the most and drinks and plays with Aphrodite during his leaves of absence, and also dines, he enjoys his holiday the most before he goes home.

Life is but a flight from the reality of death, and pleasure is the flight from the realization of approaching death. This flight from reality is the distinguishing characteristic of Middle Comedy. The poets of the Old Comedy faced the problems of life and offered solutions. They, too, wished to release men and women from trouble, but they suggested that release could be accomplished through action and through a change in ideas or in direction. The dramatists of the New Comedy did not try to solve any problems, nor did they seek escape. They presented an imitation of life with its mixture of pleasure and pain. In the transitional period the dramatists turned away from a life which was but a word, a euphemism, to picture a dream life, a festival in which men's wishes were fulfilled.

The fulfilment of this dream was discovered in myth. For the spectators, the world of the gods had all the allurements they desired—food and wine, superhuman strength and guile, and immortal youthfulness. Above all, the eroticism of the myths was especially titillating because of the religious origins of the myths. 'The covert meaning of myth and allegory', as Liddell and Scott translate Aristotle's *hyponoia*, was to be preferred to the 'foul language' of the Old Comedy [10]. For the dramatists, myths and legends provided ready-made plots and characters with the added advantage of familiarity. Invention and exposition, the initial stumbling-blocks for playwrights as Antiphanes had complained, were reduced to a minimum. The result of its popularity with spectators and dramatists was that mythological burlesque, a dramatic form inherited from Old Comedy, became in Middle Comedy the dominant type.

We know little more about these plays than the titles, but they are sufficient to indicate the myth and thus the characters and plot [11]. Adonis was a favourite with the dramatists; no less than six plays bear his name as title. Aphrodite and Dionysos were the most popular of the gods, as we might expect; Oinopion, The Wine-drinker, son of Dionysos, gave his name to two plays. Hecate, Pan, and Artemis also had plays written about them. Heracles and his adventure in Egypt with the king, Busiris, were farcical by nature. An amusing vase-painting of the sixth century portrays Heracles strangling four Egyptians, stepping on two more, while the king crouches on the altar pleading for mercy [12]. The myths of Alcmaeon, Alcestis, Andromeda, Medea, Ion, and Oedipus were common property for both tragic and comic poets. In the fourth century the comic dramatists probably combined tragic parody with mythical burlesque. The last part of Aristophanes's *Thesmophoriazusae* is an example of how amusing the combination could be if handled cleverly.

The two legends most frequently dramatized were those of Troy and Odysseus. Xuthus and Deucalion, legendary ancestors of the Trojans, Anchises, Ganymede, and, of course, Helen, her mother Leda, and the Greeks, Pandar and Achilles, appealed to the spectators' fondness for the erotic. Odysseus had been in story almost fatally attractive to women; it is not surprising to find two *Circes*, a *Nausicaa*, a *Calypso*, and three comedies about Odysseus himself.

After the dream comes the awakening. Try as they would, the dramatists could not throw the veil of illusion over the solid reality of poverty. Wealth itself provided no security against the vicissitudes of Fortune which might rob a man of all he owned.

> Any man born who considers that any possession is secure in life is vastly mistaken. Either taxes snatch everything he owns, or someone brings a lawsuit and destroys him, or going to law he loses his lawsuit and must pay a penalty, or having been chosen choregus he has to furnish gold garments to the chorus while he wears rags, or as trierarch he is strangled or he is captured while on a sea-voyage, or just walking or sleeping he is killed by his household slaves. There is nothing certain except whatever each day someone may pleasantly chance to obtain. But not this either—someone may seize the table. But when you have something between your teeth and have swallowed it, this alone you may consider security. (Antiphanes, K. 204.)

Similarly Alexis says, 'Of good things place wealth last, for it is the most uncertain possession we have' (K. 281).

Poverty means, first of all, hunger. 'Silver is the blood and soul of mortals; whoever does not hold nor own it walks dead among the living' (Timocles, K. 35). The poor man who goes to the market with four bronze coins looks at the eels and tunny and asks the price. Then he goes to the anchovies (Timocles, K. 11; cf. Eriphus, K. 3). Poverty also is naked. 'Winter is clearly the lamp of poverty; all things appear evil and unpleasant then' (Aristophon, K. 1). 'The country is the father of life for men, and it alone knows how to conceal poverty; the city is a theatre full of open misfortune' (Amphis, K. 17). 'The poor man cannot conceal his evil with the cloak of wealth, but stands transparent in his wretchedness' (Antiphanes, K. 167). Poverty is said by Antiphanes to be a teacher of character (K. 294), but Timocles thought it the wrong kind of teacher; 'Poverty forces men to do unworthy deeds contrary to their nature' (K. 28).

If poverty forced some men to work for their living, as Poverty in the *Plutus* of Aristophanes rightly claimed, and thus provided the wealthy with slaves, cooks, and courtesans, it also prompted lazy men to seek free meals. 'It is the life of gods to eat the food of others without paying for it' (Antiphanes, K. 243). 'Is there or could there be a finer craft or easier income than that of the flatterer?' asks one character. The painter and the farmer toil and struggle, but the life of the parasite is full of laughter and luxury. His greatest task is to make sport, to laugh, to joke, and to drink a lot. 'It is the second-best life after wealth' (Antiphanes, K. 144). There is divine sanction too for this livelihood; Zeus invented parasitism, and Heracles followed his example (Diodorus, K. 2). A parasite is an excellent companion, both in respect to fortune and living. He never prays that his friend will suffer financial reverses, nor is he envious of extravagance. He is a dear and reliable friend—never pugnacious, sharp-tempered, nor malignant but always good-natured, full of laughter, and cheerful in disposition (Antiphanes, K. 80). There is no more useful man than the parasite (Timocles, K. 8).

These are the specious defences proffered by the parasites themselves in defence of their lost integrity. Other characters see them clearly for what they are, 'worms of the wealthy' (Anaxilas, K. 33). Personal mockery in the style of the Old Comedy is directed at Ctesias, who knew when dinner began but not when it ended (Anaxilas, K. 31); at Chaerephon, who went to dinner in Corinth uninvited, flying in his haste (Alexis, K. 210); and, most of all, at Tithymallus, the indestructible, who would be wealthy, if he were paid by all who fed him (Timocles, K. 18; Antiphanes, K. 210; Alexis, K. 159). Old age which destroys so many pleasures, cuts off the life of a flatterer. 'No one rejoices in a gray-haired parasite' (Alexis, K. 260), and another remarks ironically, 'It's a blessed life! It is necessary for me always to be inventing new devices in order to have food for my jaws' (Antiphanes, K. 244).

While most Greeks were engaged in a fight to the death with poverty, one small group of ascetics espoused poverty. They were the Pythagoreans, a religious sect founded in the sixth century by Pythagoras. Whatever their mystic beliefs and sacred rites were, they were known to the public chiefly for their refusal to eat anything which had once been alive, and their indifference to clothes. For these few non-conformists, who rejected the standard of happiness accepted by the majority, the dramatists had nothing but ridicule. Aristophon refused to believe that their poor way of life was a philosophic choice. 'From necessity, not having a single thing, they have invented this fine pretext for their cheapness and fixed useful boundaries for the poor. When you place before them fish or meat, if they do not eat them and their fingers also, then I wish to be hung ten times' (K. 9). Another says, 'Pythagorean doctrines and subtle arguments and finely carved thoughts nourish them, these things every day, these things! One loaf of bread each, water to drink—such things!' To which another character responds, 'You speak of prison life' (Alexis, K. 221). Still another agrees with the wisdom of not eating a living thing. 'I have just now come from the market and I did not buy anything alive. I bought great dead fish and the flesh of fat lamb, not living, for that is impossible. What else? I bought baked liver too. If anyone can show that these have voice or breath, I agree that I have done wrong and transgressed the law' (Alexis, K. 27).

Although the principles and manner of life of the Pythagoreans challenged the hedonism of the theatre-going public, they constituted no threat to their welfare. There were, however, other groups in Athens who were serious menaces to happiness. These groups are amusingly summarized by Antiphanes:

> Are not the Scythians very wise because they give mare's and cow's milk immediately to their children and do not bring into their homes pesky nurses and tutors, than whom there is nothing worse after midwives, by God; they surpass everybody, after the mendicant friars, by God; that is the most wretched race if you do not wish to speak of the fish sellers . . .; after the bankers; there is no more destructive tribe than that. (K. 159.)

Women! What evils they are! Not one pleasant word survives from the Middle Comedy about the sex. 'I trust only one thing about a woman, that when she is dead she will not live again; until she is dead, I do not trust anything' (Antiphanes, K. 251). 'A man with eye disease suffers many evils, but he experiences one benefit—he does not see a woman while he is sick' (Antiphanes, K. 252). Why are women objectionable? For one thing, they cannot keep secrets. Telling a woman any affair is no different from telling the heralds in the market-place (Antiphanes, K. 253). They drink too much wine (Axionicus, K. 5; Alexis, K. 167). They talk. They chatter more than jays, doves, and nightingales (Alexis, K. 92). The grasshopper is fortunate because the female of the species is voiceless (Xenarchus, *Sleep*, K. 14).

The courtesan was an evil, but she did give pleasure—not so the wife. 'Not without reason are shrines for courtesans everywhere, but not a single one for wives in all Greece' (Philetaerus, K. 8). 'Marriage is the beginning of many evils in life,' says Anaxandrides (K. 52). It is equally bad to marry a wealthy woman and a poor one. If a poor man marries a wealthy woman, he becomes her slave. If he marries a poor woman, he has two to feed. 'A young wife is not suitable for an old man' (Theophilus, K. 6). 'Who of sound mind and body would ever dare marry, ending a pleasanter life? and is it not better for an intelligent man to be dishonoured rather than married?' (Alexis, K. 262). Naturally, a second marriage is worse than the first. The first is excusable on the grounds of innocence; the second is like walking with fore-warning into a known evil (Aristophon, K. 5). 'What did you say? Is he truly *married*? Why, I left him alive and walking' (Antiphanes, K. 221).

These jokes are stale with age and worn with use. They are the stock-in-trade of the witless playwright and no more representative of the fourth century B.C. then the fourth A.D. or of the twentieth. Far more imaginative are the gibes against the fish-sellers. One man says that any doubts he may have about the story of the Gorgon are dispelled when he goes to the market. He is turned to stone when he looks at the fish; and, if he asks the price, he is frozen stiff (Antiphanes, K. 166). Another says that it is 10,000 times easier to talk to a general and to receive a reasonable answer than to speak to the cursed fish-sellers (Amphis, K. 30; Alexis, K. 16). They do not bargain about the price and they clip their words. The fish-sellers, in turn, hate everyone but the glutton, Callimedon. They have voted to erect a statue to him, holding a crab in one hand, as a saviour of their trade (Alexis, K. 56). The chief criticism of the fish-sellers is of their exorbitant prices. 'By Athena, I am astonished that the fish-sellers are not all wealthy since they take a king's tribute. Not only do they exact a tenth of the wealth; they snatch up the whole every day' (Alexis, K. 200).

Worse than the fish-sellers are the bankers, according to the fragment quoted above. Of the bankers we hear little or nothing in the comedies. They were influential; and professional playwrights, whether citizen or alien, would hardly dare attack them openly in the theatre. However, if we look back over the list of characters, we can see how transparently the economic conflicts of the time are reflected in the dramatic conflicts of the theatre. Rich and poor man, cook and courtesan, parasite and slave, the ascetic Pythagorean, the wife, the arrogant fish-sellers, and the banker are all involved in the struggle for livelihood.

Translation obscures the connection so apparent in Greek between the means of life and life itself. In Greek the word *bios* may mean either. The uncertainty of one's livelihood has already been discussed; the playwrights were also aware of the uncertainty of life and the certainty of old age and death. 'Life is like wine. When the remainder is small, it is bitter. In old age, as in a workshop, all mortal things go bad' (Antiphanes, K. 240). 'Old age is a great evil; death is the penalty of the man who does not obtain it. We are all eager for it; but, when it comes, we try to avoid it. We are ungrateful by nature' (Antiphanes, K. 238). 'Old age is like an altar of evils; all have taken refuge on it' (Antiphanes, K. 255).

Comfort is offered the old and dying.

> Never is old age, as you think, father, the greatest of burdens. He who bears it senselessly, he is the cause. If you are content, it sometimes puts you to sleep, changing its nature auspiciously, taking away grief and bringing pleasure. But it makes grief, if you are discontented. (Anaxandrides, K. 53.)

Another says, 'No one ever dies, master, who is ready to die. Charon draws the legs struggling to live and leads unwillingly on to his ferry those who are fed and have lived in abundance. Hunger is the cure for immortality' (Antiphanes, K. 86). After all, 'death is a road we all must take' (Antiphanes, K. 53). Patient endurance is the only advice of the dramatists. 'Misfortune seems to me the lot of everyone; to bear misfortune the part of an upright man' (Antiphanes, K. 278). 'It is the part of a wise man to bear his fortunes in the right way' (Alexis, K. 252). 'If one does not endure, if one gives way to grief over the loss of livelihood or love or life, then one is close to the loss of sanity' 'Grief shares a wall with madness' (Antiphanes, K. 295; Alexis, 296).

Stripped from their context by the late anthologists, these words may sound hollow with triteness. What that context was we can guess from two words in the fragments at the beginning of the last paragraph. In the first a young man is talking to his father; in the second, a slave to his master. The role of the slave in fourth-century comedy is significant, because it differs so much from the minor role he played in fifth-century comedy. In Old Comedy, the slaves were allegorical servants such as Uproar, the attendant of War, or contemporary figures such as Nicias, Demosthenes, and Cleon, slaves of the People in the *Knights* or buffoons like Xanthias in the *Frogs*. In the fourth-century comedy the slave as a person had moved to the forefront of the action and become one of the principal characters. In the *Plutus*, for instance, Carion opens with an expository prologue; Carion dances and converses with the Chorus; Carion deals with Hermes. He manipulates the characters, changing the earlier simple plot of conflict into the complex one of intrigue. He is also prone to generalizations. His first words are, 'How hard it is, by Zeus and the gods, to be the slave of a mad master!' and his next to the last are, 'What a good thing it is to have many names' (1164).

A slave, Xanthias, in a play by Alexis addresses fellow-slaves, saying that everything is empty babbling except drinking. 'Nothing is pleasanter than the stomach. It alone is father and mother for us. The old army virtues sound arrogant, empty, dreamlike. Your spirit will grow cold at the fated time. You will possess only what you eat and what you drink. Everything else is ashes—Pericles, Codrus, Cimon' (K. 25). The hedonistic morality of the slave—the enjoyment of pleasure today because virtue will be ashes to-morrow—is typical of the morality in other fragments of Middle Comedy.

We are here faced with an insoluble problem of interpretation. A dramatist does not necessarily believe what a character in his play says; the characters themselves do not necessarily agree; the bias of the late anthologists may have created a false impression through an unrepresentative selection of quotations. We can only say that the fragments we have indicate that the bleak life of the slave coloured the tone of the Middle Comedy.

Since the direction of Middle Comedy was moving away from Old Comedy, it was natural that the characteristics inherited from Old Comedy should have been adapted to new conditions. Personal mockery was not entirely abandoned, but it was directed toward courtesans and parasites rather than pretenders, sycophants, and scapegoats. Politicians were mentioned by name, but they frequently were not Athenian politicians. International and not city politics interested the spectators. Philip of Macedon, Pharnabazus of Persia, and Dionysius of Sicily were the great powers. The growing strength of the Gauls is mentioned once, the first classical reference to the northern tribes (Ephippus, K. 5).

Plato is the only eminent man who is frequently portrayed and mocked. Aristophon wrote a play entitled *Plato*. He is sullen looking (Amphis, K. 13); he walks up and down wearying his legs and discovering nothing (Alexis, K. 147); he talks a lot (Alexis, K. 180); he likes olives (Anaxandrides, K. 19). 'You speak of what I do not know. Run, converse with Plato, and you will know bicarbonate of soda and onions' (Alexis, K. 1). What tame gibes these are in comparison with the shafts Aristophanes directed against Socrates! The picture of the clever stripling from Plato's Academy is more reminiscent of the Old Comedy. He is a Bryson-Thrasymachus-small-change-taker, with hair well cut, beared well tended, feet well shod, body well clothed. His technique is finely reasoned; he speaks nothing without consideration, and he says, 'Men of the land of Athens' (Ephippus, K. 14).

The teachings of Plato filtered through his pupils to the outside world. Allusions are made to almost all of his principal doctrines, although with none of the critical acumen of the Old Comedy. 'My mortal body has become withered, but my immortal rises to the sky'. Another character questions him: 'Is this not the disputation of Plato?' (Alexis, K. 158). 'You are clearly a man, and do you have a soul?' B: 'According to Plato, I do not know, but I guess I have.' (Cratinus, K. 10). The doctrine of the Good was less comprehensible than the doctrine of immortality. 'The good whatever it is which you expect to obtain through this means, I know this good less well, master, than the good of Plato' (Amphis, K. 6). Another tries to explain the meaning.

A: And did they not furnish hot baths?
B: Plato says the good is everywhere good, do you understand? The sweet is everywhere sweet, here and there. (Alexis, K. 152.)

Plato's belief about love was not incomprehensible, but it was incredible. 'What do you say? Do you expect to persuade me that a lover of a beautiful youth loves his fine character and cares nothing for his appearance? You are truly out of your mind. I do not believe this, nor that a poor man with many burdens does not wish to place some on the well-to-do' (Amphis, K. 15).

One of the best illustrations of the difference between Old and Middle Comedy is the difference between Aristophanes's portrayal of Socrates and his pupils in the *Clouds* and Epicrates' portrayal of Plato with his pupils.

A: What about Plato and Speusippus and Menedemus? How are they now spending their time? What thought, what argument, are they examining closely? If you know anything about it, speak clearly to me.
B: I know how to tell you about this clearly. For at the Panathenaea, seeing a crowd of youths in the Academy gymnasia, I heard words—monstrous, strange. They were marking the divisions of nature, differentiating the life of animals, the order of trees, and the genus of vegetables. And then among the boys he placed a pumpkin and asked what genus that belonged to.
A: And what divisions did they make and what is the genus of the pumpkin? Make this clear if you understand this.
B: At first, all stood without saying a word, and bending over it, they thought for a long time. And then suddenly one of the bending, thinking boys said it was a round vegetable, another grass, another a tree. Hearing this, a Sicilian doctor snorted that they were babbling nonsense.
A: They must have been terribly angry and shouted out at being scoffed at. It is not right to act that way at a discussion.
B: The boys didn't care. Plato was standing near. Very gently not at all angrily—he asked them again to define its genus, and they defined it. (K. 11.)

This is a clear, prose account of a lesson in definition without noticeable exaggeration, buffoonery, or metaphor. Compare this with Socrates hanging aloft in his basket while his pallid scholars gaze upon the ground, with the lyrics of the cloud chorus which answers the invocation of Socrates, with the farcical attempts of Strepsiades to learn genders!

Although puns and other forms of verbal humour were not unknown in the fourth century, the popular joke was the riddle. Sappho asks, 'What is feminine, enfolding a child who has no voice and yet sends a loudsounding shout over sea and land to whatever mortals she wishes, while those nearby can not hear her, being deaf although they can hear?' Another character guesses that the answer is a city, the child being the orators. Sappho replies that no orator was ever without a voice, and gives the answer—a letter (Antiphanes, K. 196). Other riddles combine allusions to fish and courtesans with an obscene innuendo (Antiphanes, K. 194).

Parody, which had been a mainstay in the Old Comedy, continued in the Middle Comedy, but it was parody of prose rather than of poetry. The antithesis of Demosthenes took the place of the airy trifles of the dithyrambic poets (Antiphanes, K. 169; Timocles, K. 12). Euripides was the favourite tragic poet of the fourth century. The dramatists were familiar enough with his works to weave lines into their plays. One long passage of tragic parody survives, and others may well have been lost with the lost mythological burlesques (Xenarchus, K. 1). On the whole, however, it seems safe to conjecture that Euripides was too well liked to be roughly handled. The following quotation from Euripides and the accompanying comment suggest that the comic and tragic poets were now kindred souls. ' "There is no man who is completely happy." By Athens, how briefly, dearest Euripides, you have placed life in a line' (Nicostratus, K. 28).

The ideas of Euripides, which had prepared the way for their own, his characters—the maidens in distress and the ragged heroes—and his plots of violent action appealed to the fourth-century dramatists [13]. One dramatist speaks of the value of tragedy, the practical lesson in patience and endurance it offers, not its aesthetic qualities. Timocles says in the *Women at the Dionysia* that the poor man looking at the beggar

Telephus bears his poverty more easily. The sick man is comforted by the madness of Alcmaeon, the blind by Phineus, the man who has lost a son by Niobe, the lame by Philoctetes, the old and unfortunate by Oineus (K. 6). In the scene in the library when Linus offers Heracles his choice of Orpheus, Hesiod, the tragedies, Choerilus, Homer, and Epicharmus. Heracles chooses Simus, author of a 'cook book'. Behind this joke lies a modicum of truth; certainly the vocabulary of Middle Comedy has more in common with Simus than Homer, Euripides, or Epicharmus (Alexis, K. 135).

The anonymous writer on comedy said that the poets of the Middle Comedy neglected poetic form, turning their attention to rhetoric and action. The surviving fragments confirm this. Only one fragment of pastoral delicacy describes a bride and husband on a summer day—ivy and plane tree, sweetsmelling flower and a light breeze, and the nightingale (Eubulus, K. 104) [14]. Metaphors are rare. A flat shallow cup is metaphorically a shield (Antiphanes, K. 112). One character speaks of the 'nurse of life, enemy of hunger, guard of friendship, doctor of exhausted hunger,' and another replies to him 'That's an unnecessarily long way of saying the short word—*table*' (Timocles, K. 13). The writers seem to have preferred the short, direct prose word to the poetic. They cared little for personification and allegory. Time perhaps is personified and Fortune (Antiphanes, K. 254; Nicostratus, K. 31; Anaxandrides, K. 4). One new personification, not to be found in Aristophanes, is *euemeria*—which means Fine Weather or Good Times or Health and Wealth. She is queen (Alexis, K. 161).

The significant images characterize life. 'Life is like dice; not always do they fall the same, nor in life does nature remain the same but it has its changes' (Alexis, K. 34).

A: Tell me, what is living?
B: Drinking, I say. You see near the wintry streams trees which are moist night and day grow tall and beautiful, but the dry trees look thirsty and parched and are destroyed, root and branch. (Antiphanes, K. 231.)

Antiphanes (K. 240) had said that life is like wine with old age the dregs; Alexis replied that man is not like wine. 'For the one as it grows old becomes unpleasant, but the oldest wine is the most desirable. The one bites, the other makes us gay' (Alexis, K. 278).

These three examples of metaphor illustrate the transition from the poetry of Aristophanes to the poetic dialogue of Menander through rhetoric. Dice and wine are the familiar accompaniments of daily life. Trees by streams are an everyday sight. The rhetorician draws his images from the ordinary rather than the grotesque, quaint, subtle, or exquisite because he does not wish his illustration to be so highly coloured that it will obscure the point nor so strange that it will be incomprehensible to the ordinary person. The structure of these fragments is rhetorical in its antithesis. Many other fragments also begin with a statement, a quotable line, followed by an explanation. Others start with a question, sometimes by one character to be answered by another; sometimes a rhetorical question is answered by the same character.

Passages which are not rhetorical would be prose, were it not for the verse form. The colloquial rhythms of speech and the quick, short dialogue of everyday life are common.

A: It is foolish even to talk about fish to the insatiable. But take these apples, maiden.
B: They're beautiful!
A: Beautiful, indeed, by the gods! For they just now arrived in Athens from the king.
B: From the Hesperides, I suppose.
A: Yes, by Phosphorus, they say these are golden apples.
B: But there are only three.
A: The scarce is everywhere fine and dear. (Antiphanes, K. 58.)

The dialogue quoted above in which Plato's Academy is described is another example of the way the speaker is prompted to continue by questions.

This trend toward everyday speech coincided with the growing interest in human character for its own sake. The titles of the plays indicate that Middle Comedy anticipated New Comedy in the portrayal of character, but in its own way. The transition from the allegorical characters of the Old Comedy to the individuals of the New was through types and professions. A brief list of some titles is our main evidence: *The Farmer*, *The Doctor*, *the Parasite*, *The Painters*, *The Lyre-player*, *The Drill Sergeant*, *The Brothel-keeper*, *The Shoemaker*, *The Goat-*

herds, *The Vine-dresser*, and *The Reapers*. Other titles of nationality, such as *The Women of Boeotia*, *The Men from Epidaurus*, *The Men from Zacynthus*, *The Thebans*, *The Thessalians*, *The Locrians*, *The Samian Woman*, may also have contained studies of character although it is difficult to be certain. Several plays about the men from Taras probably ridiculed the followers of Pythagoras. The titles of women from foreign countries may have referred to courtesans.

The fragmentary nature of Middle Comedy limits our knowledge of plot to only a few hints. The first of these hints comes from the *Life* of Aristophanes and the Argument to the *Plutus*. 'Producing this comedy as the last in his own name, and wishing to establish his son Araros with the spectators, he placed before them his last two—the *Cocalus* and the *Aeolosicon* through his son.' 'He was the first to show the manner of the New Comedy in the *Cocalus*.' The *Aeolosicon*, a word which combines Aeolus—the god of winds whose children were incestuous—and Sicon, a cook, had no chorus and was said in ancient times to have heralded the Middle Comedy; the *Cocalus* with its seduction and recognition heralded the New. It would be a mistake, however, to think that the plot of the *Cocalus* had no imitators until Menander. Suidas says that Anaxandrides was 'the first to introduce lovers and seductions.' Suidas was wrong in thinking that Anaxandrides was the first, but his statement indicates that the plot of love was used by dramatists of the Middle Comedy [15].

A fragment from the *Neottis* of Antiphanes seems to have been the prologue in the explanatory style of Euripides. It serves as an example of the kind of situation which precipitated the action of love, seduction, and recognition.

> I am a boy who has just now arrived here in Athens with my sister, having been badly treated by a trader, one of those Syrians. He chanced upon us when we were being put up for sale by a pawnbroker and bought us. He is a man unsurpassed in wickedness, the kind of man who has nothing in his house, not even anything the thrice blessed Pythagoras himself would eat outside of thyme mixed with honey and vinegar. (K. 168.)

We can guess that a youthful Athenian will fall in love with the sister, seduce her, long to marry her but be prevented by her slavery, discover through tokens that she is really the long-lost daughter of a neighbour, and then marry her.

Reviewing the conjectures and probabilities on which interpretation of the Middle Comedy necessarily rests, we can see that it was truly 'middle'. During the years of transition, the characteristics of the Old Comedy gradually diminished in importance: the chorus, the parabasis, the lyrics, the personal mockery, the political and intellectual content, the allegorical characters, and the simple plot of conflict [16]. At the same time, a New Comedy was gradually emerging: a comedy mirroring life with naturalistic characters, speaking the language of the home and market, but involved in the complexities of emotional attachments, of intrigue, and the web of circumstance. With so many changes taking place simultaneously, it is not surprising that there should be confusion of purpose, lack of integration and cohesion, a reliance upon stock-in-trade rather than freshness of invention.

This is not all that can be said of the Middle Comedy. It preceded New Comedy and thus prepared the way for Menander and later Terence and Plautus. The survival of their plays perhaps testifies to their superiority over Antiphanes, Alexis, Anaxandrides, and the others, but the later dramatists must have been indebted to the earlier explorers. In the complete history of Greek comedy Middle Comedy played a significant role; the fragments of competent dramatists should not in fairness be compared with the complete or almost complete works of geniuses.

Middle Comedy was more than a preparation for the genius to come. It had the vitality which an audience transmits to the dramatist. If the dramatists were uncertain about what was going to happen next to comedy, the spectators were uncertain too about what was to happen next to them as individuals, to their cities, to the world. There was no integration, no cohesion, after the fall of Athens, before the rise of Macedonia. The reliance of the ordinary man was upon the pleasure to-day, not the ideals of civic glory or immortal blessedness to-morrow.

Plato confirms this in his portrayal of the democratic man. The democratic man devotes his life to pleasure for which he will squander his money, work, and time (*Rep.*, VIII, 561a).

The life without order or necessity is the pleasant one. The dramatists, according to Plato, cater to the emotions and pleasures of the many who constitute their audience (*Rep.*, VI, 493d). Antagonistic as they were, philosopher and dramatist understood each other's goals and methods. The dramatists knew that Plato and his students were seeking knowledge and the Good; Plato knew that the dramatists and their audiences were seeking pleasure. One method they shared in common was the myth, which could be used by both as the image of the ideal they sought.

Wherever Middle Comedy is free from vestiges of Old Comedy, where it is in direct touch with the desires and interests of the audience, there it has the strength and sincerity of art. The life of pleasure—eating and drinking and loving; the gamble of life—wealth and poverty opposite one another like five and two on dice with chance calling the number; the enemies of life—wives, fish-sellers, and bankers; the shadows of life—sickness, old age, and death: this is a view of life we know to-day as well as the fourth-century Greeks knew it. There was no religion to bring joy. 'We are all stupid in regard to the divine and we know nothing' (Anaxandrides, K. 21). Nor was there sanity. 'Human life is completely mad' (Alexis, K. 219). There was no philosophy of hope or deliverance; Plato and the Pythagoreans were anathema. There was only the patience of endurance. That endurance should soon be made the foundation of a new philosophy by Zeno, the Stoic, and patience the foundation of a new philosophy by Epicurus is not surprising. The gods still lived, but they lived in the imagination; the myths were dreams; and the gods made sport for the amusement of men.

NOTES FOR CHAPTER 7

1. For example, H. J. Rose, *A Handbook of Greek Literature* (New York, 1934), 242, 'Passing over a number of obscurer writers, we come to what is generally called MIDDLE COMEDY, a somewhat dreary period whereof not much is known.' Moses Hadas, *A History of Greek Literature* (New York, 1950), 109. 'In any case the fragments are too slight for profitable discussion; but it is to be

doubted that these plays had as much dramatic substance as the plays of the New Comedy, which we shall consider presently.'

2. Gilbert Norwood, *Greek Comedy* (Boston, 1931) 37, n. 1, summarizes the controversy over the divisions of Greek comedy and sensibly concludes that 'the really important point is, how do works of various periods differ? not the names of the periods'. Norwood states on p. 41 that 'the main topics of Middle Comedy are eating, sex, riddles, philosophy, literature, and life', and he discusses each topic in turn. Although this discussion has been helpful to me in many ways, I question the initial judgment. 'Between the excitingly varied landscape of Old Comedy and the city of Menander stretches a desert: therein the sedulous topographer may remark two respectable eminences, and perhaps a low ridge in the middle distance, or a few nullahs, and the wayfarer will greet with delight one or two oases with a singing-bird or so; but the ever-present foreground of his journey is sand, tiresome, barren, and trickling.' [38]

3. *Comicorum Atticorum Fragmenta*, ed. Theodorus Kock (Leipzig, 1880-88), II. All references to fragments are indicated by K. in the text.

4. The parabasis of the *Acharnians* gives credence to the charges that Aristophanes was not born in Attica. The Chorus, speaking for Aristophanes, says that the Lacedaemonians wanted the island of Aegina not for its sake but for his (652). All references to Aristophanes's comedies are by line in the Oxford text.

5. *RE*, s.vv. 'Antiphanes', 'Alexis', 'Anaxandrides', 'Anaxilas'.

6. *Comicorum Graecorum Fragmenta*, ed. George Kaibel (Berlin, 1899), I, 8.

7. Cf. Aristophanes's attitude toward comedy: *Ach.* 500, 655-9; *Ran.* 686-7; *Vesp.* 1043.

8. Both the central figures and the choruses of the *Acharnians* and *Peace* are farmers; the chorus of knights speak for themselves. Cf. the parabasis of the *Clouds*, 510 ff.

9. Victor Ehrenberg, *The People of Aristophanes* (Oxford, 1943), 53-5, 110. 'Though at first distress was greatest among the agricultural population, the accumulation of great wealth in trade and business had led to the emergence of a poor class among the town working class also.' The last play of Aristophanes 'shows us the completion of the great change which we have so often noted in its earlier stages, the change from a political to an economic outlook, from the political consciousness of a citizen to the economic purpose of an individual human being' (55).

10. 'And one could see this also in the comedies, the old and the new; for in the former vulgarity was a source of amusement, in the latter rather covert meaning. They differ not a little in point of refinement.' (*Nic. Eth.*, 1128a20).

11. Cf. T. B. L. Webster, 'South Italian Vases and Attic Drama', *CQ* 42 (1948), 15-27. Mr Webster suggests that the vase paintings may represent scenes from fourth-century Attic comedy and thus provide us with information about the plays from which so few fragments survive.

12. Fig. 48, A. W. Pickard-Cambridge, *Dithyramb, Tragedy and Comedy* (Oxford, 1927).

13. Cf. Henry W. Prescott, 'The Antecedents of Hellenistic Comedy', *CPh* 12 (1917), 405-25; 13 (1918) 113-37; 14 (1919), 108-35. He assesses the influence of Euripides on the Middle and New Comedy and concludes that it has been exaggerated. The conditions of everyday life and the exigencies of the theatre account for many resemblances.

14. Cf. Norwood, *op. cit.* (above note 2), 53-4.

15. *RE*, s.v. 'Anaxandrides'.

16. For a detailed account of the comic chorus in the fourth century see K. J. Maidment, 'The Later Comic Chorus', *CQ* 29 (1935), 1-24.

CHAPTER 8

ATHENIAN NEW COMEDY: 338 TO 290 B.C.

WHEN we turn from the study of Middle Comedy to that of New Comedy, we seem at first to be emerging from uncertainty and strangeness into a world of familiar forms which we can see clearly enough to discuss with some degree of certainty. We are no longer dependent solely on scattered fragments, because substantial portions of three plays have been recovered in papyri [1]. We are no longer reading the lines of mediocre dramatists but the poetry of Menander, revered in antiquity as a great artist. The dominant form of play is no longer the strange mythological burlesque but the familiar plot of young lovers in adversity finally reunited. The Middle Comedy had no influence beyond its time; New Comedy was the source for the plays of Plautus and Terence and through them it influenced the development of comedy in the Renaissance [2]. One further result of these differences is that scholars have taken little note of the Middle Comedy, while they have devoted much time to the texts and criticism of New Comedy [3].

Some of these differences can be seen, on closer examination, to be more apparent than real. Even though we have large parts of three plays by Menander, we still have no complete play. Of the other dramatists we have only fragments. Like Aristophanes, Menander stands alone. Without the works by his rivals for comparison, the judgment of the quality of his achievement is necessarily partial. The plot of young lovers who are separated and reunited may be familiar to us, but the cause of separation is linked in all the extant plays with the strange practice of exposing new-born children to die.

The borrowing of Greek plots by Roman authors increases our knowledge to some extent, but the evidence of Roman comedy must be used with great caution [4]. Not one of the Greek originals of an extant Roman comedy is extant. Thus we have no reliable method of comparing the latter with the former to see how closely Plautus and Terence translated the Greek plays. Scholars who work with Roman comedy necessarily discuss the problems of translation and adaptation and try to evaluate the nature and degree of originality of Plautus and Terence. But to conjecture what Plautus and Terence may have done to their sources seems to me far less hazardous than to conjecture what the sources were like before they were translated and adapted. Since we do have substantial portions of three Greek plays, our statements about Greek comedy should be based on Greek sources, referring to Latin comedies only to confirm generalizations.

The process of transition, which made the Middle Comedy so confused, was completed by the time Menander started to write. Few traces of Old Comedy survive in New Comedy. The Dionysiac spirit has gone and all that was associated with it. The chorus is only a band of revellers who entertain the spectators between the acts; it is not an integral part of the design, nor does it have a role in the action. With the subordination of the chorus, the parabasis disappeared, and with it the hymns to the gods, the political advice, the personal comments of the poet, and the satire of individuals. The ecstasy of Dionysos which showed in songs of joy and delight in nature, the rollicking fun which showed in the gay treatment of the divine and in the fantasies of Cloud-cuckoo-land, the earthy pleasures of natural processes, the disgust for all unnatural vices—all these elements of the Old Comedy so closely linked with Dionysos were gradually discarded during the fourth century and by the time of Menander had practically disappeared.

In their place New Comedy took on new and distinctive elements. The characters are upper middle-class citizens, usually of Athens, and the immediate circle such citizens would daily encounter—slaves, tenant farmers, and hetairae. The goal of the citizens is happy marriage for the young people. The difficulties are the legal requirement of citizenship for both members of the marriage, the economic necessities of a dowry for the bride, the social restraints which prevented young people of good families from meeting and falling in love, the exposure of children because of poverty or illegitimacy, and the opposition of parents. The plot was a simple reversal of the situation from bad to good accomplished by a series of recognitions. The scene was usually a street before two or three houses. The diction was clear and realistic. The psychological effect was a dramatic illusion that the spectator was seeing 'life' and hearing people he knew speaking naturally to each other. The emotional effect was that he felt pity for those in adversity and reassurance in the ordered goodness of the world when they achieved happiness.

The causes for these radical changes were both many and complex. No one cause can be singled out as *the* important one; nor can any one except theoretically be disentangled from the others. Old and Middle Comedy, Euripidean tragedy, Aristotelian criticism, Theophrastean psychology, and Athenian politics and economics all had a share in moulding the form of New Comedy, and all were interrelated. In what follows I shall try to indicate the accumulative power of the mould rather than the direct assignment of one characteristic of New Comedy to one specific source. The point of discussing influences and sources, in my opinion, lies not in saying that Menander 'borrowed' the plot of violation and the exposed child from Aristophanes or from Euripides but rather in showing what in this plot interested Menander so much that he selected it for special emphasis [5].

Aristophanes was said to have anticipated the New Comedy in his last play, the *Cocalus*, produced by his son [6]. All that we know of this play is that it had for its plot a violation and recognition. The loss of this play is most regrettable. It would have been very illuminating to compare the way Aristophanes handled the plot with the way Menander did. We can compare Menander's handling of an *agon* with Aristophanes's, because remnants of the *agon* of Old Comedy can be discerned in the scene which gives its title to *The Arbitrants* by Menander. The pattern is familiar. The contestants prepare for battle and choose a judge. The loser-to-be opens the argument with a speech frequently interrupted by his opponent. Then the opponent speaks. The judge decides. The victor and loser respond appropriately. But Menander has adapted the device to his own texture. The parts are not marked off by a variety of metres; this section is in iambic metre like the rest of the play. The object of the conflict is a babe in arms, a mute witness to the struggle and a tender appeal to the pity of the spectators. The judge is by an ironic twist of fate the baby's own grandfather. We have only to compare this scene with the contest between Cleon and the Sausage-seller for the favour of the People or between Aeschylus and Euripides for the favour of Dionysos to see how tradition becomes innovation. The poets of New Comedy had received from their predecessors a rich heritage of characters, plots, and technique which gave scope for their individual selection and emphasis.

This inheritance from Old Comedy was transmitted, of course, through the Middle Comedy. In this process of transmission much of what seems 'new' in New Comedy may well have been anticipated. It is easier to trace the gradual loss of the distinctive features of Old Comedy than to see the gradual growth of New Comedy. We do know that two dramatists wrote in both the period of Middle Comedy and of New Comedy; they were Eubulus and Alexis. Alexis, in fact, lived into the third century. His influence is significant both because he was a prolific dramatist and because he was the uncle of Menander. In the light of our limited knowledge of Middle Comedy perhaps the most we can say is that it may have contributed to the presentation of home and family life and to an emphasis upon love as a motive.

Intertwined with the development of comedy is the continuous influence of Euripides from his first production in 455 B.C. [7]. By the end of the fourth century Euripides had a double entry into comedy: his tragedies had proved so popular that they were frequently performed and were available to the public in written form; and the comic poets had quoted and parodied his poetry and burlesqued his characters and plots. Menander admired Euripides [8]. One character in a play by Philemon says, 'If the dead had accurate perceptions, as some say, I would strangle myself to see Euripides' [9].

Of the extant tragedies of Euripides, the *Ion* exhibits so many features later found in New Comedy that the comic poets might seem to have deliberately imitated it. In both, a god speaks a long explanatory prologue; the plot depends on the antecedent action of the exposure of an illegitimate baby with birth tokens; Athenian citizenship is of vital importance; a man admits having violated a woman during Bacchic rites; the theme is the nature of justice; and the ending is happy not only because the identity of the child is revealed and child and mother united but also because the world is said to be under the guidance of a just god. The total of similarities is striking. Whether the comic poets deliberately imitated Euripides or wrote like him because they and their auditors shared his tastes and interests is less important than the changes the comic poets made.

The Greeks had too sensitive a feeling for literary form to confuse tragedy with comedy. If we compare the *Ion* with Menander's plays, we can see clearly the distinctions in form [10]. First of all, the characters in the *Ion* are mythical and legendary; Hermes speaks the prologue; Athene appears as the *dea ex machina*; Creousa and Xuthus are legendary while Ion is the eponymous hero of the Ionians. The time is long ago, and the place the sacred temple of Delphi. The characters in the comedies are fourth-century Athenians; if a god speaks a prologue, he is really an abstraction like Misapprehension; the illegitimate children have human, not divine fathers. The action takes place in the streets of Greek cities like Athens or Corinth. The most important difference is that of tone. At every point Euripides emphasizes the cruelty involved in the situation. Creousa and Ion both comment on the cruelty of Apollo's violation of Creousa. Creousa has been cruel to expose Ion, and she is cruel again in her jealous rage and plot to kill the boy her husband so joyfully has received as his son. Such violent passions do the characters have that the audience is continuously made fearful, fearful that Ion will be killed by his mother, fearful that Creousa will be killed by her son. In the New Comedy the cruelty of violation and exposure is toned down as much as possible by directing the spectator's attention to palliative circumstances—the drunkenness of the violator, the poverty of the father, the shame of the mother—so that we pity the parents as well as the child. Moreover, the danger which makes recognition imperative is the danger to a happy marriage, not to life itself.

This difference—the nature of the danger involved—is the basic difference between tragic and comic irony. It is tragic irony that Creousa may unwittingly kill the very son she seeks or Ion kill the mother he has longed for. It is comic irony that Charisius should be outraged because his wife has borne a child as a result of his own violation of her before their marriage or that Polemon should be jealous of Glycera's affection for Moschion, who turns out to be her brother.

These differences between tragedy and New Comedy are clearly marked by Aristotle in his *Poetics*. While a few tragic poets, he says, go outside history or legend for their characters and invent fictitious ones, most of them start with a familiar story (*Poetics*, 1451b). The comic poets, however, construct their plots in accordance with probability and then give the characters appropriate names, a creative process unlike both that of the tragic poets and the iambic or satiric poets who write about individuals. New Comedy is thus distinguished both from Old Comedy and from tragedy.

New Comedy is distinguished both from Old Comedy and from tragedy in respect also to structure. Old Comedy, as we have seen, had a structure based on conflict and consequences. Tragedy, according to Aristotle, has a structure based on a reversal of fortune and a recognition (*Poetics*, 1452a). He describes the emotional effect of various kinds of reversal; the truly tragic reversal is the change from good fortune to bad as a result of some flaw in the character of a man predominantly good. The plays of Euripides which end unhappily are the most tragic although the spectators prefer a happy ending. This happy ending is appropriate to comedy where enemies are reconciled and no one is slain. The change of fortune in a comedy, thus, is from bad to good.

The extent of Aristotelian influence on New Comedy can not be accurately judged [11]. That Aristotle may possibly have affected comedy we can surmise because he was the teacher of Theophrastus, who was the teacher of Menander. Aristotle's critical theories were probably well known to the dramatists. The difficulty here in my opinion is not so much with the specific relations between Aristotle and Menander as the relations between critical theory and poetic creativity.

The *Characters* of Theophrastus was published three years after the performance of Menander's first play, so that the *book* can hardly be said to have influenced New Comedy, but Theophrastus was the teacher of Menander and his interest in the ludicrous details of men's characters may well have affected the youthful dramatist [12]. Whatever may have been the exact nature and extent of the philosopher's influence upon the dramatist, we do have evidence that the educated men at this time thought it worth their while to observe the ways of ordinary men and to make nice distinction—between apparently similar traits. Theophrastus, for instance, describes two kinds of talking too much and three kinds of closeness with money. The repeated types in New Comedy would not have been boring to those spectators who delighted in observing the subtle details which made each character an individual within the type.

Comedy, tragedy, and philosophy helped to shape the new form of comedy, but the most potent formative influence was the condition of the world in which the dramatists lived. Athens had lost her political independence at Chaeronea in 338 [13]. After the death of Alexander in 323, the city revolted against Macedonian rule, but she was defeated and her sea-power destroyed in 322. A Macedonian garrison was installed. In 317 Demetrius of Phalerum was appointed viceroy of Athens, a position he held until 307. Demetrius favoured the wealthy and the aristocrat, relieving them of duties which had taxed their resources and transferring the expenses of dramatic choruses to the state. He also was instrumental in stopping the *theorica*, a fund which paid the wages of working-men during the days of festivals so that they could attend the theatre without loss of pay. Although working-men were still free to attend the theatre if they wished, few could afford to lose a day's pay. The result was a change in the composition of the audience which the dramatist was seeking to please. The majority of the spectators now were the leisured and educated, rendered prosperous by the economic policy of the ruler and by peace and left free for cultural pursuits by their loss of political freedom and responsibility.

Most of the playwrights were also without political responsibilities in Athens. Like the playwrights of the Middle Comedy, they were almost all foreigners. The chief rivals of Menander—Diphilus and Philemon—were from abroad, Diphilus from Sinope and Philemon from Syracuse. One Apollodorus came from Gela, another from Carystos. Some of the other playwrights may have been Athenians—most were too insignificant to have their birthplaces recorded—but only Menander is definitely known to have been an Athenian.

This difference between foreigner and citizen may partially explain a curious fact about New Comedy: on the one hand it existed as a homogeneous body of similar plays; and on the other hand Menander's plays are easily distinguishable from those of his contemporaries. For the homogeneity we have the evidence of Latin comedy; for the distinctiveness of Menander we have the evidence of the extant fragments and of ancient critics.

New Comedy was homogeneous, first of all, because it was unlike Middle Comedy. Evidence based on the fragments has already been presented; and this evidence is seconded by the choice of plays for translation made by Latin dramatists. So far as we know, they selected plays from only the New Comedy [14]. No comedy of an earlier period was apparently sufficiently like the later ones to be to their taste or to the taste of the audience. Secondly, the plays of Menander, Philemon, Diphilus, and lesser dramatists were similar to each other, if we may judge from the Latin comedies. Did Plautus and Terence wish the 'typical' plot of New Comedy—the long-lost child and a recognition? Then they could find one by Menander or Diphilus, by Philemon or Apollodorus. Did they wish something different? The same dramatists could supply them. Similarities in plot, characterization, and technique are marks of the whole body of comedy. There is no indication that Menander differed from his contemporaries in these respects [15].

The themes, however, as they have been preserved to us in the Greek fragments are markedly different. The fragments of the dramatists of New Comedy aside from Menander are hardly distinguishable from those of Middle Comedy. Once more we read of fish and fish-sellers, of cooks and parasites, and of courtesans. Once more the philosophers seek 'the good' and the characters speaking find it in 'pleasure'. The suffering of poverty is contrasted with the instability of wealth. Nothing is secure; everything changes. The life of man is wretched; death is the only doctor for its ills.

Two fragments only, both by Philemon, indicate concern for new ideas. In one Philemon contrasts the nature of beasts with men (K. 89). Each genus of beast has but one character: the lions are stalwart; the rabbits are cowardly; the foxes are audacious dissemblers. If there were thirty thousand foxes, they would all have one nature. But men have as many different characters as they have bodies. In the other fragment Philemon is concerned with the definition of the just man: 'The just man is not the one who is not unjust, but the one who is able to do an injustice and does not wish to' (K. 94).

These same themes of character and justice are prominent in the comedies of Menander. In fact, his distinction as a dramatist lies in the intelligence and sensitivity of his comments on human behaviour. The very number of extant fragments testifies to this. Over eleven hundred fragments from the works of Menander have been preserved, while less than three hundred from the works of his nearest rival, Philemon, have survived [16]. Quintilian's estimate of the two dramatists may be quoted as one example of ancient criticism.

> Now, the careful study of Menander alone would, in my opinion, be sufficient to develop all those qualities with the production of which my present work is concerned; so perfect is his representation of actual life, so rich is his power of invention and his gift of style, so perfectly does he adapt himself to every kind of circumstance, character and emotion. . . . Indeed, such is his supremacy that he has scarce left a name to other writers of the new comedy and has cast them into darkness by the splendour of his own renown. Still, you will find something of value in the other comic poets as well, if you read them in not too critical a spirit; above all, profit may be derived from the study of Philemon, who, although it was a depraved taste which caused his contemporaries often to prefer him to Menander, has none the less deserved the second place which posterity has been unanimous in awarding him. [17]

Menander's superiority may be ultimately traced to the superiority of genius over talent, but many lesser differences between Menander and the other comic poets have contributed to Menander's greatness. Menander was an Athenian citizen. He was the nephew of Alexis, a prominent comic poet. He was a friend of Demetrius, ruler of Athens. He was a student of Theophrastus. Whatever the reasons, the fact is that his are the plays which have survived, and necessarily his are the plays we must study. They may be considered, I think, as representative of New Comedy in kind but not in quality.

'Menander and life, which of you two imitated the other?' [18]

Aristophanes of Byzantium asked this question, thus emphasizing with hyperbole the impression of realism his comedies have made upon readers ancient or modern. Every element would seem to contribute to this impression. The characters are human beings. Gone are the animals which enlivened the Old Comedy, and almost gone are the gods and abstractions. If a god or abstraction does speak in the New Comedy, it is as the prologue. For example, Misapprehension, in *The Girl Who Gets Her Hair Cut Short*, tells the audience of antecedent action and explains the underlying meaning of the play, but she does not play a role as Dionysos did in the *Frogs* or Dicaeopolis in the *Acharnians*.

The human beings represented are also realistic because they are not eccentric in social status, profession, or character. They are ordinary citizens of a Greek town or village. The professions or trades they follow are the ordinary ones of the day—soldier, cook, charcoal-gatherer, or merchant. This man may be inclined to avarice, that to jealousy, but these traits are not exaggerated beyond human recognition. Moreover, we see these human beings in their family relations [19]. What is important is their position as father or sister or husband or son and the emotions involved in their relations under stress of unusual circumstance. It is not man as citizen but man as human that Menander studies.

We see these characters in their native environment—the street just outside their houses. The ancient theatre was unable to produce scenes laid in the interior of a house, unquestionably a limitation on the degree of theatrical realism which Menander could achieve, but in view of the climate, the structure of Greek houses, and social customs, more conversation and action took place in the streets than we to-day are used to. No one in antiquity implied that Menander's plays seemed to them implausible because the scene was a street. The entrances to the scene-building lent verisimilitude to the fiction of the houses. All the action was confined to the visible area of the close vicinity. For example, we are through our imaginations taken into the houses. We hear of the remorse of Charisius or the anger of Niceratus as they displayed these emotions within their homes. But our imaginations are not called upon to picture the scene-building as first the house of Trygaeus and then the cave of War. The characters do not create the scene; they live in it.

Their speech also is realistic. The colloquial idiom, the simple, clear vocabulary, the pauses, repetitions, broken sentences—all the marks of everyday speech are there. No fantastic metaphors or playful joke or parody are inappropriately assigned the characters. This difference in style was noted in antiquity as the most prominent point of contrast between Aristophanes and Menander.

> Moreover, in his [Aristophanes's] diction there are tragic, comic, pompous, and prosaic elements, obscurity, vagueness, dignity, and elevation, loquacity and sickening nonsense. And with all these differences and dissimilarities his use of words does not give to each kind its fitting and appropriate use; I mean, for example, to a king his dignity, to an orator his eloquence, to a woman her artlessness, to an ordinary man his prosaic speech, to a market-lounger his vulgarity; but he assigns to his characters as if by lot such words as happen to turn up, and you could not tell whether the speaker is son or father, a rustic or a god, or an old woman or a hero.
>
> But Menander's diction is so polished and its ingredients mingled into so consistent a whole that, although it is employed in connexion with many emotions and many types of character and adapts itself to persons of every kind, it nevertheless appears as one and preserves its uniformity in common and familiar words in general use. . . . [20]

The realism of the plots is open to more question than the realism of character, setting, and dialogue. The exposure of children and their recognition decades later can hardly have been common, but may not have been as improbable in the fourth century as they would be to-day. One critic in defence of the typical plot says,

> At a time when the selling of prisoners of war as slaves was frequent, piracy not uncommon, and the exposure of unwanted children not unknown, it is probable enough that many hetairai had taken to their profession because of such an accident and not impossible that some of them were recognized and rescued. . . . Similarly, we have to explain one or two particulars incidental to the society which Menander depicts—for example, the Athenian law of citizenship, the general disorder and unrest of the age;

> we do not have to explain the conduct of his men and women: that is common to humanity. [21]

Granted the improbability of the antecedent action, the immediate action is convincingly real. The characters come and go in a natural way, preparing meals, ordering the slaves, seeking help. No one rides aloft on a beetle or rows over the river Styx.

Menander has succeeded in creating an illusion of reality so compelling in its surface verisimilitude that we momentarily suspend judgment about the nature of the reality being rendered. His realism was in line with the realism of the arts during the late fourth century. Praxiteles, Scopas, and Apelles were realists in a similar way. Philosophy, too, had taken the direction of the naturalist.

> The realities of time and place are also carefully observed; we shall find extraordinarily few instances where the relation between real time and acted time is disregarded; normally act ends are carefully arranged to cover journeys to harbour or market-place and distant journeys are no longer undertaken within the limits of the play. [22]

So convincing is this realistic illusion that when a character speaks to the audience, he seems to destroy the illusion. He should speak only to other characters. We have forgotten we are an audience; when the character speaks to us, our attention is drawn back to ourselves, and we are reminded we are watching a play. This address to the audience is a remnant of the Old Comedy, a lingering on of the old attitude that dramatist, character, and spectator all readily admit that a play is being performed. I wonder which of the two attitudes is the more realistic [23]. Is not the Old Comedy the more honest? Is the dramatic illusion not the opposite of realism, a pretence, a fiction which can be only momentarily sustained?

The truth is that the realism we have been discussing is not a likeness to life but a likeness to convention. The characters are conventional types, with conventional names and conventional masks. The playwright had a stock of all three from which he could draw. Did he want a young man? He could take from his stock a jealous soldier, choose the name Polemon, and ask the mask-maker for the appropriate mask. The plot was a formula. Numerous changes could be rung, but the fictitious and romantic pattern was the same. The separated are united: children separated from parents, husband from wife, lover from mistress are brought together at the end of the play. The causes of separation may vary and the means of uniting may change, but the formula is always the same. Similarly, the dialogue fits the type of character. The soldier speaks one way; the old man another. But, at the same time, the dialogue has qualities which are recognizably Menander's. The scene is also conventional. Two or three houses may be represented; the houses may be in Athens or Corinth or a village; but these changes are all within the conventional pattern.

What then is *real*? The answer lies, I think, in Menander's view of life as we find it preserved in the three plays. Menander had artistic integrity. He used the conventional characters and plots because what he had to say could best be expressed by working within the conventions. Menander had faith in the value of the individual. Each man's character determines his action. There are forces outside of man which influence the *outcome* of his action, forces of justice and enlightenment. Even if a man's character leads to an evil action, the forces of good are strong enough to overcome this evil.

This faith of Menander's is expressed directly by the characters. Misapprehension, the Prologue of *The Girl Who Gets Her Hair Cut Short*, tells the audience that she has caused Moschion to burn with passion for Glycera contrary to his own nature in order that their true relation as brother and sister may be revealed. 'Therefore,' she says, 'if anyone is displeased by this and considers it a public dishonour [the word *atimia* meant in Athens the loss of civil rights] let him change his mind. Through the help of God even the evil turns into good in the very process of happening' [24]. This process of evil turning into good is exemplified in *The Arbitrants*. Davus is doing evil when he tries to keep for himself the birth tokens of the baby he has found, but this very action calls attention to the tokens which are recognized by Onesimus, slave of Charisius, the baby's father.

The good achieved is a combination of recognition and justice. The recognition of long-lost relatives is only the obvious form of enlightenment. Far more significant is the recognition of self-knowledge. When Charisius recognizes the foundling baby as his, he recognizes that he has been as dishonourable as the wife he has been treating with such scorn. He is guilty of the same offence as she is, and he has added unkindness whereas his wife is forgiving. Through this self-knowledge justice is achieved—the same forgiveness for the same act. And ultimate justice closes the play when the baby is proved to be the result of their union. Similarly, Polemon recognizes how wrong he has been in his jealousy and rage and how generous Glycera is to forgive him. The person like Smicrines, who refuses to admit his own responsibility, who blames Necessity for his actions, who does not see that his own character (*tropos*) is determining the action, is ridiculous in his blindness and must be brought to enlightenment before the play can end happily. Niceratus must recognize that the child he plans to kill is his grandson before he can be freed from his rage and the harm that rage can do. Demeas must be taught the harm his jealousy may cause, when Moschion, his adopted son, rebels against the suspicions Demeas has harboured.

All the plays are concerned with justice. The initial injustice which must be righted is the exposure of a child. Such an exposure was unjust because the baby was made to suffer for the wrongs of his parents; moreover, if he were rescued and grew up, he was deprived of his civil rights. This meant loss of freedom and livelihood for man, loss of the possibility of a suitable marriage for a woman. Injustice within the action of the play resulted from insufficient perceptions into the character and motives of others. Polemon misjudges Glycera's motives in kissing Mochion and cuts her hair in his anger. He wrongs her in thought and action, because he thinks he has been wronged. Charisius leaves his wife Pamphila in moral indignation. He wrongs her by living next door with a mistress because he thinks his wife has wronged him.

The arbitration scene which gives the title to *The Arbitrants* was considered one of Menander's finest scenes by ancient critics. Certainly it has preserved for us evidence of his strong interest in justice. Justice is not a simple matter, easily discerned. Davus has a just claim to his discovery: the baby, represented by Syriscus, has a just claim to his birth tokens.

Davus and Syriscus argue skilfully in behalf of their claims. The facts are agreed upon. Two questions of justice are involved. Do the tokens belong to the finder or to the baby? Does the baby belong to the finder or to the man who wishes to raise him with love? The judge chosen is Smicrines, ironically the baby's grandfather, but more significantly a man whose character has already been demonstrated to be miserly. He is disgusted with the extravagance of Charisius his son-in-law. Such a man might decide for the finder because of his own attitude toward money. On the other hand, Smicrines is visiting his daughter because he thinks she is being treated unjustly by her husband. The husband is using her dowry for a mistress, and that is not right. The dowry is the gift of the father to his son-in-law and rightfully belongs to the wife. Smicrines's sense of justice and goodness wins out over miserliness when he judges that the birth tokens belong to the baby and the baby to the man who cares for him.

Menander's view of life is comic not because it is joyous but because it is satisfying. His comedies present us with an illusion of life or with life itself, depending upon our own faith. He says that life is ordered and that the order is good. Evil only appears to be evil; its outcome will be good. The blind can learn to see; the slave can be freed; the lover will be loved. This is a reassuring belief. We need not wonder at Menander's popularity through the centuries nor that St Paul should have quoted from his plays.

With Menander, Greek comedy may be said to end if by comedy we mean new plays of literary value produced in Athens. After him no comic poet of stature composed for the theatre. But the theatre itself continued to function [25]. Contests of comic poets and comic actors were held at the City Dionysia until about 120 B.C. and at the Lenaea until after 150 B.C. [26]. Although no record for the performance of old comedies exists for the Lenaea, they were performed at the City Dionysia from 311 until at least 155 B.C. The spirit of comic enjoyment was still alive even if the spirit of comic creation no longer resided in Athens.

The spirit of comic creation moved out to other centres of civilization—to Sicily, Alexandria, and Rome—and revealed itself in the minor forms of the mime, dialogue, and fictitious letter. Sicily had been a home of the mime from the sixth-century Epicharmus through fifth-century Sophron. Sophron is hardly more than a name to us, but he was famous in antiquity [27]. The third century was a period favourably inclined to the mime. Rhinthon and Sopater were popular writers of the century [28]. Theocritus, a native of Sicily who travelled to Alexandria, is the best known to moderns of the ancient mime writers [29]. He raised the mime to a literary level—Idylls XIV and XV are masterpieces of realistic characterization—but these idylls, like his pastoral dialogues, were dramatic only in form. He did not intend them for the theatre. The other prominent mime writer of the third century is Herodas of either Cos or Miletus [30]. His satirical character sketches show clearly the continuing strength of centuries of comic tradition from Hipponax and Aristophanes to Menander.

Comic prose was late in developing. The two prose writers especially deserving of mention, Lucian and Alciphron, both lived in the second century A.D. Lucian is one of the major Greek writers [31]. His dialogues are delightful because of his wit and his sympathetic amusement at the foibles of mankind. His dialogues, while they have the freshness of the newly minted, are also enriched by his thorough knowledge of the ancient comic poets. Alciphron wrote fictitious letters. Their groupings are reminiscent of the Middle Comedy: letters of fishermen, farmers, parasites, and courtesans [32]. The last category contains correspondence supposedly exchanged by Menander and his mistress Glycera.

The diffusion of the Greek comic spirit throughout the ancient world helped to keep alive the memory of 'classical' comedy. These later authors also had a function in the future history of comedy since they were the intermediaries between the ancient comic poets and the literary men of the Renaissance. In the Renaissance Epicharmus was unknown, but Theocritus, who honoured him as the 'originator of comedy', was well known [33]. The comedies of Aristophanes were accessible to scholars of the sixteenth century, but were too difficult to read to have a wide audience or much influence [34]. The spirit of Aristophanic comedy was really transmitted through Lucian, who was popular with the early circle of classicists—Erasmus and Sir Thomas More—and with later satirists [35]. Menander was just a name, but the Latin translations and adaptations of New Comedy were read and performed in schools, colleges, and courts. They were adapted to convey propaganda or to delight the audiences in the public theatres [36].

Greek comic poetry may be said to have its beginning with Susarion and its end with Menander. It may also be said to have no discernible beginning and no foreseeable end. As I said in the first chapter, from one point of view the fountainhead of comedy is internal and not external. Comedy is born anew with every clown and spectator. If we notice in the theatre or literature to-day characters, plots, technique, or jests which remind us of ancient comedy, the likenesses may be traced to a common source for all artists—our common humanity. The comic spirit of any time or nation may be one of revelry, purification, fantasy, or faith in the goodness of man and his ordered world [37].

At the same time hardly a century of the twenty-two since Menander's death has passed without some conscious effort on the part of theatrical men, literary men, or scholars to revive the ancient comic poets. Productions, translations, adaptations, borrowings, allusions, anthologies, histories, criticisms all have contributed to keeping alive the memory of what was distinctive in the Greek comic spirit. Revival is perhaps the wrong word for so buoyant a spirit. That spirit bobs up in a college swimming-pool, in a leading article in the *Times Literary Supplement*, in a drawing-room comedy by one of our greatest living poets. The flurry of excitement not long ago about the meaning of the *Ecclesiazusae*—a flurry which halted the scheduled production of the play in New York—indicates the living force of Aristophanes's ideas. I wonder sometimes if we are right in hoping that we can revive Aristophanes; perhaps we should hope Aristophanes can revive us.

NOTES FOR CHAPTER 8

1. Menander (trans. and ed. Francis G. Allinson, Loeb Classical Library, London, 1930).

2. George E. Duckworth, *The Nature of Roman Comedy* (Princeton, 1952), p. 24 and *passim*.

3. Only a few of the many significant works can be cited here. For the general reader I recommend Gilbert Norwood, *Greek Comedy* (Boston, 1931), chap. vii; Philip Whaley Harsh, *A Handbook of Classical Drama* (Stanford University, California, 1944), chaps. vii and viii; Ph. E. Legrand, *The New Greek Comedy* (trans. James Loeb, London, 1917). For specialized studies see Norman W. DeWitt, 'Epicurus and Menander', *Studies in Honour of Gilbert Norwood* (ed. Mary E. White, Toronto, 1952), pp. 116-26; A. W. Gomme, 'Menander', *Essays in Greek History and Literature* (Oxford, 1937), pp. 249-95; A. Körte, 'Menandros', *RE*; C. R. Post, 'The Dramatic Art of Menander', *Harvard Studies in Classical Philology*, XXIV (1913), 111-45; Levi Arnold Post, 'Aristotle and Menander', *Transactions of the American Philological Association*, LXIX (1938), 1-42; Levi Arnold Post, 'Menander in Current Criticism', *Transactions of the American Philological Association*, LXV (1934), 13-34; T. B. L. Webster, *Studies in Menander* (Manchester, 1950).

4. Duckworth has an excellent discussion of this problem, pp. 52 ff., 59-60.

5. For the formative influences on New Comedy see Duckworth, pp. 33-8; Webster, pp. 153-94; Henry W. Prescott, 'The Antecedents of Hellenistic Comedy', *Classical Philology*, XII (1917), 405-25, XIII (1918), 113-37; and XIV (1919), 108-35.

6. *Vita Aristoph.*, I. 69.

7. See authorities cited in note 5.

8. Quintilian, *Institutio Oratoria* (trans. and ed. H. E. Butler, Loeb Classical Library, London, 1922), X, i, 69.

9. K. 130.

10. Cf. C. R. Post, pp. 126 ff.

11. Webster has an illuminating chapter entitled 'Menander and Philosophy', pp. 195-219.

12. *Ibid.*, pp. 212-17.

13. William Scott Ferguson, *Hellenistic Athens* (London, 1911), chap. ii.

14. Duckworth, p. 24.

15. *Ibid.*, pp. 30-1.

16. *Ibid.*, p. 26.

17. Quintilian, X, 1, 69-72 (trans. H. E. Butler).

18. Quoted by Norwood, p. 314, n. 6.

19. This fact has been observed by a number of critics. See, for example, Gomme, p. 264.

20. Plutarch, 'Summary of a Comparison between Aristophanes and Menander', *Moralia* (ed. and trans. Harold North Fowler, Loeb Classical Library, London, 1949), x, 467.

21. Gomme, p. 274.

22. T. B. L. Webster, *Studies in Later Greek Comedy*, (Manchester, 1950), pp. 114-15.

23. Victor Ehrenberg, *The People of Aristophanes* (Oxford, 1943), p. 30.

24. *The Girl Who Gets Her Hair Cut Short*, lines 47-50.

25. Sir Arthur W. Pickard-Cambridge, *The Dramatic Festivals of Athens* (Oxford, 1953), pp. 125-6.

26. *Ibid.*, p. 125.

27. Norwood, pp. 77-9.

28. *Ibid.*, 73-7.

29. Theocritus (ed. and trans. A. S. F. Gow, Cambridge, 1950).

30. *Herodas: The Mimes and Fragments* (notes by Walter Headlam, ed. A. D. Knox, Cambridge, 1922).

31. The works of Lucian are available in eight volumes edited and translated by A. M. Harmon (Loeb Classical Library, London, 1927).

32. *The Letters of Alciphron, Aelian and Philostratus* (ed. and trans. Allen Rogers Benner and Francis H. Fobes, Loeb Classical Library, Cambridge, U.S.A., 1949).

33. Theocritus, *Epigram* XVIII.

34. See my article, 'Greek Comedy on the Sixteenth Century English Stage', *Classical Journal*, XLII (1946), 169-74. In preparing this article, I found particularly helpful Arthur Tilley, 'Greek Studies in England in the Early Sixteenth Century', *English Historical Review*, LIII (1938), 221-39, 438-56. Louis E. Lord, *Aristophanes, His Plays and His Influence* (Boston, 1925), is also recommended.

35. Francis G. Allinson, *Lucian, Satirist and Artist* (Boston, 1926), pp. 143 ff.

36. It is almost possible to trace the history of English comedy by tracing the varied ways Latin comedy was used in the sixteenth century: adapted to the parable of the Prodigal Son, used as a thin

disguise for an attack on the doctrine of transubstantiation, adapted to English characters and setting for the school and college actors, and a plot borrowed with additions by Shakespeare himself.

37. An interesting topic for speculation is the cycle of a dramatic form. I think the pattern which emerges from the history of Greek comedy can be found again (with variations, of course) in the history of English comedy. In both, the main trend is from many religious and secular minor forms of comic play toward satiric attacks on the contemporary world through a confused period of romance to a 'realism' which is actually conventional. This is an hypothesis which obviously needs full development and considerable supporting evidence. My interest in this subject owes much to the lectures of Professor Rhys Carpenter and particularly to his share in *Art: A Bryn Mawr Symposium*, *Bryn Mawr Notes and Monographs*, IX (1940), 76-177.

INDEX